LEST CUDWORTH FORGETS.

ALEX CLARK   **JOHN HAYHOE**

Published by

The Cudworth Local History and Heritage Group

The Library

Barnsley Road

Cudworth

Barnsley

South Yorkshire

S72 8SY

Printed by

Adlard Print & Reprographics Ltd.

The Old School

The Green

Ruddington

Notts. NG11 6HH

www.adlardprint.com

ISBN 0 9549832 0 3

The Cudworth Local History and Heritage Group has produced this book in conjunction with the restoration of the War Memorial situated in the grounds of the St. John the Baptist Church, Cudworth.

The Group wishes to thank Alex Clark, John Hayhoe, and Linda Laughton for the many hours spent in researching and compiling the information included in the book. Thanks are also expressed to Don Clark for assistance with typing, Marion Hodge for proof reading and to Tony Turner for looking after the administration associated with producing this book.

It has not been possible to include the details of all the local war casualties. Most of the parents are no longer with us, some siblings and descendants move away, and after so many years memory plays tricks on those who are left to pass on what they know.

Appeals have been made from time to time for help from the relatives of the casualties. We are very grateful to all those who responded and gave us so much information and allowed us to copy personal letters and photographs.

Relatives may be almost anywhere in the world and may not have read our appeals for information.

When a young person is killed (and there were so many) there are no descendants to remember them.

Newspaper photographs published on war-quality newsprint do not reproduce well and some incidents did not get reported in the press at all due to wartime security censorship.

These are some of the handicaps under which the book has been written

Thus, whilst every effort has been made to make this book as accurate as possible the authors and publishers apologise for any errors or omissions and do not accept responsibility for anyone using the information contained therein for the research of their own works.

Relatives and friends of the people remembered contributed with the loan of personal letters and photographs for which we shall be forever grateful.

Dedication.
This book is dedicated to Tony Mullaney, Bob Murgatroyd, Ken Gorman, Margaret Ogley and Arthur Stringer, being Members of the History Group who have died since the Group was formed in November 1996. They were founder members and continued to play an active part in the Group's activities and development.

Acknowledgements.

Barnsley Chronicle.
Barnsley Archives.
Cudworth Library.
St. John the Baptist Church, Cudworth.
The Commonwealth War Graves Commission.

Barnsley Metropolitan Borough Council.
British Legion.
Cudworth West Green Partnership.
The Methodist Church, Cudworth.
The Lottery Heritage Initiative.

Cover Picture.
Aerial View of Cudworth. By G.J. Alliott, Local Historian.

Cudworth St. John the Baptist Church and the Cemetery can be seen in the lower right-hand corner of the front cover.

Contents

CHAPTER 1.

HISTORY GROUP.

THE CHURCH.

THE MEMORIAL.

THE RE-DEDICATION.

CUDWORTH LOCAL HISTORY AND HERITAGE GROUP

Brief History.

The Group was formed in November 1996 to promote a wider understanding and knowledge of local history and to preserve and store any historical information for the benefit of present and future generations. This includes the collection, categorising, archiving and displaying of materials that are considered to be part of the heritage of Cudworth.

Meetings are held in the Cudworth Library and membership is free to anyone who supports the aims of the Group.

One of its main objectives over this period has been to create an archive of local photographs, documents and information relating to Cudworth. These photographs have been used for displaying at local exhibitions, history fairs and in the window of Cudworth library.

In 1997, the Group received a grant from the Arts Council of England National Lottery Fund through their A4E Express scheme, plus some additional sponsorship from Corridor Arts to produce a CD ROM covering aspects of Cudworth local history. Copies were distributed free to local schools and libraries in the Barnsley area.

In 2003, the Group received a grant from Awards for All to purchase a computer and software for the purpose of digitising the existing archive of photographs and documents and future contributions. At a later date it is planned to include these on a CD, which will be available to the general public.

Cudworth War Memorial Renovation.

The most recent project was the renovation of the Cudworth War Memorial, situated in the grounds of St. John the Baptist Church, Cudworth. The Memorial was erected in 1920 and over the years names had been damaged. The stonework had become dirty and was being eroded due to weather conditions.

After discussions with local stonemasons it was agreed that the Memorial should he cleaned and the names engraved on to new granite panels to be fixed over the existing names and inscriptions. This should preserve the Memorial for future generations. Military rank and any medal awards would be added, plus additional names and details that were originally omitted, but had since become available.

After agreement with the Church Faculty a successful application for funding was submitted to the Countryside Agency, through the Local Heritage Initiative. Members of the History Group have spent a lot of time researching records from the War Graves Commission, Imperial War Museum, British Legion, reference books, local cemeteries, etc. to obtain the additional information for inclusion on the War Memorial.

The Memorial renovation was completed in June 2004, the work being carried out by Hopkinson Memorials Ltd., Staveley, at a cost of £6,400.

In addition to the renovation of the War Memorial, the funding included provision for two publications relating to the men and women who lost their lives in the wars. The first is a limited edition "Book of Remembrance", which lists all the names on the Memorial in chronological order of the date they died, with their service, regiment, rank and number and the place where they are buried or commemorated. This has been given to local schools, churches, armed services, the British Legion and libraries/archives.

ST. JOHN THE BAPTIST CHURCH, CUDWORTH.

From 1234 Cudworth had been in the Parish of Royston and became part of the newly created Parish of St. Paul, Monk Bretton in 1839. In 1893 the Parish of Cudworth was created with St. John the Baptist Church being built at the highest point in Cudworth at that time.

Built of Huddersfield Stone, the new structure consisted of a nave and chancel, with a north aisle, organ chamber and vestries. It has large tracery windows at the east and west ends, a bell-turret over the chancel arch, and a Westmorland Slate roof that was recently renewed.

Internally the church has a lofty and well-lit appearance. The north aisle is divided from the nave by an arcade with four arches of simple character rising from octagonal piers. The organ chamber is separated from the chancel by a lofty arch carried on shafted responds, with carved caps and corbels. The ceiling is open timbered, unvarnished pitch pine with moulded principals and curved ribs. The seating consists of pitch pine pews. The chancel fittings are of oak. There is a low chancel screen, with panel work and an alabaster coping. The sacrarium is raised above the nave by five steps. The original pulpit was of richly carved Caen Stone.

The Church has a capacity of two hundred and sixty and cost two thousand, five hundred and thirty pounds with all but three hundred pounds being raised prior to the consecration.

The Archbishop of York (Dr. Maclagan) consecrated the Church on Thursday the 29th of June 1893 assisted by the Vicar of Monk Bretton the Reverend W.R. Hannam and the incumbent of Cudworth the Reverend C.F. Husband.

A new Altar was dedicated in the year 2000 in memory of Father J.C.K. Brumpton who had been a very popular priest in Cudworth from 1953 to 1966. The Altar was a gift from his family in remembrance of his love for St. John's.

Under the care of Father David Nicholson, the church in Cudworth today is very active and flourishing with a well-attended daily mass.

Cudworth Churchyard War Memorial.

In ever grateful remembrance of the Men of Cudworth who gave their lives in the Great War.

MARCH 2004

JUNE 2004

THE FIRST WORLD WAR.

The need for a War Memorial began as early as 1916 when family and friends of the men who had lain down their lives for King and Country expressed the wish for some form of War Memorial to remember them. On the 15th of November 1916 a Working Committee was appointed for the Churchyard Memorial registered under the War Charities Act.

In September 1917 it was recorded that the scheme and particular form of the Memorial met with the approval of Cudworth men serving at the Front. A public subscription was to be raised and a decision was made that a contribution of three shillings and six pence per household within the township would "provide a worthy memorial that would speak for generations to come of the sacrifice made by our brothers". The secretary of the committee at this time was the Rev. H.I. Robinson and the treasurer was Mr. F. Parkinson.

By September 1918 one hundred and seven pounds, seventeen shillings and seven pence had been raised and more than one hundred pounds was still required to erect the monument. The Hon. Secretary of the committee, the Rev. H.I. Robinson was appointed as the Vicar of Carlton-juxta Snaith.

The approval of the Church faculty for erecting the Memorial was obtained in November 1919 and the completion of the work by the Sculptor was awaited.

In spite of strikes and great poverty, over £300 was raised for the erection of the War Memorial before the unveiling. This did not include the cost of the inscription of the names of the one hundred and sixty one Cudworth men, which was to be carried out after the unveiling.

The unveiling ceremony took place on the evening of the 22nd of July 1920 and was preceded by a procession assembled at the Pond.

The Cudworth Old Brass Band led the procession. Mr. W.D. Armitage was the Master of Ceremonies. The Mayor of Barnsley, Col. W.E. Raley, O.B.E. was dressed in his robes and chain of office and was supported by the Vicar, the Reverend F. Richardson, Reverend Father O'Shaughnessy, Reverend F. Gordon Mee, County Councillor J.

Newton J.P. (chairman of the Urban District council), who presided over the ceremony, members of the Urban District Council, members of the Memorial Committee, followed by relatives and friends of the fallen and the general public.

The Memorial was covered by a Union Flag and after a making a speech the Mayor carried out the unveiling. The Vicar read out the Roll of Honour followed by the sounding of the Last Post. The Three Minutes Silence was ended with the awakening notes of the Reveille. The ceremony closed with the singing of "O God our help in ages past."

On Sunday the 1st of August 1920 the memorial was formally dedicated by the Reverend R.H. Gilbert, Rector of Hemsworth and Rural Dean. Assisting in the service were the Reverends F. Richardson (Vicar of Cudworth), R.A. Russell (assistant priest), and the Reverend F. Gordon Mee (Wesleyan Minister) who read the Roll of Honour.

THE SECOND WORLD WAR.

The council meeting minutes of July/August 1947 record the attendance of members of the Memorial Trust Fund committee who reported on the amount of money standing to the credit of the fund but intimated that in the opinion of their committee it was no longer representative of the township and had no authority and suggested that the council should call a Township meeting for the following purposes: -

- To decide whether or not a War Memorial is desired, if so, what form should the memorial take?

- If a memorial is desired, to appoint a representative committee to submit schemes and to outline a future policy and to be prepared to carry that policy out.

- To decide how the money already in the trust fund is to be used.

It was resolved that a Township meeting be called for the 18th of September next in the Cudworth Village Club at 7. 30pm and that the clerk arrange for posters to be posted throughout the Township.

Council minutes were researched up to the 26th of April 1950 and no further reference to the War Memorial was found.

The names of Second World War men and women were added to the base of the memorial erected for the First World War. No record has been found of when this was carried out, who the organisers were, or of the re-dedication of the memorial.

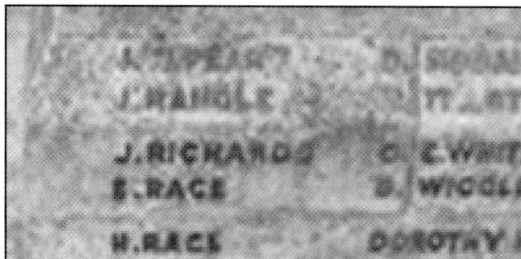

PART OF BASE (note missing letters)

THE RESTORATION OF THE WAR MEMORIAL.

During the Millennium Year, the Cudworth Local History and Heritage Group were engaged in a photographic survey of Cudworth, which was being conducted by Donald and Alex Clark. The idea behind the survey was to take photographs, in different directions, at road junctions and village boundaries that would give a pictorial record of Cudworth in the year 2000.

It was at this time that the group realised the War Memorial was in great need of restoration. It was evident upon inspection that the stone into which the lead lettering had been placed had become a casualty to corrosion causing the letters to stand proud; and some of the letters were missing.

Alex Clark teamed up with John Hayhoe, who had already been researching the names on the Memorial, to carry out further investigation. Linda Laughton assisted with genealogical investigations to determine where they had lived in Cudworth and their family connections. The research revealed forty-one men whose names had not been included (thirty-five in WW1 and six in WW2). Tony Turner took the pressure off the researchers by taking care of all the paper work and organisation of events

The group talked to friends within the community to obtain memories of the men who had fallen and their families, and took part in publicising the restoration project at various functions in the village.

Stonemasons advised that the restoration of the Memorial in its present form would be time consuming and costly and only last for approximately another eighty years. The consensus of opinion was that granite panels should be fitted.

Members of the group then carried out visits to see work carried out by the various stonemasons before a final decision was made.

Members of the group are shown going to contact the local church officials after examining the War Memorial at Huntington, near York.

Work started on the Memorial in October 2003 with the cleaning of the crucifix. The granite panels were fitted in April 2004 and work progressed through May and was completed by the end of June 2004.

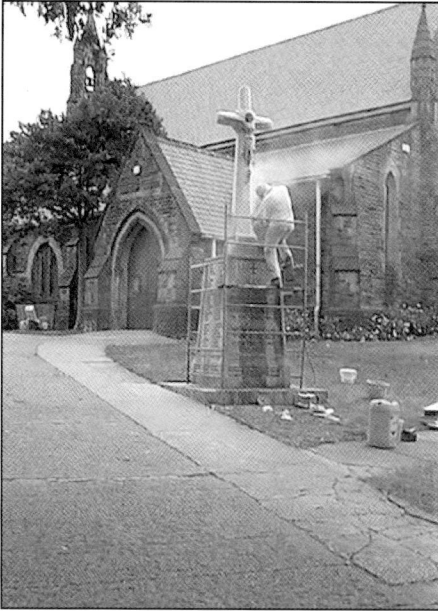

CLEANING THE CROSS

**MEMORIAL PREPARED
TO ACCEPT GRANITE PANELS**

FIRST PANEL FITTED

CLEANING LAST PANEL

The names on the base of the War Memorial recording those who died in the Second World War showed deterioration to such an extent that they had to be removed and added to the new panels to be fixed to the Memorial.

The names for the First World War have been left behind the granite panels as an historical record.

DEDICATION PANEL

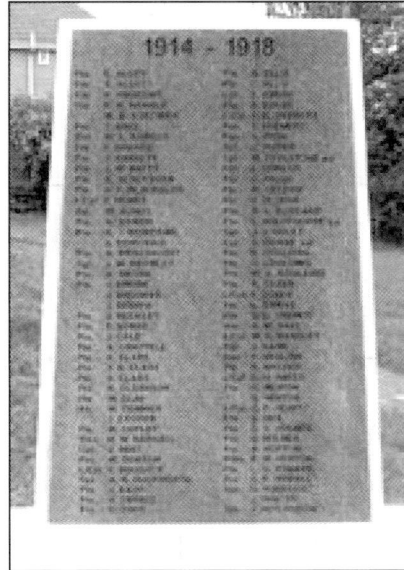

NORTH FACE

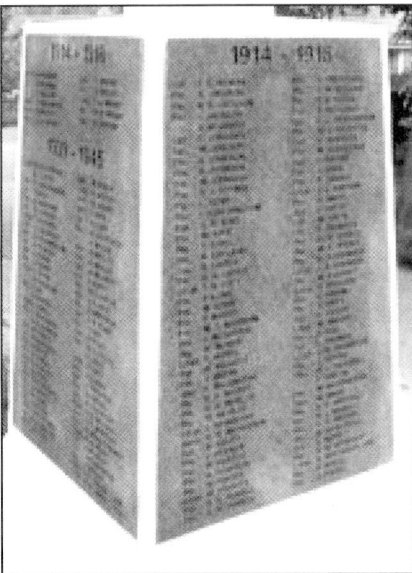

SOUTH & EAST FACES

The wording of the dedication has not been modified to suit the political correctness of the present era. (After W.W.2. only a small letter 'S' was added to the word 'WAR'.)

Although Nurse Dorothy Hirst was added to the memorial for the Second World War, the dedication panel was not changed to include women. Her Christian name was included in the Roll of Honour as a mark of respect and this principle has been followed on the renovated memorial.

THE CHURCHYARD

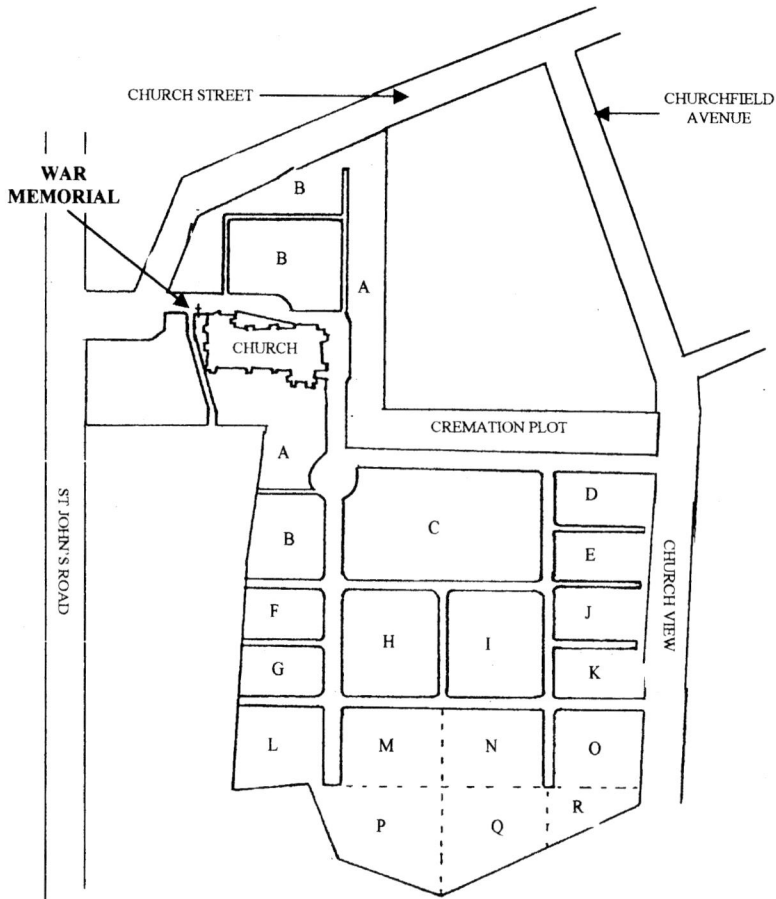

FIRST AND SECOND WORLD WARS.

GRAVES FOR THIS PERIOD ARE TO BE
FOUND IN SECTIONS A, B, C AND D.

Pte. T. BALL	SE5. 3. 5	Dvr. W.L. BARKER	B. 4. 38
Pte. W. BONDS	ASE. 2. 12	Cpl. A. BRADSHAW	D. 4. 10
Pte. P. BURKE	AS. 4. 5	L/Bdr. D.P. CULLEN	J. 1. 7
Spr. L. DAY	D. 5. 3	Gnr. W. EVERETT	C. 10. 39
Pte. T. FARMERY	B. 4. 24	Pte. G. FROST	B. 3. 32
Pte. W.A. GOULDING	AS. 4. 9	Pte. L. GRIEVE	B. 2. 44
Pte. W.H. GROCOTT	C. 6. 14	Pte. S.G. GRUNDY	B. 3. 8
Pte. G. HARPER	AS. 4. 2	Pte. G. HEATON	B. 10. 16 *
Cpl. J. HEATON	B. 9. 10 *	Sgt. M.G. HUDSTON	C. 8. 37
Spr. F. HUTCHINSON	B. 1. 40	AC. J.E. HYDE	D. 8. 77
Gnr. E. KIRK	D. 9. 10	Gnr. B. LISTER	AS. 3. 6
AB. R. MIDGLEY	B. 8. 34	Fusilier. E. RACE	C. 10. 3
L/Cpl. H. RACE	C. 10. 3	Pte. J. SHEA	B. 10. 12
Pte. T. SWANN	B. 7. 21	Pte. H.J. TUCKWELL	B. 10. 18
AB. H. WILLIAMSON	B. 3. 38		

* Buried in same grave.

RE-DEDICATION OF THE WAR MEMORIAL

The re-dedication of the Cudworth War Memorial took place at St. John the Baptist Church in Cudworth on Monday the 20th of September 2004, commencing at 3 p.m.

The Lord Bishop of Wakefield, the Right Reverend Stephen Platten, assisted by the Rural Dean of Barnsley, the Reverend Allan Briscoe Vicar of St. Peter's, and the Vicar of the Parish of Cudworth, the Reverend Father David Nicholson, conducted the service.

In addition to the members of the Local History Group, Church members and members of the general public, there were a number of distinguished guests and representatives from various organisations who attended the ceremony including:

Her Majesty's Lord-Lieutenant for South Yorkshire, Mr. D.B. Moody.

The Mayor and Mayoress of Barnsley, Councillor Roy Millar and his wife Christine.

The Member of Parliament for Barnsley Central, Mr. Eric Illsley.

Barnsley Council Leader, Mr. Steve Houghton.

Cudworth Councillors, Mr. Joe Hayward and Mr. Charles Wraith.

Lt/Colonel Julian Fox, Captain David Morris from the East and West Riding Regiment, Fontenay (D.W.R.) Company.

Major Deeds from the Light Infantry. (K.O.Y.L.I.).

Officer R Parker, Flt. Sgt. C. Scott (Standard Bearer) and cadets B. Beardshall and B. Reynard from the Air Training Corps.

British Legion Members from the Royston and Grimethorpe branches.

Area Forum Officer and representatives from the Cudworth and West Green Partnership,

Cudworth Library and Barnsley Archives.

Staff and children from the Cudworth Primary Schools.

Front row. Alex Clark, Florence Whittlestone, Gerald Alliott and Marion Hodge
Back row. Jack Thompson, Gwen Hampson, John Hayhoe, Cliff Gorman and
Tony Turner.

Members of the Group arrived early to welcome guests, show people to their seats and distribute the 'Order of Service'.

The Bishop of Wakefield entered the Church as the congregation sang, "Praise to the Lord, the Almighty, the King of Creation".

Father Nicholson welcomed everyone to the Service of Re-dedication and led the Act of Reconciliation for past sins.

There followed a reading from the Book of Wisdom of Solomon, Chapter 3 verses 1 to 9 by Monica Street, a member of the Parochial Church Council.

After the Hymn "Tell out, my soul" the Rural Dean Reverend Alan Briscoe, read the second lesson from St. John's Gospel, Chapter 15 verses 12 to 17, before Father David led the Prayers. After the Prayers everyone joined in singing "All people that on earth do dwell".

Then the Right Reverend, the Lord Bishop of Wakefield, and Father David gave thanks to the members of the Cudworth Local History and Heritage Group for the work in getting the Memorial renovated and providing additional names not included when the Memorial was first dedicated in July, 1920. They also paid tribute to all the men and women who lost their lives. Then followed the Hymn "O God our help in ages past".

On completion of this Hymn the Altar Party, followed by the Distinguished Guests and the rest of the congregation, moved in silence to the newly renovated War Memorial for the Act of Re-dedication and our own act of Commitment.

The Reverend Father David Nicholson reads out the names that have been added to the War Memorial.

The Lord Bishop of Wakefield, the Right Reverend Stephen Platten carries out the act of Re-dedication.

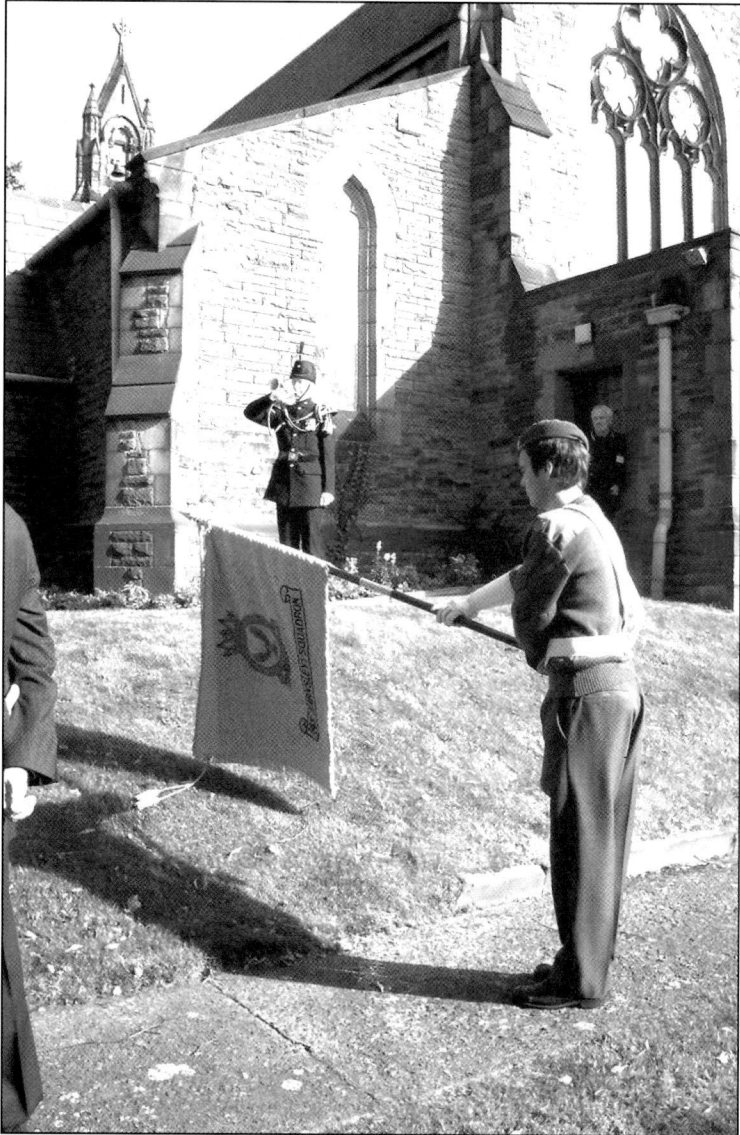

Bugler John Goose sounds the Last Post and
Flt. Sgt C. Scott of the Air Training Corps lowers the
Standard of the Barnsley Squadron.

Mr. A.L. Plunkett of the Royston Branch lays a wreath on behalf of the British Legion.

Florence Whittlestone lays a wreath on behalf of
the Cudworth Local History and Heritage Group.

The Re-dedication service ended with a Blessing by the Bishop and the singing of the National Anthem. The Altar Party then returned into the Church.

The clergy, distinguished guests and members of the congregation adjourned to the Valley Centre on Manor Road, Cudworth for a buffet reception.

People arrive at the Valley Centre

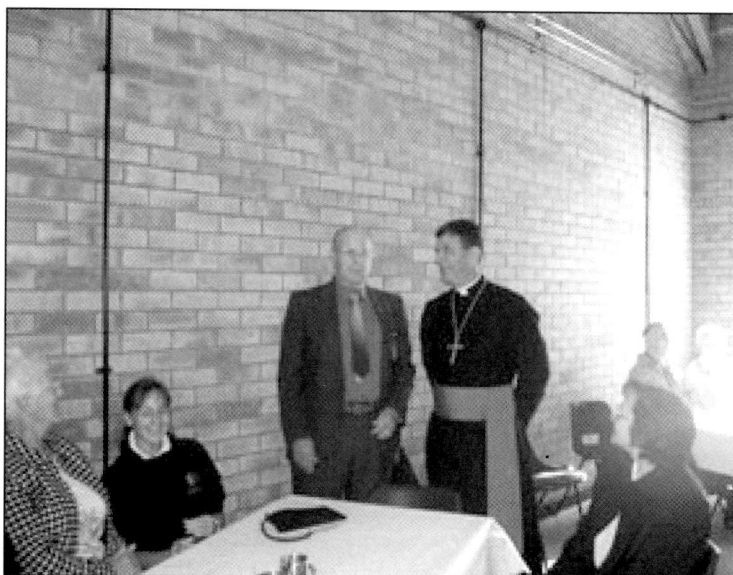

The Bishop talks to Don and Eileen Clark and Maureen Hayhoe as they gather for the Buffet Reception.

CHAPTER 2.

CHRONOLOGY

OF

WORLD WAR ONE.

World War 1 Calendar

1914   ***June***: Archduke Franz Ferdinand of Austria was assassinated in Sarajevo on June the 28th.

July: The German government issued blank cheques to Austria, offering support for the war in Serbia. Austria gave an ultimatum to Serbia. Serbia accepted all but two points. Austria refused to accept a compromise and declared war. Russia began mobilization to defend their Serbian ally. Germany demanded Russian demobilization.

Aug: Germany declared war on Russia. France mobilized to assist Russian ally. Germans occupied Luxemburg and demanded access to Belgium territory, which was refused. Germany declared war on France and invaded Belgium. Briton declared war on Germany then on Austria. Dominions within the Empire, including Australia automatically involved in the battle of Tannenburg between Central Powers and Russia. Russian army encircled.

Sept: British and French troops halted German advance just short of Paris and drove them back. First Battle of the Marne, and of Aisne. This was the beginning of trench warfare.

Oct-Nov The First Battle of Ypres. Britain declared war on Turkey.

1915   ***April-May:*** Gallipoli offensive launched by British and Dominion troops against the Turkish forces. Second Battle of Ypres. The first use of poison gas by the Germans. Italy joined the war against Austria. German submarine sank ocean liner Lusitania, later bringing USA into the war.

Aug-Sept: Warsaw evacuated by the Russians. Battle of Tarnopoi. Vilna taken by the Germans. Tsar Nicholas II took supreme command of Russian forces.

1916   ***Jan:*** Final evacuation of British and Dominion troops from Gallipoli

Feb: German offensive against Verdun began, with huge German losses for very little territorial gain.

May: Naval battle of Jutland between British and German Imperial fleet ended inconclusively, but put a stop to further German naval participation in the war.

June: Russian (Brusilov) offensive against Ukraine began.

July-Nov: The first Battle of the Somme, a sustained Anglo-French offensive that won very little territory and lost a huge number of lives.

Aug: Hindenburg and Ludendorf took command of the German armed forces. Rumania entered the war against Austria but was rapidly overrun.

Sept: British used an early design of tanks on the Western front.

Nov: Nivelle replaced Joffre as commander of the French forces. The Battle of Ancre took place on the Western Front.

Dec: French complete recapture of Verdun fortifications. Austrians occupied Bucharest.

1917   *Feb:* Germany declared unrestricted submarine warfare. Russian Revolution and Tsarist rule overthrown.

March: British seizure of Baghdad and occupied Persia.

March-April Germans retreated to the Siegfried Line (Arras-Soissons) on the Western Front.

April-May: USA entered the war against Germany. Unsuccessful British and French offensive. Mutinies among French troops Nevelle replaced by Petain.

July-Nov: Third Ypres offensive, including the Battle of Passchendaele.

Sept: Germans occupied Riga.

Oct Nov: Battle of Caporetta saw Italian troops defeated by Austrians.

Dec: Jerusalem taken by British forces under Allenby.

1918   *Jan:* US President Woodrow Wilson proclaimed Fourteen Points as a basis for a peace settlement.

March: Treaty of Brest-Litovsk with Central Powers ended Russian participation in the war with substantial concessions of territory and reparations. Second Battle of the Somme began with German Spring offensive.

July-Aug: Allied counter offensive, including tank attacks at Amiens, drove Germans back to the Siegfried Line.

Sept: Hindenburg and Ludendorff called for an armistice.

Oct: Armistice offered on the basis of the Fourteen Points. German naval mutinies occurred at Kiel and Wilhelmshaven.

Nov: Austria-Hungary signed armistice with the Allies. Kaiser Wilhelm II of Germany went into exile. Provisional government under social democrat Friedrich Ebert formed. Germany agreed armistice on the 11th of November. Fighting on the Western Front stopped.

1919   *Jan:* Peace conference opened in Versailles.

May: Demands presented to Germany.

June: Germany signed a peace treaty at Versailles on the 29th of June 1919 (ratified in Paris on the 19th of January 1920).

Peace treaties with other Central Powers were signed as follows:

Austria - Treaty of St German-en-Laye, on the 10th of September 1919 (ratified in Paris on the 16th of July 1920).

Bulgaria - Treaty of Neuilly, in November.

1920   Hungary - Treaty of Trianon on the 4th of June 1920.

Turkey - Treaty of Sevres on the 10th of August 1920. This was not ratified and was superseded by the Treaty of Lausanne on the 4th of July 1923 (ratified the same year).

CHAPTER 3.

WORLD WAR ONE

CASUALTIES.

THE MEN WHO MADE THE SUPREME SACRIFICE
IN THE FIRST WORLD WAR.

ALLEN ERNEST. 14587 Private 2nd Battalion Duke of Wellington's (West Riding Regiment).

Ernest Allen was born in Cudworth and in 1921 when His Majesty's Stationery Office published "Soldiers who Died in the Great War 1914-19", his parents, Isaiah and Annie Allen lived at 12 Brook Street, Fryston, Castleford. He had enlisted at Castleford.

Aged 19, he died on Thursday the 6th of May 1915 of wounds received in France and Flanders and was buried in the Bailleul Communal Cemetery Extension in Northern France. The grave reference is II. A. 132.

ALLOTT ARTHUR. 10501 Private 2nd Battalion York and Lancaster Regiment.

Arthur Allott, the son of Mathew Allott, was born in the Blackburn district of Sheffield and resided at School Terrace, Cudworth with his sister Mrs Horner, his father having been killed in a mining accident at the Jordan Colliery, Meadow Hall, Sheffield. He enlisted at Pontefract a few months before the outbreak of the war.

His death, at the age of 23, was announced in the Barnsley Chronicle under the heading of *"CUDWORTH BOMB THROWER KILLED. TWELVE MONTHS OF WARFARE."* *Private Allott was killed in action on August 9th 1915 in France. A message of sympathy has been received from their Majesties the King and Queen*

Private Allott is remembered on the Ypres (Menin Gate) Memorial, Panels 36 and 55.

His brother Private Thomas Allott was wounded at Ypres.

ANDREWS HENRY. 22098 Private 8th Battalion King's Own Yorkshire Light Infantry.

Henry Andrews was the husband of Mary Ann Andrews (remarried Mary Ann Pickard) of 54 Snydale Road, Cudworth. His parents were Thomas and Ann Andrews of 49 Market Street. He was employed as a miner at Brierley Colliery, enlisting with the K.O.Y.L.I. in October 1914 at South Kirkby.

Having served in Salonika, Egypt and France he was killed in action, at the age of 30, in the Ypres Salient on Thursday the 30th of June 1917. He is remembered with honour on the Tyne Cot Memorial in Zonnebeke on Panels 108 to 111.

ARNOLD RICHARD HENRY. 4095 Private 1st/5th Battalion King's Own Yorkshire Light Infantry.

Richard Henry Arnold was the son of John and Sarah Arnold of 19 Jackson Street, Cudworth (1915) and later 39, Charles Street (1918). His father was a railway guard.

Private Arnold was killed in action on the Somme on the 5th of July 1916. He is remembered with honour on the Thiepval Memorial, Pier and Face 11C and 12A.

AUSTWICK WALTER A.

We failed to locate a W.A. Austwick in the Commonwealth War Graves Commission records or "Soldiers Who Died in the Great War".

The C.W.G.C. website listed 12 men with the surname Austwick but none with the initials W.A. W.H. was in the King's Own Scottish Borderers and W.N. was in the Essex Regiment but both men have no next of kin or place of residence given. Ambrose Austwick served in the Durham Light Infantry and also has no next of kin etc.

The most likely candidate is 13/1344 Private A. Austwick who died on the 18th of May 1917 and had served in the 13th Battalion of the York and Lancaster Regiment, but no reference is given to his next of kin, place of birth or residence. He was buried in the Albuera Cemetery, Bailleul-Sire-Berthoult in grave reference South. C. 16. "Soldiers Who Died In The Great War" lists 13/1344 Pte. A. Austrick as born in Shafton and enlisting at Silkstone.

The 1918 Cudworth Electoral Roll lists several Austwick families in the village but no evidence to connect W.A. Austwick with any particular family.

BALL THOMAS. 152969 Private Scottish Horse (formerly 2nd Life Guards).

Thomas Ball was the husband of Grace Ball of 147 Barnsley Road, Cudworth and the son of Thomas and Harriet Ball. He was born in Castleford and enlisted at Hoyland.

He served in the South African Campaign from 1899 to 1902. Other Regiments with which he served were the Household Cavalry and the Imperial Camel Corps.

At the age of 36, Private Ball died of wounds in the V.A.D. Hospital, Cupar, County Fife, on the 6th of January 1918 and was buried on the 10th in the Cudworth Cemetery, grave reference SE5. 3. 6. No service was held because he had not been baptised.

BARKER WILLIAM LEONARD. T/293465 Driver Heavy Transport, Royal Army Service Corps.

William Leonard Barker was the husband of Lucy Barker and lived at 14 Methley Street, Cudworth.

Private Barker died of wounds on the 17th of March 1920, aged 31, and was buried in the Cudworth Cemetery in grave reference B. 4. 38.

BARNES FRED. 22684 Private 1st/5th Battalion Prince of Wales's Own (West Yorkshire Regiment).

Fred Barnes, born in Halifax Nova Scotia, was the son of Hy Barnes of 4 Quarry Street, Cudworth. He enlisted at Barnsley and was formerly Private 1219 in the York and Lancaster Regiment.

Private Barnes was killed on Friday the 28th of July 1916, by a large shell explosion at the rear of the dugout. His grave is in the Blighty Wood Cemetery at Authuile Wood on the Somme. The grave location is II. K. 9.

BASSETT THOMAS. 2493 Private 1ˢᵗ/5ᵗʰ Battalion 9ᵗʰ Platoon York and Lancaster Regiment.

Thomas Bassett resided in Cudworth at 5 George Street, Pontefract Road, Cudworth. He was a member of the Boys Brigade and the football team at St. John's.

Enlisting at Barnsley, Private Bassett was killed in action on Saturday the 10ᵗʰ of July 1915 at 18.30 hours by a bursting shell in the trenches. His Memorial is on the Ypres (Menin Gate) Memorial Panel 36 and 55.

BATTY JAMES WILLIAM. 15321 Private 9ᵗʰ Battalion York and Lancaster Regiment.

James William Batty was born in Cudworth but at the time of enlisting at Mexborough, he resided in Swinton.

Private Batty was killed in action on the Somme on Saturday the 1ˢᵗ of July 1916. He is remembered with honour on the Thiepval Memorial, Pier and Face 14A and 14B.

BLACKBURN ARNOLD. 201244 Private 2ⁿᵈ/4ᵗʰ Battalion York and Lancaster Regiment. (Hallamshire Battalion) (Territorial Force)

Arnold Blackburn was the youngest son of George Arthur and Elizabeth Blackburn of 11 Bow Street, Cudworth. He worked at the Sheffield Telegraph newspaper.

Enlisting in 1914, Private A. Blackburn was reported as missing on the 3ʳᵈ of May 1917 but was recorded as being killed in action on Saturday the 5ᵗʰ May. He was 18 years old. His memorial is to be found on Bay 8 of the Arras Memorial, located in the Faubourg-d'Amiens Cemetery.

BLACKBURN HUGH POTTS. 51411 PRIVATE 11ᵗʰ Battalion Prince of Wales's Own (West Yorkshire Regiment).

Hugh Potts Blackburn was the eldest son of George Arthur and Elizabeth Blackburn of 11 Bow Street, Cudworth. He worked in the family dairy business.

He enlisted at Sheffield and died of wounds on Saturday the 22ⁿᵈ of September 1917, at the age of 21, after being admitted unconscious to the 47ᵗʰ General Hospital in France and failed to recover. He is buried in the Mont Huon Military Cemetery at Le Treport, grave reference IV. N. 4A.

BONDS FRANK. 240500 Lance Corporal 1ˢᵗ/5ᵗʰ Battalion King's Own Yorkshire Light Infantry.

Frank Bonds, the son of Iden and Ann Bonds of 13 St. John's Cottages Cudworth was born in Monk Bretton and baptised there on the 7ᵗʰ of August 1898 aged 3.

He worked at Grimethorpe Colliery and enlisted at South Kirkby in 1914.

Reported as missing on 5ᵗʰ of July 1916, he was last seen going over the top with his Captain on a scouting mission. Private Bonds was killed in a land mine explosion at the age of 20.

He is remembered with honour on the Thiepval Memorial and his brother's headstone in Cudworth Cemetery.

BONDS WILLIAM. 14/1327 Private 14th (Service) Battalion (2nd Barnsley Pals) York and Lancaster Regiment.

William Bonds, the son of Iden and Ann Bonds of 13 St. John's Cottages Cudworth.

Private Bonds died of wounds 0n the 23rd of March 1919 at the age of 34, and is buried in Cudworth (St. John the Baptist) churchyard, grave reference ASE 2. 12. His brother, Frank is remembered on his headstone.

BOWEN ARTHUR. 13/100 Private 13th (Service) Battalion (1st Barnsley Pals) York and Lancaster Regiment.

Arthur Bowen was married with two children and lived at 17 The Brickyard, Shafton. He worked at Grimethorpe Colliery and enlisted in October 1914.

He was washing at 6 pm, on Friday the 11th of August 1916, when an enemy rifle grenade exploded nearby and a piece of shrapnel entered his heart. He died at the age of 33 was buried in grave III. K. 15 at the St. Vaast Post Military Cemetery, Richebourg-l' Avoue, Pas de Calais.

BOWERING G.J. 5611 Private 1st/5th Battalion King's Own Yorkshire Light Infantry.

Private G.J. Bowering enlisted at Doncaster and was killed in action on Tuesday the 12th of September 1916. He is buried in the Lonsdale Cemetery, Authuille. His grave reference is IX. A. 4.

BOWERING J.

The C.W.G.C. website has 6 soldiers called Bowering with the initial "J" but no conclusive identification can be made.

BROADHURST GEORGE. 14/406 Private 1st/5th Battalion York and Lancaster Regiment.

George Broadhurst was the husband of Doris Broadhurst of 5 Lockwood Lane, Goldthorpe and the son of Albert and Jessie Broadhurst of 9 George Street, Cudworth. He was born in Royston and enlisted at Barnsley.

Private Broadhurst was killed in action on the 12th of April 1918 and is buried in the Aire Communal Cemetery, grave reference II. B. 23.

BROMLEY JOHN WILLIAM. 14/284 Sergeant 14th (Service) Battalion (2nd Barnsley Pals) York and Lancaster Regiment.

John William Bromley was born in Caistor, near Grimsby. Married to Alice, they had a young son named James and lived at 35 Garden Cottages, Cudworth.

He enlisted in the 14th Battalion of the York and Lancaster Regiment at Barnsley on the 21st of January 1915 and was posted to 'B' Company. Prior to this he worked as a stoker at New Monckton Colliery.

Having previous experience serving in the South African War with the Lincolnshire Regiment he was promoted to Sergeant on the 5th of February 1915.

The 14th Battalion joined the 12th and 13th Battalions of the York and Lancaster Regiments *(Sheffield City Battalion and 1st Barnsley Pals)* and the 11th East Lancashire Regiment *(Accrington Pals)* at Penkridge Bank Camp, Cannock Chase to form the 94th Infantry Brigade (31st Division). They were transferred, first to Ripon Camp, then to Hurdcott Camp before finally embarking from Devonport for Port Said in Egypt on board H.M.T. Andania. After two months in Egypt the threat of a Turkish attack had diminished and the Division was ordered to the Western Front to take part in the planned offensive on the Somme. John Bromley was a member of two companies from the 14th Battalion that accompanied the 13th Battalion on board H.M.T. Megantic for the voyage to Marseilles. (Pictures of the H.M.T. Andania and the H.M.T. Megantic are included with the information on Corporal R. Roberts of the 13th Battalion York and Lancaster Regiment).

The Battle of the Somme commenced with the attack on the village of Serre on the 1st of July 1916. 'B' Company fought on the left of the British Line. The attack started at 07.30 hrs. Very early in the attack John Bromley received bullet wounds to the knee and foot. It is thought that he lay in a shell hole all day and that he was brought back or able to crawl back to his lines when darkness fell. On the 2nd of July he was admitted to the 19th Casualty Clearing Station at Beauval.

Sergeant Bromley died of wounds on the 17th of July 1916 in N[o.] 2 Stationary Field Hospital as a result of serious wounds received in the "Big Push" on the 1st of July at the Somme. He is buried in the Abbeville Communal Cemetery, grave reference IV. E. 8.

BROOK ARTHUR. 205092 Private 1st/5th Battalion West Yorkshire Regiment. (Prince of Wales's Own)

Arthur Brook was born in Cudworth, the son of Walter and Elizabeth Ann Brook of 6 Prospect Street.

He enlisted at Barnsley and at the age of 19 was killed in action on the 9th of October 1917. He is remembered on the Tyne Cot Memorial at Zonnebeke, Panels 42 to 47 and 162.

BROOKES J.

The name "Brookes J" gives 37 hits on C.W.G.C. website, many in Yorkshire regiments, but with no conclusive evidence that connects any of them to Cudworth.

BROOKS JOHN. 27264 Private 11th Battalion East Lancashire Regiment.

John Brooks was born in Wigan and lived with his wife at 4 Pinfold Cottages, Darfield Road, otherwise known as the Back Row. Working as a miner at Grimethorpe Colliery he enlisted at Barnsley.

An appeal by his wife was made in the local press, for information concerning his fate, as he had not been heard of for over a month. John Brooks had been killed in the Battle of Serre on Saturday the 1st of July 1916 at the age of 27. He is remembered with honour on the Thiepval Memorial Pier and Face 6C. He formerly served with the 1st Barnsley Pals, changing regiments as part of battlefield regrouping.

BUCKLEY JOSEPH MITCHELL. 240551 Pte. 1st/6th Duke of Wellington's (West Riding Regiment)

Joseph Mitchell Buckley was the third son of George G. (a carting contractor) and Emily Buckley. The 1891 census shows them living at 7 Wilkinson's Yard, Worsbrough with Joseph 3 years old. The family history shows them moving first to Barnsley and then to Cudworth in the early nineteen hundreds where they lived at 4, 6 and 8 The Green, Lower Cudworth the family having increased to 9 children. They left Cudworth in 1918 to live in Doncaster and Harriet, the only daughter returned to live at Cudworth in 1922.

The C.W.G.C. records show George G. Buckley "living at 8 Skellow Road, Carcroft, Doncaster and Joseph Mitchell being a native of Worsboro Dale".

"Soldiers Who Died in the Great War" record Joseph Mitchell Buckley as *"living in Clayton West and enlisting at Huddersfield (Doncaster)"*.

Private Buckley died on Thursday the 9th of May 1918 at the age of 31 and was buried in grave reference IX. B. 60 in the Boulogne Eastern Cemetery, France. His headstone states "Born at Darley Villa Worsborodale".

BURKE PETER. 240659 Private 2nd/5th Battalion King's Own Yorkshire Light Infantry.

Peter Burke was the son of Peter and Sarah Burke of 17 Starmer Street, Cudworth.

Private Peter Burke enlisted at South Kirkby and died of wounds at home on Sunday 15th April 1917 at the age of 57. His wife Louisa, who died in March 1928 at the age of 62 and his son Thomas who died, age 23, on the 19th of March 1926 are buried in the same grave in the Cudworth Cemetery, reference AS. 4. 5.

The date of his death in the Commonwealth War Graves Commission records and the date on the grave are the same, confirming that it is the same person.

CALE JOHN. 24382 Private 2nd Battalion York and Lancaster Regiment.

John Cale was the son of Thomas and Emma Cale of 226 Barnsley Road, Cudworth. He was born in Cudworth and baptised on the 2nd of April 1893.

He enlisted at Barnsley.

Aged 21 and single, he was killed in action on Wednesday the 12th of October 1916 and is remembered on the Thiepval Memorial and also on the Roll of Honour in the Cudworth West End Working Men's Club.

CHAPPELL ALBERT. 19750 Private 8th Battalion King's Own Yorkshire Light Infantry.

Albert Chappell was born in Sheffield, his father Edward, lived at 15 The Avenue, Newtown, Cudworth. His wife Annie remarried and became Annie Jaques, living at 103, Barnsley Road. He worked at Grimethorpe Colliery and enlisted at Pontefract.

He was killed on the Somme on Saturday the 1st of July 1916 aged 23 and is remembered with honour on the Thiepval Memorial.

CLARE HENRY. 14/19 Private 14th (Service) Battalion (2nd Barnsley Pals) York and Lancaster Regiment.

Henry Clare was born in Royston, married with two children and lived at 193 Barnsley Road, Cudworth. He worked as a miner at Brierley Colliery.

Killed in action on the Somme on Sunday the 4th of June 1916, aged 26. He was brought in from no-man's land having been killed, probably by shrapnel from British shells that fell short. He is buried at Sucrerie Military Cemetery at Colincamps.

CLARE JABEZ BENJAMIN. 4431 Private 1st/5th Battalion King's Own Yorkshire Light Infantry.

Jabez Clare, one of four brothers, was born in Carlton in the spring of 1898. He worked in the mines as a pony driver.

The Barnsley Chronicle reported; "*Amongst the heavy Cudworth casualties is Pte Jabez B. Clare. Enlisting when only 17 years of age in the 1st / 5th K.O.Y.L.I., Pte Clare spent his first day in the trenches on his eighteenth birthday. In civil life he lived with his father and sister at 201, Victoria Terrace, Pontefract Road, Cudworth. The official intimation was received by his sister (Mrs. Philips) at the address mentioned on Friday last and a letter received from his Quartermaster Sergeant reads: - "It is with very deep regret I have to inform you of your brother's death on July 8th. Pte. J.B. Clare was killed in action whilst doing his duty nobly for his King and country. He was fearless of any work that was given him to do, also a promising lad with a career suddenly ended. In might be some consolation to know he suffered no pain being instantly killed. He was buried in the soldiers' cemetery just behind the line. Please accept our deepest sympathy in your great loss of a good brother. Believe me, yours sincerely, Quartermaster-Sergeant Firth." Pte. Clare has two brothers out in France. His brother Thomas is a stretcher-bearer in the Barnsley Battalion, whilst the other brother Philip Henry, was a Sergeant in the 2nd Barnsley Battalion, but sacrificed his three stripes to go out with the Royal Engineers before the Battalion was ready. Another brother, Rev. Joseph Clare is a Methodist Minister having been elected secretary of the Christian Endeavour Society, Osceola, Iowa.*"

On the 5th of July 1916, Private J.B. Clare was buried at Serre Road Cemetery No 2 in grave reference V. C. 14. He is also remembered on the gravestone of his parents, Joseph & Betsy Clare in Cudworth Churchyard, where his age is given as 18 years and 6 months.

CLARE SIDNEY. 46877 Private 7th Battalion Leicestershire Regiment.

Sidney Clare was born in Woodstone, Lincolnshire but resided in Cudworth.

He enlisted at Mexborough and was killed in action on Friday the 22nd March 1918. Private Clare is remembered on the Pozieres Memorial, Somme, Panels 29 and 30. Also remembered on the memorial within the Cudworth Methodist Chapel.

CLARKSON REUBEN. 1831 Private 1st/4th Battalion East Lancashire Regiment.

Reuben Clarkson was born in Cudworth, he enlisted at Padiham in Lancashire. Private Clarkson was killed in action at Gallipoli on Friday the 4th of June 1915 and is remembered with honour on the Helles Memorial in Turkey. Panels 113 to 117.

CLAY WILLIAM. 14/510 Private 6th Battalion York and Lancaster Regiment.

William Clay was born in Bucknall, Stoke on Trent, Staffordshire, the son of Mr T and Rebecca Clay of 23 Somerset Street, Cudworth. He enlisted at Barnsley and was killed in action on Tuesday the 9th of October 1917. He is remembered on the Tyne Cot Memorial on Panels 125 to 128.

CONNICK WILLIAM. KW/183 Able Seaman Nelson Battalion RN Division RNVR.

William was the son of Thomas Connick of 84 Chapel Street, Leigh in Lancashire and resided at 62 Lunn View, Cudworth. Employed as a miner at Grimethorpe Colliery.

Formerly in the York and Lancaster Regiment, he was killed in action at the age of 23 on Sunday the 6th June 1915 in Gallipoli. He is remembered on the Helles Memorial in Turkey. Panels 8 to 15.

COOPER JONAS.

COPLEY WILLIAM. 1451 Private 1st/5th Battalion York and Lancaster Regiment.

William Copley was born in Featherstone, lived at 36 Bloemfontein Street, Cudworth and was employed as a miner at Grimethorpe Colliery.

He enlisted at Barnsley and had been wounded and gassed three times before being killed in action on Friday the 7th of July 1916 at the age of 22. He is remembered with honour on the Thiepval Memorial on Pier and Face 14A and 14B.

A family member of William Copley examines the Memorial Book at The Thiepval Memorial.

DARNELL WILLIAM HENRY. SS/114438 Stoker 1st Class H.M.S. "Good Hope".

William Darnell was killed in action on the 1st of November 1914 and is remembered with honour on the Portsmouth Naval Memorial on Panel 4.

The Battle of Coronel.

H.M.S. Good Hope was a cruiser, launched in February 1901 at the Fairfield Govan shipyard. She was a member of the 6th Cruiser Squadron and was used as the Flagship of Rear-Admiral Craddock in the hunt for the Admiral Graf Spee.

On the 29th of October 1914 one of the Squadron, a light cruiser H.M.S. Glasgow was despatched to Coronel to gather intelligence on the German Squadron. On the 1st of November the Glasgow located German vessels. The Spee formed a battle line including the Scharnhorst, Gneisenau, Leipzig and Dresden. The British Squadron was composed of The Good Hope, Monmouth, Glasgow and Otranto. The British Squadron still had the opportunity to slip away in the poor light, but Rear-Admiral Craddock did not want to risk losing the Spee during the night so the British ships turned towards the German ships.

The British Squadron was highlighted by the setting sun to their rear, and the Germans were hard to see in the failing light. At approximately 19.30 hrs., the German cruisers opened fire from a range of about 6.5 miles. The third salvo from the Scharnhorst hit H.M.S. Good Hope, knocking out her forward 9.2-inch gun causing a sheet of flame. Monmouth was also hit by the third salvo from the Gneisenau setting her forward turret on fire. The German gun crews maintained rapid and accurate fire. Both the leading British cruisers received over 30 hits, whilst the British reply was ineffectual. The visibility deteriorated such that the Germans had to aim at the fires on board the British ships and the British could only aim at the flashes from the enemy guns.

Leipzig and Glasgow engaged each other and the Dresden opened fire on the Otranto, which quickly pulled out of line and fled. This enabled the Dresden to join the Leipzig in her attack on the Glasgow.

Craddock closed the range to just over 3 miles to bring his 6-inch guns into range. The Spee saw this as an attempt to launch a torpedo attack and steamed to increase the range.

At 19.50 hrs H.M.S. Good Hope suffered a magazine explosion that crippled the ship, which drifted out of sight and sank soon after. There were no survivors.

H.M.S. Monmouth was on fire and listing to port. H.M.S. Glasgow had been hit five times and on seeing that the Monmouth was beyond help fled to avoid certain destruction and to warn the approaching H.M.S. Canopus to turn back. The Monmouth, unable to fire, was still flying her White Ensign. The newly arrived German ship, the Nűrnberg, found her and finished the Monmouth off with close range gun fire, seventy-five gun flashes being observed by the Glasgow. Once again there were no survivors.

The German Squadron detached the Leipzip and Dresden to find H.M.S. Glasgow and H.M.S. Otranto that were heading for the Falkland Islands whilst the rest of their cruisers returned to Valparaiso to coal and provision.

Britain had suffered its first defeat for over one hundred years with the loss of two armoured cruisers and nearly 1600 crew. The only damage to the Germans was two hits on the Scharnhorst and four hits and three wounded on the Gneisenau.

DENT JAMES. 13/266 Corporal 13th (Service) Battalion (1st Barnsley Pals) York and Lancaster Regiment.

James Dent was born in Belle Green, Cudworth and baptised on the 25th of April 1894. He was the son of John and Annie Dent.

He enlisted at Barnsley and was killed in action on the 28th of June 1918. Corporal Dent is remembered with honour on the Ploegsteert Memorial at Comines-Warneton near Hainaut, Belgium, Panel 8.

DOBSON WILLIAM. 44046 Private 2nd Battalion York and Lancaster Regiment.

William Dobson was born in Oldham, Lancashire the son of Martha and Frederick Dobson of 2 Pontefract Road, Cudworth and the first husband of Florence Hellewell, 62 Redhill Avenue, Barnsley.

He enlisted at Barnsley and was killed in action, at the aged of 29, on Thursday the 21st of March 1918. Private Dobson is remembered with honour on the Arras Memorial on Bay 8.

DOUGHTY FRED. 13/1253 Lance Corporal 13th (Service) Battalion (1st Barnsley Pals) York and Lancaster Regiment.

Fred Doughty was born in Shafton on the 19th of November 1889. He was the oldest son of William and Mary Jane Doughty who went to live at 20 Pontefract Road, Cudworth. He had five brothers Willie, Victor, Bernard, Laurence and Harold. They lived at 212 Pontefract Road,

Cudworth. He was a miner and enlisted at Barnsley on the 30th September 1914.

He served with the British Expeditionary Forces in Egypt. Lance Corporal Doughty was killed in action on Wednesday the 7th of June 1917. Aged 28, he was killed at the Battle of Oppy Wood and is buried in the Albuera Cemetery, Bailleul-Sire-Bethoult, grave D11.

DUCKWORTH ALBERT ROBINSON. PLY614/S Private Nᵒ· 4 Company Plymouth Battalion R.N. Division Royal Marine Light Infantry.

Albert Duckworth was born on the 16th of April 1890, the son of Henry and Mary Duckworth who lived with relatives in Cudworth. He worked as signalman on the Hull & Barnsley railway at Hemsworth. He was one of three Barnsley Lads who enlisted with Jack Clegg at Manchester on the 10th of November in 1914. Aged 24 he was 5 ft 6½" tall.

From the 12th of May 1915 until the 26th men of the Plymouth Battalion were supposedly 'resting' at Cape Helles, but were found employment digging communication trenches and building roads. On Thursday the 13th of May 1915 while they were in the process of constructing a makeshift bath in the so-called 'rest Camp' at Cape Helles, a Turkish shell fell on a section of No. 4 Coy. Plymouth Bn., wounding several and killing PLY 614/S Pte. Albert Duckworth age 25. Pte. Duckworth, of Cudworth, had distinguished himself at 'Y' Beach during the withdrawal & was rewarded with a 'Mention in Despatches'. Pte. Horace Bruckshaw, No. 4 Coy. wrote of the fatal incident : - *"Soon after we had completed our rough and ready toilet a big shell dropped right in amongst us knocking out seven or eight. Duckworth, the man who did such good work in the landing was blown to atoms"*. Harold Benfell, in his letter to the Barnsley Chronicle on the 10th of June 1916, also wrote of 'Y' Beach and his comrades, Hitchin & Duckworth: - *"Pte. R. Duckworth, of Cudworth, and Pte. S. Hitchin, of Royston were both in my section. Both of them met their fate while close to my side. We went to Port Said, Egypt, and awaited the great landing on the 25th of April when we again were engaged in one of the most trying positions of the Peninsular. We numbered about 1,100, and after a struggle up the high cliff at 'Y' Beach we began a hard fight with the Turks. All that night I had my work cut out carrying ammunition and it was then when Pte. Hitchin fell."* Further comments are made about the lack of Battle Honours for the Corps of Royal Marines at 'Y' Beach whilst others received them for the campaign.

Private Duckworth is remembered on the Helles Memorial in Turkey on Panels 2 to 7.

EADY JOHN. 48633 Private 8th Battalion Machine Gun Corps (Infantry).

John Eady was born in Cudworth in the spring of 1889. He enlisted at Pontefract.

Private Eady was killed in action on Wednesday the 24th of April 1918. He is buried in the Adelaide Cemetery at Villers-Bretonne near Somme. The grave reference is II. J. 18.

EBBAGE HARRY. 24006 Private 9th Battalion King's Own Yorkshire Light Infantry.

Harry Ebbage was born in the first quarter of 1895; his parents were Harry and Margaret Ebbage who lived at 18 Market Street, Cudworth. He was employed as a miner at Grimethorpe Colliery and enlisted at Barnsley.

Private Ebbage was admitted to N[o.] 5 General Hospital in France badly wounded in the thigh. Poison set in and his leg was amputated. He lived for only a few hours after the operation, dying on Wednesday the 7th of June 1916, aged 21.

He is buried in grave reference A. 24. 3. of the St. Sever Cemetery at Rouen.

EDER GEORGE. 13/290 Private 13th (Service) Battalion (1st Barnsley Pals) York and Lancaster Regiment.

Born in Halifax, George Eder, known locally as Dick, was the son of Mr & Mrs John Eder of Guest Yard, Cudworth. He was a miner at Grimethorpe Colliery.

Private George Eder was one of the first to join the 1st Barnsley Battalion. He was killed in action on Friday the 10th of August 1917, three days before his 23rd birthday, by a shell explosion. His grave is located in the Beehive Cemetery at Willerval, reference A. 9.

ELLIS ALFRED. 14/1010 Private 14th (Service) Battalion (2nd Barnsley Pals) York and Lancaster Regiment.

"B" Company.

Private Ellis was born in Cudworth and lived at 6 Sidcop Road, Cudworth and Ash Cottage, Shaw Lane, Cudworth. No further details have been confirmed.

ELLIS CHARLES HENRY. 28271 Private 14th (Service) Battalion (2nd Barnsley Pals) York and Lancaster Regiment.

Charles Henry Ellis was born in Knottingley, the son of H and E Ellis of 3 Higham Lane, Barugh Green.

He enlisted at Barnsley and was killed in action on Sunday the 11th of March 1917 at the age of 27. Private C.H. Ellis is buried in grave XXII. A. 8A of the Etaples Military Cemetery, Pas de Calais.

EMERY EDWARD. 5068 Corporal 1st Battalion Royal Munster Fusiliers.

Edward Emery was born in Carlton, the son of Edward and Mary 153 Moor Bottom, Cleckheaton, Huddersfield. He lived at Starmer Street, Cudworth and worked at Grimethorpe Colliery.

Enlisting at Barnsley in November 1914, he went to Salonika, then Egypt and on to France. At the age of 20 he died of wounds on Wednesday the 5th of July 1916 and is buried in the Bethune Town Cemetery, grave reference V. F. 53.

EVANS ERIC. 81610 Private 15th Battalion Durham Light Infantry.

Eric Evans was born and resided in Cudworth, he enlisted at Barnsley and was formerly Private 42299 in the York and Lancaster Regiment and was transferred to the Durham

Light Infantry. He was killed in action on the 29th of May 1918 and is remembered with honour on the Soissons Memorial at Aisne.

EVERETT CHARLES ERNEST. 81608 Lance Corporal 15th Battalion Durham Light Infantry.

Charles Everett was born in Southwark, London and resided in Cudworth with his mother, Sarah, at 34 Market Street, Cudworth.

He enlisted at Barnsley.

He was mentioned in despatches in the London Gazette on the 21st of December 1917.

Lance Corporal Everett was killed in action on Friday the 26th of April 1918 and is remembered on the Tyne Cot Memorial on Panels 128 to 131, 162 and 162A.

Lance Corporal Everett had previously served as Private 14/486 in the 14th (Service) Battalion (2nd Barnsley Pals) York and Lancaster Regiment.

FARMERY THOMAS. 241371 Private 1st/5th Battalion King's Own Yorkshire Light Infantry.

Thomas Farmery lived at 20 Somerset Street, Cudworth.

At the age of 43 he died of wounds on Wednesday the 27th of March 1918 and is buried in the Cudworth Cemetery, grave reference B. 4. 24.

The reference given is taken from the Commonwealth War Graves Commission records but the Cudworth burial records state B. 4. 26.

FENN ALBERT. 14/317 Private 13th (Service) Battalion (1st Barnsley Pals) York and Lancaster Regiment.

Albert Fenn was born in Havercroft and died of wounds at the age of 26. His death was reported in the Barnsley Chronicle as follows: -

PRIVATE ALFRED FENN

"Another Cudworthian to forfeit his life in the war is Private Alfred Fenn, who died of wounds on September 3rd, 1916. He enlisted in the 2nd Barnsley Battalion a year ago, at which time he was working at Monckton Main Colliery. He leaves a wife and three children with whom the deepest sympathy is felt in their great loss. They reside at 85, Victoria Terrace, Cudworth.

From the 1-2 London Casualty Clearing Station, B.E.F., Mrs. Fenn has received a kind and sympathetic letter from the Sister-in-Charge. "With deep regret I have to write of your husband's death. He was brought in this morning suffering from severe wounds in the abdomen and chest. Everything possible was done for him, but the injuries were too serious and he quickly sank. You will be comforted to know that he suffered very little pain; he was too weak to feel it, and he did not speak at all. He will be buried, with a service in the Cemetery near where he will rest with many of his fallen comrades." -- Captain H. Quest wrote: "Please allow me to offer you my most heartfelt sympathy in your great bereavement. I knew your husband very well and I can assure you that he always did his duty. This last time in the trenches he was put in charge of a few men and he performed his work very creditably indeed, and the company has lost the services of a very good man. It was a German machine gun, which brought about his end. He was one of a party with myself doing some work in 'No Man's Land' and when the enemy opened with machine gun fire your husband was unfortunately hit through the stomach and through the thigh. He was brought back to our lines by Sergt. Hadfield, of my Company, and taken to the dressing station where he received treatment and afterwards passed on to an advanced hospital where he died twelve hours later. He has been buried in a Military Cemetery behind the firing line, and may his soul rest in peace. The officers and men of the Company join me in expressing their most heartfelt sympathy towards you.""

The Commonwealth War Graves Commission gives his resting place as the Merville Communal Cemetery extension in Northern France reference I. A. 8.

FISHER GEORGE. 121953 Sapper 252nd Tunnelling Company, Royal Engineers.

George Fisher was born in Cudworth and enlisted at Darfield.

Sapper Fisher died of wounds on Wednesday the 5th of April 1916 and was buried in the St. Sever Cemetery, Roune Seine-Maritime in plot reference A. 19. 13.

FOULSTONE WILLIAM. M.M. 240658 Corporal 2nd/5th Battalion King's Own Yorkshire Light Infantry.

William Foulstone was born in Wombwell to Thomas and Betsy. He and his wife, also named Betsy, had a daughter, Marion L. Foulstone. They resided at 31 Garden Cottages, Pontefract Road, Cudworth.

He was employed as a miner at Monckton Colliery and enlisted at South Kirkby.

Corporal William Foulstone was killed in action on Tuesday the 27th of November 1917 and is remembered with honour on Panel 8 of the Cambrai Memorial at Louverval in France.

William Foulstone was awarded the Military Medal for Bravery and "Gazetted" in the London Gazette on the 13th of March 1918.

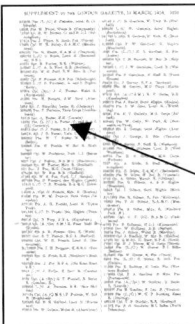

240658 Cpl. W. Foulstone, York. L.I. (Barnsley).
9607 Cpl. J. Fowler, R.A.M.C. (Blackburn).

Supplement to the London Gazette 13 MARCH 1918. 3233

FOWLER ERNEST. 3869 Private 1st/4th Battalion King's Own Yorkshire Light Infantry.

Ernest Fowler was single, the son of Ward and the late Emily Fowler who lived at 5 Sidcop Road, Cudworth.

At the age of 22 Private Fowler died of wounds on Monday the 20th of December 1915 as the result of being gassed at the Front. He is buried in the Lijssenthoek Military Cemetery at Poperinge in Belgium, grave reference II. D. 18.

His death was announced at the Cudworth council meeting on the 29th of January 1916 and reported in the Barnsley Chronicle on the same day as follows: -

CUDWORTH SOLDIER FATALLY GASSED.

COMMANDING OFFICER'S FINE TRIBUTE.

Pte. E. Fowler, whose parents reside at Cudworth, has died in Hospital from the effects of gas poisoning. The deceased was in the 4th Battalion K.O.Y.L.I.

In a letter to the parents Lieut. Colonel H.J. Haslegrave says: *"It is with deep regret I have to inform you that your son, Private E. Fowler, of the Battalion under my command has died from the effects of gas poisoning. The Germans sent over clouds of gas in the early morning and your son was one of the many who were gassed. Please accept my sincerest sympathy in this your sad bereavement of great loss. Your son was a brave lad and stuck it to the last, and he has died the death of a hero - fighting to uphold the honour and glory of the country he loved so dear, against an enemy who have to resort to do all kinds of scientific and mechanical devices in order to destroy man. Everything possible was done by the Doctor immediately and he was removed in the ambulance to the Casualty Clearing station where he died later. A record has been kept of his place of burial, and I hope at some future date to be able to tell you the exact spot where the body lies".*

From the hospital in France the rev. A.B. Brookes (Chaplain) wrote: *"I am very sorry indeed to inform you of your son's death. He was severely injured in the firing line and from the first there was no hope of his recovery. Everything possible was done for his comfort by the medical staff here, and I, too, did all I could for him. He was scarcely ever conscious and he passed peacefully away without feeling pain. I buried him later the same day in the Military Cemetery and his grave will be marked with a cross bearing his name. Please accept my deepest sympathy."*

FROST GEORGE. 340 Private 13th (Service) Battalion (1st Barnsley Pals) York and Lancaster Regiment.

George Frost was the son of Kate Frost who lived at 101 Barnsley Road, Cudworth.

Private Frost died of wounds on Wednesday the 22nd of May 1918 and was buried in the Cudworth Cemetery, grave reference B. 3. 32, on the 27th of May. He was 30 years of age.

GELDER WILLIAM. 14/153 Private 14th (Service) Battalion (2nd Barnsley Pals) York and Lancaster Regiment.

William Gelder was born in Cudworth and worked as a Platelayer on the Midland Railway at Cudworth. He enlisted at Barnsley.

The Commonwealth War Graves Commission records state that William Gelder was the son of S.A. Gelder of 160 Barnsley Road, Cudworth. The Barnsley Independent newspaper of 1917 gives his father's name as Robert Henry Gelder. S.A. Gelder could be his mother?

Both the C.W.G.C. and "Soldiers who Died in The Great War" list William Gelder serving with the 2nd Battalion York and Lancaster Regiment however his Army number 14/153 denotes that he was in the 14th Battalion, also known as the "2nd. Barnsley Pals". The low number shows that he must have been one of the first to join the "2nd local" Battalion. The report of his death in the Barnsley Independent in 1917 sheds some light on this. *"He was wounded in the knee and shoulder in the big push last July and was in Norwich Hospital for a time. He returned to the front to join the 2nd/5th Battalion Local Territorials as a machine gunner".*

Private Gelder was 21 years old, and single, when he died of wounds on Thursday the 19th of April 1917. His place of rest is in the Philosophe British Cemetery at Mazingarbe, grave reference II. N. 8.

GLOVER DAVID. 14/1401 Private 14th (Service) Battalion (2nd Barnsley Pals) York and Lancaster Regiment.

David Glover, age 34, was the son of the late Mr & Mrs W.H. Glover, native of Barnsley. The photograph is from a Barnsley Chronicle feature and bears the caption Pte. D. Glover (Cudworth, killed).

As with William Gelder the C.W.G.C. record states that he was in the 2nd Battalion York and Lancaster Regiment but "PALS" by Jon Cooksey lists him as being a member of the 14th Battalion.

Private Glover was single when he was killed in action on Wednesday the 16th of August 1916. He is buried in Auchonvillers Military Cemetery, grave reference II. G. 4.

GODDARD ARTHUR LISTER. 14451 Private 4th Battalion Coldstream Guards.

Arthur Lister Goddard was born in Barnsley, the son of Arthur Lister and Hannah Goddard of 156 Barnsley Road, Cudworth. At the time of his father's death in 1909 the address was given as 199 Barnsley Road.

Working as a miner at Brierley Colliery, he enlisted at Sheffield on the 2nd of January 1915 and was first in action at Loos in 1915.

Private Goddard is listed as dying of wounds on Monday the 19th of June 1916 and his resting place is the Wimereux Communal Cemetery, near Boulogne, grave reference I. N. 8A. He is also remembered on the Roll of Honour in the Cudworth West End Working Men's Club.

The minutes of the Cudworth Council Meeting state – *"He died at Base Stationary Hospital, Wimereux, near Boulogne. News was conveyed to his mother Mrs Bolton. He contracted kidney trouble after 10 months in the army. He would have been 21 on Friday 16th June. He played football for St. John's Football Club, and attended the Bible Class held by the Rev. Bell."*

GOLDTHORPE LEWIS. M.M. 7380 Private 10th Battalion Worcestershire Regiment.

Lewis Goldthorpe was the first husband of Minnie Lazenby of 171 Snydale Road, Cudworth. The address at the time of his death may have been 157 Snydale Road as stated in the 1915 Electoral Roll. He was the son of Joseph and Lydia Goldthorpe of Flash House, Thurlstone.

A Cudworth resident remembers that Lewis Goldthorpe lived in a shop across from the Dorothy Hyman Stadium. After his death his wife married Wallace Lazenby of Low Cudworth and lived on Moorland Terrace. They had four children, one of whom they named Lewis after Minnie's first husband.

Private Goldthorpe was killed in action on Friday the 13th of July 1917 at the age of 37. He is buried at the Croonaert Chapel Cemetery, Heuvelland, Belgium. The grave reference is C. 10.

His Majesty the King in the supplement to the London Gazette on 17th of September 1917 graciously approved the award of the Military Medal for Bravery in the Field to Private Lewis Goldthorpe. (9607)

town).
41183 Spr. W. Glynn, R.E. (St. Helens).
103170 Spr. A. T. Godden, R.E. (Reading).
7380 Pte. L. Goldthorpe, Worc. R. (Cudworth).
18380 Cpl. D. Gordon, H.L.I. (Musselburgh).

**Supplement to the London Gazette
17th SEPTEMBER 1917. 9607**

GOLEY JOHN JAMES. 8170 Sergeant 2nd Battalion Cheshire Regiment.

John James Goley was born in Cudworth, the son of Patrick (deceased) and Margaret Goley. He went to reside in Stockport and enlisted at Chester.

Sergeant Goley was killed in action on Sunday the 3rd of October 1915 and is remembered with honour on the Loos Memorial, Panels 49 and 50. He was 28 years old,

GOOSE GEORGE. M.M. 13/393 Corporal 13th (Service) Battalion (1st Barnsley Pals) York and Lancaster Regiment.

George Goose was married to Alice and had three children. A report in the Barnsley Chronicle gives their address as 4 Church Street, Cudworth but they lived at 71 St

John's Road, Cudworth at the time of the compilation of the Commonwealth War Graves Commission records. His father was Harry Goose who lived on Royston Lane.

Born in Skinningrove, Cleveland, he worked as a miner at Grimethorpe Colliery and enlisted in 1914.

He was awarded the Military Medal for Bravery in June 1917, which was graciously approved by His Majesty the King in the supplement to the London Gazette on 21st of October 1918 (12407).

Corporal Goose was killed in action on Monday the 30th of September 1918, at the age of 30, and lies at rest in the Strand Military Cemetery, Comines-Warneton, 13 kilometres south of Ypres in Belgium. The grave reference is VIII. D. 9. He is remembered on the Roll of Honour in the Cudworth West End Working Men's Club.

Supplement to the London Gazette OCTOBER 1918. 12407

GOULDING BERTRAM. 30052 Private 39th Coy Machine Gun Corps (Infantry)

Bertram Goulding was born in Cudworth, the son of Harry George and Elizabeth Goulding. He was baptised on the 25th of June 1893. Prior to joining the army he worked as a lampman at Grimethorpe Colliery.

He was attested for the army on the 9th of December 1915 and recorded as being 5 feet 6 inches tall. He was approved on the 24th of January 1916 and enlisted at Barnsley as 24289 Private, 3rd Battalion York and Lancaster Regiment.

At the age of 23, Private Bertram Goulding was killed in action, in Mesopotamia, on Saturday the 14th of April 1917. He is buried in Iraq at the Baghdad (North Gate) War Cemetery, grave reference XIX. B. 8.

GOULDING ORLANDER. 13/386 Private 1st Battalion York and Lancaster Regiment.

Orlander Goulding was the husband of Daisy, nee Fearn, of 44 Snydale Road, Cudworth. His parents were William and Elizabeth Goulding of Red Brick House, Lower Cudworth. He was born in Cudworth and baptised on the 17th of September 1893.

Private Orlander Goulding was 24 when he died of wounds in Salonika, on Saturday the 21st of July 1917. He is buried in grave G. 4. 3. at the Sarigol Cemetery, Kriston, Greece.

GOULDING WILLIAM ARTHUR. 240316 Private 1st/5th Battalion York and Lancaster Regiment.

William Arthur Goulding was born in Cudworth and baptised on the 16th of May 1897. He was the younger of the two sons of William and Elizabeth Goulding of Red Brick House, Lower Cudworth.

He worked as an apprentice to John Allen of Cudworth and enlisted at Barnsley.

Private William Arthur Goulding died of wounds in the Fairfield Court Hospital in England on Sunday the 10th of June 1917 at the age of 21. His coffin was borne to the train at Eastbourne by six privates of the Cavalry Command Depot and he was accorded a full military funeral, with a firing party in attendance, at Cudworth Cemetery on the 14th of June. His resting place is grave reference AS. 4. 9.

GREEN EDWARD. 17211 Private 7th Battalion Northamptonshire Regiment.

Edward Green was born in Cudworth, the son of Edward (a publican) and Annie. He was baptised on the 2nd of August 1887. He enlisted at Northampton.

Private E. Green was killed in action on Monday the 27th of September 1915 and he is remembered with honour on the Loos Memorial, Panels 91 to 93.

GREEN FREDERICK. G/15410 Lance Corporal Royal Fusiliers.

Fred Green was the son of James and Sylvia Green of 53 Bloemfontein street, Cudworth and the brother of Annie Green. He worked at Grimethorpe Colliery and enlisted in January 1915.

Formerly 73690 of the Royal Field Artillery he first went out to Salonika and then to France. He returned home on furlough at Whitsuntide 1917.

He returned to the front and was killed in action on Wednesday the 22nd of August 1917, aged 24. He is remembered with honour on the Tyne Cot Memorial at Zonnebeke, Panels 28 to 30 and 162 to 162A and 163A.

The Roll of Honour in the Cudworth West End Working Men's Club also bears his name.

The Commonwealth War Graves Commission records give his age as 24 but a report in the Barnsley Independent on the 29th of September 1917 says that he was 26 years old.

GRIEVE LANGFORD. 54151 Private 83rd Training Reserve Battalion, York and Lancaster Regiment.

Langford Grieve was the first husband of Margaret Happs of 7 Princess Street, Hoyland Common. Born in Cockermouth in 1893, he was 25 years old when he died on Thursday the 14th of November 1918.

Private Grieve was buried in the Cudworth Cemetery, grave reference B. 2. 44, on the 19th of November.

GRUNDY SAM GEORGE. 13/350 Private 13th (Service) Battalion (1st Barnsley Pals) York and Lancaster Regiment.

Sam George Grundy was born in Clay Cross, Derbyshire, on the 3rd of March 1883 and was christened Samuel two days later.

He and his wife Anne lived at 1 Eveline Street, Cudworth.

The minutes of Cudworth Council meeting for June 1915 record that *"George Grundy, a soldier stationed at Silkstone, formerly of Cudworth, committed suicide at Cudworth Police Station. On Tuesday he caused a disturbance while quarrelling with his wife Anne Grundy of Eveline Street, Cudworth. An inquest is to be held."*

Private Sam George Grundy is remembered in the Commonwealth War Graves Commission "Debt of Honour" and "Soldiers Who Died in the Great War".

Private Grundy died on Tuesday the 22nd of June 1915 at the age of 32; he was buried in the Cudworth Cemetery, grave reference B. 3. 8.

HALL A. W.

HANDLEY WILLIAM HENRY. 34250 Lance Corporal 2nd Battalion Prince of Wales Volunteers South Lancashire Regiment.

William Henry Handley was born in Hoyland and resided with his parents George and Mary at 12 Bow Street, Cudworth.

He enlisted at Barnsley and was killed in action on Monday the 27th of May 1918. He is remembered with honour on the Soissons Memorial at Aisne in France.

HANN JOHN. 17721 Private 1st Battalion York and Lancaster Regiment.

John Hann was born in Newcastle in 1881. He was married to Eliza Ann (nee Wassell) and had a daughter named Lavinia. They lived with his mother-in-law, (see C.E. Wassell), at 18 Charles Street, Cudworth.

Certified Copy of an Entry of Marriage.

He enlisted at Pontefract soon after the war commenced and originally served as Private 153361 in the West Yorkshire Regiment.

He died of wounds on Wednesday the 5th of May 1915 and is remembered on the Ypres (Menin Gate) Memorial, Panels 36 and 55.

HARLOW THOMAS HENRY. 312511 Gunner R.G.A. (Territorial Force) West Riding Heavy Battalion.

Thomas Henry Harlow was born in Sturston, Ashbourne, Derbyshire. He lived with his wife and five children at 63 Bloemfontein Street, Cudworth.

He was employed as a miner at Grimethorpe Colliery and enlisted at Durham in January 1915 and joined the 142nd (Durham) Heavy Battery R.G.A. He had previously served for seven years with the Royal Field Artillery.

Gunner Harlow was killed in action on the 9th of September 1917, hit by a shell burst. He is buried in the Bard Cottage Cemetery at Ypres in Belgium, grave reference IV. F. 43.

HARPER GEORGE. 14/52 Private 13th (Service) Battalion (1st Barnsley Pals) York and Lancaster Regiment.

George Harper was born in Worsborough in the third quarter of 1895. He was the son of John and Annie Harper who lived at 136 Barnsley Road.

He was the husband of Lucy Harper of 10 Guests Yard, Cudworth and they had two children. At the time of compiling the Commonwealth War Grave Commissions records Lucy had moved to 221 Barnsley Road, Cudworth.

It was reported at the Cudworth Council meeting on the 1st of July 1916 that Private Harper had been wounded in both legs and the left shoulder and was still in Hospital in France. He died of wounds on the 8th of February 1917 in the Ontario Military Hospital in Keir Torlus, Kent, at the age of 27.

He was buried in Cudworth Cemetery on the 13th February 1917 in grave reference AS. 4. 2.

HAYES CHARLES HENRY. 14/54 Lance Corporal 14th (Service) Battalion (2nd Barnsley Pals) York and Lancaster Regiment.

Charles Henry Hayes was the son of Alfred Hayes of 8 Star Terrace, Cudworth. At the time of his death he resided at Back Denton Row, Kingstone, Barnsley.

Lance Corporal Hayes was killed in action on Saturday the 5th of May 1917 and is buried in the Orchard Dump Cemetery, Arleux-en-Gohelle in France, grave reference VII. H. 12. His name appears on the Memorial Plaque within Kingstone Church, Barnsley.

HEATON GEORGE. 13/271 Private 13th (Service) Battalion (1st Barnsley Pals) York and Lancaster Regiment.

George Heaton was born in Cheddleton in Staffordshire. He was the husband of Mary (Martha) and the father of four children who lived at 5 Somerset Street.

Private Heaton died of wounds in England on the 10th of February 1915. He was given a Military Funeral in Cudworth Cemetery, held during a snowstorm (Vicar's note), grave reference B. 10. 16. The Church Magazine for February 1915 gives the cause of death as "Died of Apoplexy". He was 37 years old.

The name of G. Henton appears on the original War Memorial, of whom there is no trace. A member of the Heaton family contacted the group with the information that their relative, George Heaton was not on the War Memorial. The 1881 British Census lists under Cheddleton, Staffs. a George Heath aged 2. He was the Great Grandson of a John Shenton. He is believed to be George Heaton (Henton). George Heaton's name has been added to the refurbished memorial to ensure that, in case our research has failed, no disrespect is given to G. Henton.

HEWITT CHARLES ERNEST. 13/506 Lance Corporal 4th Battalion York and Lancaster Regiment.

Charles Hewitt was born in Hemsworth to John W. and Mary Hewitt who are recorded to have lived at Burton Road, Monk Bretton (C.W.G.C.), 26 Charles Street, Cudworth (Barn. Chron.) and 26 Church Street, Cudworth (Barn. Ind. 16.06.1917).

He married Mary Alice in 1910 at Grimethorpe and lived at 18 Princess Street, Cudworth; they had three children. He was employed as a deputy at Grimethorpe Colliery and was reported in the Barnsley Independent as being one of the first to enlist in the Barnsley Battalion. He served with the British Expeditionary Forces until the 1st of July 1916 when he was killed in action at the age of 28.

Lance Corporal Hewitt is remembered with honour on the Thiepval Memorial, Pier and Face 14A and 14B, and also the Plaque of Remembrance in the West End Working Men's Club.

HILL GEORGE. 267863 Private 2nd/6th Battalion Duke of Wellington's West Riding Regiment.

George Hill was born in Leeds, he was the adopted son of Thomas Reynolds of 44 Churchfield Terrace, Cudworth. He enlisted at Elland.

Private Hill died of wounds, at the age of 24, on the 14th of April 1918. He is buried in the Boulogne Eastern Cemetery, grave reference VIII. I. 189 and remembered on the Roll of Honour in the West End Working Men's Club.

HOLMES GEORGE STANLEY. 36912 Private 1st Battalion Northumberland Fusiliers.

George Stanley Holmes was born in St. John's Cottages, Cudworth. He lived with his parents, Thomas and Annie, at 145 Barnsley Road, Cudworth. His father was a Colliery Banksman. George was baptised on the 22nd of November 1896.

He enlisted at Barnsley and was 5 feet 6 inches tall, when attested on the 10th of December 1915. He was approved on the 22nd of February 1917 and was attached to the 1st Training Reserve Battalion on the 23rd of February 1917 and then the York and Lancaster Regiment (40934).

Private Holmes was 21 years old when he was killed in action on the 27th September 1917. He is remembered with honour on the Tyne Cot Memorial Panels 19 to 23 and 162.

HOLMES VICTOR. 14/695 Private 14th (Service) Battalion (2nd Barnsley Pals) York and Lancaster Regiment.

Victor Holmes was the son of Henry and Mary Ann (deceased) Holmes of 12 Ibbott Street, Cudworth. He was the youngest of five boys, all of whom served in the forces. Employed at as a miner at Grimethorpe Colliery, he enlisted at Barnsley at the age of 17 but was sent home as being too young and re-joined as soon as possible.

Private Victor Holmes was killed in action on the 1st of July 1916 at the age of 19. His father received a very touching letter from Sergeant A. Totty; in it he explained that an exploding shell had killed Victor. He is remembered with honour on the Thiepval Memorial, Pier and Face 14A and 14B.

HORTON A. (TOM). 3/4423 Private 2nd Battalion York and Lancaster Regiment.

Tom Horton was married to Lily who had remarried by the time the records were compiled becoming Lily Asprey living at 9 Duke Street, Castleford.

Private Horton was killed in action on Monday the 9th of August 1915 aged 37. He is remembered with honour on the Ypres (Menin Gate) Memorial, Panels 36 and 55.

HORTON ERNEST WILLIAM. S/10177 Rifleman 9th Battalion Rifle Brigade, Kings Royal Rifles.

William Horton was the son of William H. Horton who, according to the C.W.G.C. records, lived at 15 Pembroke Street, Mansfield, Nottinghamshire. A Cudworth resident remembers them living at Garden Cottages, Pontefract Road, Cudworth.

The Original War Memorial gave the name as W. Horton, but an extract from Barbara Wilson's (nee Dodd) father's diary states "*that E.W. Horton was killed in action at the Battle of Hooge in Belgium on the 9th of August 1915 while serving with the Kings Royal Rifles. A Memorial Service was held at the Wesleyan Chapel, Cudworth on the 15th of September 1915*". He was 28 years old.

Private William Horton is remembered with honour on the Ypres (Menin Gate) Memorial, Panels 46 to 48 and 50. He was named on the Vicar's Roll of Honour in November 1915.

HOWARD LAWRENCE GEORGE. 24078 Private 8th Battalion York and Lancaster Regiment.

Lawrence George Howard was the son of George and Lucy Howard 9 St. George's Terrace, Pontefract.

Private Howard was killed in action on Saturday the 1st of July 1916. He is buried in the Blighty Valley Cemetery, grave reference V. E. 38.

HOWELL ERNEST KIRTLAND. WR/44106 Pioneer Royal Engineers.

Ernest Howell was the son of Samuel Henry and Ellen Howell of 273 Sticker Lane, Bradford,-the Electoral Roll of 1913 gives them living at 6 Low Cudworth.

At the age of 24 he died of wounds on Sunday the 29th of February 1920 and is buried in the Bradford (Bowling) Cemetery, grave reference C. 381.

HUBBARD DAVID. 3829 Sergeant 1st/5th Battalion King's Own Yorkshire Light Infantry.

David Hubbard was the son of John Hubbard who, according to C.W.G.C. records, resided at 76 High Street, Stoke-on-Trent.

He enlisted at South Kirkby and was killed in action, at the age of 26, on the 4th of October 1915. Sergeant Hubbard is remembered with honour on the Ypres (Menin Gate) Memorial on Panel 47.

HUNTER JOHN.

HUTCHINSON FRED. 151187 Sapper Railway Transport Depot Royal Engineers (Longmoor).

Fred Hutchinson was born in Ecclesfield to Joseph and Ann Hutchinson, Jeffcocks Houses, Ecclesfield. He resided in Cudworth and enlisted at Barnsley.

Sapper Hutchinson died of wounds in the Westminster London Hospital on Saturday the 6th of June 1916, at the age of 35, and was buried in Cudworth Cemetery on the 10th of June. Grave reference B. 1. 40.

HYMAN CHARLES ERNEST. 9813 Lance Corporal 1st Battalion Grenadier Guards.

Lance Corporal Charles Ernest Hyman was born at Mount Sorrell, Leicestershire in 1882. He lived at 19 Garden Cottages, Cudworth and worked as a gas regulator at Royston.

He enlisted at Nottingham and was reported as missing in the Vicar's letter in August 1915.

He died of wounds in a military hospital, at the age of 33, on the 24th of June 1915 and was buried in the Etaples Military Cemetery in France. The grave reference is II. B. 2.

JACKSON ARTHUR. 165025 Private 1st Battalion York and Lancaster Regiment Labour Corps.

Arthur Jackson was born in Sheffield and resided at 100 Snydale Road, Cudworth. His father, Herbert Jackson, lived at 235 Pontefract Road, Cudworth.

He enlisted at Sheffield and was formerly 17623 Private in the 1st Battalion of the York and Lancaster Regiment.

Private A. Jackson received wounds to the head and died at home on the 17th of October 1917. He is buried in the City Road Cemetery in Sheffield in grave reference Y "C" 14279.

JACKSON HERBERT EDWARD. 32602 Private 1st/7th Battalion Lancashire Fusiliers.

Private H. Jackson originally served as Private 174217 in the Royal Field Artillery.

Herbert Jackson was born in Normanton and lived at 63 Snydale Road, Cudworth with his parents Joseph and Caroline Jackson.

At the age of 20, he was killed in action on Sunday the 28th of October 1917 and was buried in the Coxyde Military Cemetery at Koksijde, Belgium, in grave reference IV. J. 10.

JACKSON JAMES. 240417 Private 1st/5th Battalion York and Lancaster Regiment.

James Jackson was employed as a miner at Monckton Colliery and lived at 2 George Street, Cudworth.

He enlisted at Barnsley and had previously been wounded on the 10th July 1915. He returned to France in February 1916 and was reported missing on the 7th of July 1916.

Private J. Jackson had been killed in action on this date, although a report in the Barnsley Chronicle on the 28th of October 1916 said he was missing. Aged 23, he is remembered with honour on the Thiepval Memorial Pier and Face 14A and 14B.

His father & brother were serving in France at the same time.

JAMES J. W.

JOBURNS EDWARD. 15320 Corporal 6th/7th Battalion Royal Scots Fusiliers (15th Division).

Edward Joburns was the son of William and Mary Anne Joburns of 42, Pontefract Road, Cudworth. He was born in Brownhills, Staffordshire on the 14th of April 1888. He was employed as a miner at Monckton Colliery and enlisted at Barnsley on the 28th of December 1914. He served with British Expeditionary Force from April 1915.

A report in the Barnsley Chronicle on the 23rd of October 1915 states: -

"A CUDWORTH SOLDIER IN GREAT ADVANCE."
"GERMANS MOWN DOWN LIKE MEAT."

"Private Ed. Joburns, who lived with his parents at 42, Pontefract Rd., previous to enlisting in the Royal Scots Fusiliers, has sent a very interesting letter to his father and mother describing the recent victory at the battle of Loos, and requests that it be published in the ""Barnsley Chronicle."" Private Joburns is now attached to the 7th service Battalion Royal Scots Fusiliers, B. Company, 45 Brigade, 15th Division, and in the course of his letter he says his regiment did not know the big battle was coming off until they received orders to pack up. They obeyed, and at 4 a.m. on the Saturday their big guns began blazing away at the German trenches: Orders to "Stand to" were received and at 6 o'clock the order to "charge" came. Every man worked like a nigger and the Germans were simply mown down like wheat. We were 48 hours without food and as our water had been finished we felt like dropping asleep, but there was not one shirker. "One Man cried 'Mercy, comrade', but I remembered poor Will Horton and without hesitation I put my bayonet straight through the Hun" " Private Horton, to whom the letter refers was killed recently."*

The death of Edward Joburns was announced in the Barnsley Chronicle as a dual bereavement because his brother, William, had been killed just over three months earlier.

"CUDWORTH PARENTS DUAL BEREAVEMENT."

"Mr. and Mrs. Joburns, 42, Pontefract Road, Cudworth, have received official intimation that their second son, Corporal Edward Joburns, has been killed in action after being out in France 18 months. Edward joined the Royal Scots Fusiliers in December, 1914, was wounded in June last, after having been home on leave the previous January. He was 28 years of age, single, and lived with his parents. Before enlisting he worked at Monckton Colliery, Royston. His eldest brother was killed in April last when with the 2nd Barnsley Battalion, and there is a third brother, the youngest, now in France with the R.F.A.

In a letter to his parents, concerning Edwards death, the O.C. writes: " He was a good and brave soldier and all his comrades wish me to convey to you their deepest sympathy in your sad loss. I am sure he would have wished for no better end than to die fighting for his country, and I am sure you will agree with us when I say he did his duty and gave of his best. 'Greater love hath no man than that he lay down his life for a brother.' We do not know the day or the hour when we may be called upon to answer our last Roll Call, but we put our trust in Him, Who is our Maker, to guide us to victory. I hope you will find help and comfort in knowing that your son is at rest with many of his comrades in a soldiers' grave, after doing his duty."

Sam Joburns, who is a bombardier in the R.F.A., has this week written to his distressed parents saying that when he was informed of the loss of his second brother he has not been the same man. "It is hard for us to lose Will and Ted (he writes), but we must put our trust in God and rest assured that he will not leave us comfortless. Ted has done his duty nobly and well. 'Greater love hath no man than this, that he lay down his life for his friends.' He has given his life in order that the loved ones at home may be kept safe. Rest assured, mother, that we shall meet them where there will be no more wars. He fought the good fight, and he kept his faith! May God give you and Dad strength to bear this terrible blow"?

Corporal Edward Joburns was killed in action on Saturday the 12th of August 1916 and is remembered with honour on the Thiepval Memorial Pier and Face 3C.

JOBURNS WILLIAM. 14/162 Corporal 14th (Service) Battalion (2nd Barnsley Pals) York and Lancaster Regiment.

William Joburns was the son of William and Mary Anne Joburns of 42, Pontefract Road, Cudworth

Corporal William Joburns worked as a miner at Monckton Colliery. He enlisted at Barnsley in March 1915.

A report in the Barnsley Chronicle on the 20th of May 1916 states:

"CUDWORTH CORPORAL KILLED"
"SHOULD HAVE BEEN MARRIED LAST EASTER"

"The late Corporal Wm. Joberns (sic), whose photo appears in this issue, was killed in action on Friday, April 28, the cause of his instantaneous and painless death being a "whiz-bang" shell. Before joining the Second Barnsley Battalion, the deceased worked at Monckton Colliery, resided with his parents at 42, Pontefract Road, Cudworth, and was very highly respected in the village. For many years he had been identified with the Wesleyan cause in Cudworth, being a teacher in the Sunday school and a prominent member of the Wesley Guild. He was fond of music and took part in competitions with the Brotherhood Male Voice Prize Choir. At the present time two of his brothers are on active service in France, one belonging to the Royal Scots, and the other to a West Yorkshire Regiment. Preparations had been made for Corporal Joberns, who was aged 29, to be married at Easter last year, but it was put off on account of the war and consequently much sympathy is being expressed to the bereaved young lady as well as to his parents. On the day of his death his fiancée received a letter in which he referred to Easter time, saying it was the most miserable Easter that he and his comrades had ever seen. "I would willingly," he wrote, " have given 10s. to have been with you in Chapel yesterday, singing 'Christ the Lord is risen to-day'. Easter time was ever in my thoughts yesterday, and I only hope it will be the last Easter that I will spend so far away. I felt that the presence of God was with me, and though I was not at Cudworth, still I felt quite happy and confident in the love of Christ. If it be God's will that I shall return to you I want to return back safe and sound: but we shall have a tremendous time before us. I shall be in it, and it will be the only way to finish the war, because trench fighting will never finish it, I feel certain of it, and I am afraid that many of our brave lads will fall in it and England will be astonished when they read of it. But it is bound to come off sooner or later, but my trust is in God and I am not afraid. I may return back safe in limb and body, but if it be God's will whether I live or die I am the Lord's."

Lieut. W. Hirst, No.1 Platoon, A. Company, writing to the late Corporal Jobern's parents, says: -- "As his platoon commander, I beg you and your family to accept the sincerest sympathy of Officers N.C.O.'s and men of A Company in your sad bereavement. As senior corporal in No.1 Platoon your son held a position of some responsibility and at all times I found him keen and enthusiastic in carrying his work. His conduct was always exemplary and his principles of the best. One of his great traits was his cheerful disposition, which proved a fine asset, as it was impossible for the men to become down-hearted when he was about; his cheery words helped the men considerably and many were the laughs he raised by his witty remarks on occasion when things were not of the brightest. His loss to the company is a serious one and will be severely felt, he was quite a favourite with us all and it is hard to realise that he is gone. He has now been laid to rest alongside other lads of our Battalion in a cemetery behind the firing line, and a small wooden cross suitably inscribed denotes the place."

Corporal W. Joburns was buried in the Sucrerie Military Cemetery in grave reference I. I. 93.

JOHNSON JOSEPH. 3/223 Private 1st Battalion King's Own Yorkshire Light Infantry.

Joseph Johnson was born in Christchurch, Wakefield. He enlisted at Pontefract.

Private J. Johnson was killed in action on Friday the 1st of October 1915. He is remembered with honour on the Loos Memorial Panels 97 and 98.

The Barnsley Chronicle dated the 29th Jan 1916 reports as follows:

"CUDWORTH SOLDIER MISSING."
"THE WORST FEARS ENTERTAINED."

"Private Joseph Johnson of the 1st Bn., K.O.Y.L.I., is missing and it is feared that he has been either severely wounded or killed, nothing having been heard of him since the first instant. Private Johnson's home was at 4, Queen's Rd., Cudworth, where he was a boot and shoemaker prior to the war. He was a native of Wakefield and was 24 years of age. One of his comrades (J. Francis) has written to Mrs. Johnson expressing the firm opinion that her husband has been killed. "I was not many yards from your husband when we were coming out of a trench. We were being relieved at the time and the trench was crowded with men, when the Germans started to send high explosive shells knocking the trench to pieces. A panic followed: some of our men lost their heads and ran into the open, and it was at this point that I missed your husband (my chum) and nobody seems to be able to enlighten me as to his whereabouts. We had not been in the same trench since, nor do I think we shall, but if we do I will certainly do all in my power for you. It is a great pity it should have occurred when your husband was expecting coming home shortly. I am glad to say Mr. Gratton got out of it alright, but he was very lucky indeed, as were all of us who escaped.""

JOHNSON SHEPLEY. 73446 Gunner 119th Battery Royal Field Artillery.

Shepley Johnson was the son of Joseph and Harriet Johnson who lived at 13 Albert Street, Cudworth.

He was killed in action on Tuesday the 10th of April 1917 and was buried in the Bois-Carre British Cemetery grave reference I. A. 17. Gunner S. Johnson is named on the Roll of Honour in the Cudworth West End Working Men's Club.

JOHNSON WALTER. 2831 Private 3rd Battalion Coldstream Guards.

Walter Johnson was born in Sharlston, Wakefield and resided in Cudworth. A miner at Grimethorpe Colliery, he enlisted at Sheffield.

He was listed as missing in the Vicar's letter of the August 1915 Church magazine.

The Barnsley Chronicle on the 5th of February 1916 reported:

"ANOTHER CUDWORTH HERO."
"BURIED BY THE GERMAN MILITARY AUTHORITIES."

"Official intimation has been received of the death of Private Walter Johnson, 3rd Coldstream guards, which occurred so long ago as October 21st, 1914. He was buried by the German military authorities at Ebrenfriedof, near Poelcapelle, Belgium. He lies in the Ebrenfriedof British Cemetery.

The news of his death was received through the American Embassy.

Called up at the beginning of the war, Private Johnson went to France in September 1914, and was last heard of on October 18th, the following month, at St. Julien, Belgium. The deceased was 34 years of age and leaves a wife and two children who reside at 90, Barnsley Road, Cudworth, when war broke out the deceased man was working at Grimethorpe Colliery. He is named on the Roll of Honour in the Cudworth West End Working Men's Club".

Private Walter Johnson was buried at the Poelcapelle British Cemetery in grave reference IA. C. 4.

The 1901 census shows Walter Johnson, born in Wakefield, living in the Administrative County of London, with the occupation of a Private in the Coldstream Guards. Being employed as a miner when enlisting in 1914 and entering action so early in the war suggests that he was in the Army Reserves.

JOYNER BERNARD J. 3667 Private 1st/6th Battalion Black Watch (Royal Highlanders. 6th Perthshire Battalion Territorial Force).

Bernard Joyner was born in Barnsley to Henry and Elizabeth Joyner. He worked as a miner at Grimethorpe Colliery and enlisted at Barnsley.

Private Joyner was killed in action on Sunday the 30th of July 1916 and is remembered on the Thiepval Memorial Pier and Face 10A. His name is engraved on his parents' grave in Cudworth Cemetery as an act of remembrance.

The Barnsley Chronicle reported his death as follows:

"He was only 19 years of age and joined the forces 13 months ago, at which time he was a junior clerk at Grimethorpe Colliery and at the same time studying with Mr. H.N. Horton at Barnsley for the professional career of organist. The deceased soldier was the youngest son of Mrs. H. Joyner of Cudworth, and a brother of Madame Amy Joyner of Hopwood Street, Barnsley, the well-known vocalist. Lieut. R.L. West, commanding the 3rd Co. of the same Regt. as Pte. Joyner, has written Madame Joyner a letter, which was received on Tuesday; - "the news I have to send will come as a great shock if it has not already reached you. Your brother was killed in action on July 30th while taking part in an attack on the German lines. I would like to convey to you and to all who are near and dear to him the very deep and sincere sympathy of all officers and men who remain. We are proud to have had such a lad in our ranks. He died a noble death doing his duty bravely and well in the face of the enemy, for the sake of those he loved and for the sake of his country."

KEMP LEONARD. 2313 Private 7th Battalion Royal Munster Fusiliers.

Leonard Kemp was born in Sidcop, Cudworth and baptised on the 17th of February 1895. He was a member of the St. John's Boys Life Brigade.

Enlisting at Barnsley on the 3rd of September 1914, he formerly served as Private 15992 Kings Own Yorkshire Light Infantry.

His death was reported in the Barnsley Chronicle as follows:

"Mr. & Mrs. Leonard Kemp, of 48, Bow St., Cudworth, have received intimation from the War Office that their son, Private Leonard Kemp, who enlisted in the Royal Munster Fusiliers on September 3rd last year, has been killed in action in the Dardanelles on September 15th. The deceased soldier was a bright lad and would have celebrated his coming of age on November 14th next. Most of his training was spent at the Curragh Camp in Ireland, previous to going to the front.

Just a week before he met with his death (September the 8th) Private Kemp wrote to his mother and father the following encouraging letter: - Dear mother and father, -In answer to your kind and loving letter I was pleased to hear you are well at home, only for you having rheumatism. Never mind dad, I hope it will not be long before you are well again. I am pleased to be able to tell you that I am in the "pink", and still in the race. You say you like to hear when I am "in the pink"; well, I shan't tell you a lie when I say so, because I hope never to feel any worse than what I feel today. I received your letter yesterday (on the 7th) and I am able to send you a letter back on our Arthur's birthday, and wish him many happy returns of the year, and hope he lives to be 90! You say you always think when you lock the door at night that you lock it now on two of us; but never mind, better days are in store, as you said in your last letter to come. I have still got that letter, and hope to show it you before long. Trust in the Lord, and everything will come right. We have been in the trenches 14 days before we got relieved, and now we are having a rest beside the seaside. It's very fine, I'll tell you to go in and have a dip it makes you forget you are fighting the Turks. The Turks don't give us much peace when we are fighting them, and we don't give them much; they seem as eager as us to finish the war. There are some crack shot snipers in the Turks; but you should hear them shout when they get caught - "Haller" ("Allah") that is what they say. You say my mother is always thinking of me, well she is sure to do, but you don't want to study too much mother that is what puts old age on folks. Cheer up and sing - " He's been a long time gone for the wood!" So I think this is all this time, with heaps of love to all at home from your son Leonard. Keep smiling until you hear from me again. Good night, and God bless you all".

Much sympathy is expressed locally towards the sorrowing parents and family who also have another son (Joseph Kemp) serving in the Kings Royal Rifles".

Killed in action on Wednesday the 15th of September 1915, he is remembered with honour on the Special Memorial, Panel D6, in the Greenhill Cemetery in Turkey.

KENCHINGTON ISAAC. 2826 Private 1st/5th Battalion King's Own Yorkshire Light Infantry.

Isaac Kenchington was born in South Kirkby and was employed as a miner at Grimethorpe Colliery. He was married, with children, to Sabrina Kenchington and lived at Pinfold, Darfield Road, Cudworth.

Enlisting in South Kirkby, he was killed in action on Wednesday the 8th of December 1915. Private Kenchington is buried in the Bard Cottage Cemetery at Ypres, Belgium in grave I. L. 8.

KING GEORGE RICHARD. 8/12748 Sergeant 10th Battalion York and Lancaster Regiment.

George King was born in Ashton-under-Lyne, in Lancashire. His wife remarried and became Lavinia Roebuck, living at 5 Court, 4 House, Burleigh Street, Barnsley. He enlisted at Pontefract in September 1914.

A Barnsley Chronicle report announcing his death stated:

"A CUDWORTH SERGEANT FALLS."
"LEAVES A WIFE AND SEVEN CHILDREN."

"A painful shock has been created in Cudworth on the receipt of the intelligence that Sergeant G. R. King, Y and L, of 16, Somerset Street, died of wounds on July 20th 1917, his injuries having been received a week previously. He was 35 years of age and the distressing feature is that he leaves a wife and seven children. Sergeant King was well known in the district and before enlisting in September. 1914 he worked at Grimethorpe Colliery. The first intimation of his having been wounded was conveyed by a letter to the bereaved widow by Chaplain R. S. Watson who said her husband was considered dangerously ill and had been wounded in the right groin".

He is buried in the Hazebrouck Communal Cemetery, Nord France, grave reference III. D. 33.

KIRK WILFRED. 13/555 Private 'B' Coy. 13th (Service) Battalion (1st Barnsley Pals) York and Lancaster Regiment.

Wilfred Kirk was born in New Whittington, Staveley, Derbyshire. A miner at Monckton Colliery, he enlisted at Houghton.

Wounded at the Battle of Serre, a gunshot to the left side of his chest punctured a lung; he succumbed to a severe haemorrhage on Monday the 31st of July 1916. Private Kirk received a Full Military Funeral.

Private W. Kirk's death was reported in the Barnsley Chronicle.

"Private Wilfred Kirk B Co., 1st Barnsley Battalion has succumbed to wounds received in action. He was 23 years of age, married with no children, and his home was 11, Wells Street, Cudworth. His wife, Mrs. Kirk, now resides at 19, Bridge Street, Barnsley. The deceased soldier formerly worked at Houghton Main Colliery. His brother, Horace Kirk, is in the machine-gun section of the same battalion, and a third brother in the K.O.Y.L.I. has returned wounded. Mrs. Wilfred Kirk has received two letters of condolence from No. 2 Stationary Hospital, France. The sister wrote: "Your husband had a severe haemorrhage from the chest; he gradually sank and passed away peacefully. I know that it will be a terrible blow to you and his mother for he often spoke of you both to me. The Chaplain (Rev. E. Milner-White) forwarded the following; "Dear Madam. - By now you will have heard the sad news of your husband's death in hospital from wounds. Despite the short time here I knew him well and the suddenness of it was a great shock. He was buried in the lovely cemetery of Abbeville on August 2nd, with military honours, and a church service. How tenderly cared for are the graves you will see by the photo. If you wish, I can send, in two months time or so, a photo of the actual grave and the cross already standing upon it. The French folk covered the grave with flowers. It will be some consolation in your grief to remember that by giving his life freely for others, he has followed very nearly the example of his Saviour and has won the declared and lasting praise of God-'Greater love has no man than this, that he lay down his life for his friends.' The prayers on the card were used at the funeral, and at a memorial celebration of Holy Communion in the hospital chapel. May they be blessed by your use, too, to the eternal happiness of one who fought and died gallantly for Right"."

Private W. Kirk is buried in Abbeville Communal Cemetery in grave reference VI. F. 8.

KIVELL THOMAS. 16651 Private 8th Battalion East Lancashire Regiment.

Thomas Kivell was born in St. John's, Ashton-under-Lyme in Lancashire. His parents were James and Ann Kivell of 11 Somerset Street, Cudworth.

At the age of 23, Private Kivell died of wounds, in the United Kingdom, on the 3rd of November 1914 and is buried in the Wardour Roman Catholic Cemetery in Wiltshire.

LAYLAND ROBERT. 40217 Private 8th Battalion York and Lancaster Regiment.

Robert Layland, the son of Ada and Robert Layland of 316 Barnsley Road, Cudworth, was born in Barnsley.

Private Layland, aged 19 and single, was killed in action on Sunday the 16th of June 1918 and is buried in the Barenthal Military Cemetery at Vicenza on the Asiago Plateau in Italy. The grave reference is, Plot 1, Row A, Grave 12.

LISTER BEN. 15324 Gunner 107th Coy. Royal Garrison Artillery.

The minutes of the Cudworth Council Meeting in June 1916 recorded:

"An inquest was held on Ben Lister, 32, Miner of 107 Barnsley Rd., who died in Barnsley Becketts Hospital that previous day. He had been a gunner in the Royal Garrison Artillery, and had been discharged on a time expired reason. He had been at the front since the beginning of the war and had not been wounded. He came home on April 27, and recommenced work on May 2 at Grimethorpe colliery. He went to work in the morning and came home at 10 o'clock. He had been emptying a tub of muck on a flat sheet when he fell as if he had twisted his muscles. He was working with Tom Hutchinson and Ben Ashton. He went to see Dr. Walsh, who told him to go home and go to bed. His wife called Dr. Eskrigge as she was worried about her husband, who examined him but did not express any opinion. He was informed by M.Goodyear that he had a vacant bed at Becketts. He was then taken to Hospital, when she visited her husband he was sinking and died the following day". Verdict - Death from Bright's disease (Kidneys)".

Ben Lister's wife's Christian names were Jessie May, her address is given in the Commonwealth War Graves Commission records as 2 St. Stephen's Square, Bayswater in London. His parents were William and Charlotte Lister of Monk Bretton.

Gunner Lister died on Thursday the 15th of June 1916 and was buried on the 20th in grave AS. 3. 6. at Cudworth Cemetery.

LISTER GEORGE HENRY. 81589 Private 15th Battalion Durham Light Infantry.

George Henry Lister was the son of George and Harriet Lister of "Struan," Aniaby Park Road, Hull. He resided at 12 Crosby Street, Cudworth, was 21 years of age and single. He worked as an engine cleaner with the Hull and Barnsley Railway at Cudworth.

He enlisted at Mexborough in February 1915 and was discharged in February 1916. He was recalled to the colours on the 25th of July 1917 as Private 44764 in the 14th Battalion of the York and Lancaster Regiment and was transferred to the Durham Light Infantry with whom he was serving when killed.

Private Lister was killed in action on Tuesday the 28th of May 1918. He is remembered with honour on the Soissons Memorial at Aisne in France.

LOFT THOMAS DIXON. 13637 Lance Corporal 1st Battalion Coldstream Guards.

Thomas Dixon Loft was the son of Mary H. Loft who later married Joseph H. Hight of 10 St. Lukes Street, Hull. He was born in Beverley in 1894 and lived with Hy and Elizabeth Ann Loft at 6 Crosby Street, Cudworth. (Parents address in 1925).

Lance Corporal Loft was killed in action, age 23, on Tuesday the 31st of July 1917 and is remembered with honour on the Ypres (Menin Gate) Memorial Panel 11, and the Methodist Chapel in Cudworth.

LOWE JOSEPH. 14/1317 Private 14th (Service) Battalion (2nd Barnsley Pals) York and Lancaster Regiment.

Joseph Lowe was born in Worsborough in 1896. He was the son of John Henry and Elizabeth Lowe who moved to 228 Pontefract Road, Cudworth. He enlisted at Barnsley.

Private J. Lowe of "A" Company died of wounds on Thursday the 29th of June 1916 and was buried in Doullens Communal Cemetery, near The Somme, grave reference I. B. 3.

LOWE WALTER. 4708 Private 1st/4th Battalion King's Own Yorkshire Light Infantry.

Walter Lowe enlisted at Wakefield.

The Barnsley Chronicle reported his death as follows:

"Private Walter Lowe of the 4th K.O.Y.L.I. whose home address was 324 Barnsley Road, Cudworth was killed in action on July the 7th. He was 20 years of age, and prior to enlisting in March 1915 worked at the Brierley Colliery. He went to France in December of last year. In a letter to the father of the dead soldier, the officer commanding No. 8 Platoon writes of him: - "He was a bright and cheerful soldier. Always did his duty, under fire or on parade. You will always have the satisfaction of knowing that he died like a Briton. He was killed instantly by a piece of shrapnel in the head and suffered no pain. At the time of death he was acting as a runner and was only a few yards away from me. I have today seen his brother in the 5th K.O.Y.L.I., and informed him of your loss". Captain George Thompson also writes to the mother asking her to accept his deepest sympathy in her sad bereavement. Concerning the circumstances of Private Lowe's death he writes: - " He was killed by a piece of shell while on duty in our front line trenches at a very critical stage of the proceedings, and fell doing his duty like a British soldier as he always did"."

Private Lowe was killed in action on the 7th of July 1916 aged 20.

The 1918 Electoral Roll records a William Lowe living at 324 Barnsley Road, this is presumably his father.

MAHER PATRICK. 12568 Private "B" Coy 9th Battalion York and Lancaster Regiment.

Patrick Maher was born in Droylsden, Ashton-under-Lyme in Lancashire. He lived with his wife, Ethel, at 72 Manor Road, Cudworth. Employed at Grimethorpe Colliery, he enlisted at Pontefract in 1914.

Private Maher had been in France since 1915 and died of wounds on Sunday the 2nd of July 1916. He is buried in the Puchevillers British Cemetery, near Somme in France, in grave reference I. A. 17.

MARSDEN WALTER THOMAS. 12836 Private 7th Battalion King's Own Yorkshire Light Infantry.

Walter Thomas Marsden was born in Barnsley on the 6th of November 1898 to George and Sarah Marsden. His wife was Minerva Marsden who was also a native of Barnsley. The Commonwealth War Graves Commission records show his wife's address as 16 Ida Terrace, Stourton, Leeds at the time they were produced.

Private Marsden enlisted at Pontefract and died of wounds at the age of 37 on Thursday the 20th of April 1916. He is buried at Etaples Military Cemetery in grave reference V. B. 6.

McGUIGAN JOSEPH. 13/1282 Private "B" Coy 13th (Service) Battalion (1st Barnsley Pals) York and Lancaster Regiment.

Joseph McGuigan was born in Wombwell in 1895 the son of Mrs. L. McGuigan, 58 Eliott's Terrace, New Scarborough, Wombwell.

Private McGuigan was killed in action on Friday the 1st of December 1916 at the age of 21. He is buried in the Euston Road Cemetery at Colincamps on the Somme, grave reference IV. Q. 6.

McNAB WILLIAM. 503769 Sapper 11th Field Company Canadian Engineers.

William McNab was born in Lancashire.

"A CUDWORTH CANADIAN KILLED"
"FORMER GRIMETHORPE BLACKSMITH."

The death in action in France is reported of Sapper William McNab, who formerly resided at 229, Victoria Terrace, Cudworth. The deceased went to Canada five years ago, being up to then engaged as a blacksmith at Grimethorpe Colliery. He was single, 39 years of age, and was a son of the late Finlay McNab of Cudworth. He had enlisted in the Canadian Regiment. Mrs. McNab, who resides at Moorthorpe, has received the following letter from Major H. L. Trotter: - "I am very sorry indeed to have to inform you of the death of your son, who was killed in action on April 9th. Sapper McNab was one of a party of three who accompanied the attacking infantry, to take charge of consolidation when the enemy's position was captured. That's what has to be done in order to repel a counter-attack. As soon as an enemy position is captured certain men are sent to work, under the direction of the sappers, to dig a trench and prepare the place for defence. Your son was with Corpl. Scenion and Sapper Maeers. They all got to their work, and they succeeded in doing a lot of useful work. They then helped to beat off an enemy counter-attack. A machine gun bullet or a piece of shrapnel killed your son. His comrades went next day and carried in his body and buried him with military honours beside four others of his friends. I wish to offer you my most sincere sympathy in your loss. May it be of some comfort to you to know that your son died like a hero, with victory in sight and that he took a leading part in the greatest battle of this Great War. The exact location of the cemetery will be sent to you officially. We are putting up a cross and are fencing off the little plot for our own boys."

Sapper McNab was killed in action on Monday the 9th of April 1916 and lies at rest in the Zouave Valley Cemetery plot reference II. D. 18.

The Commonwealth War Graves Commission records show his age as 37 and his mother's address at the time the records were compiled as 238 King's Terrace, Cudworth, King's Terrace may be part of Pontefract Road.

McNEIL HAROLD. 265906 Lance Corporal 10th Battalion Prince of Wales's Own (West Yorkshire Regiment).

Harold McNeil was born in 1895 and resided in Cudworth. He enlisted at Bramley, Leeds.

Lance Corporal McNeil was killed in action on Thursday the 28th of March 1918 and is remembered with honour on the Arras Memorial, Bay 4.

MEGGITT WALTER. 241925 Private 2nd/5th Battalion York and Lancaster Regiment.

Walter Meggitt was the son of John Meggitt of 10 Somerset Street, Cudworth. He enlisted at Barnsley.

Private Meggitt was killed in action on the 3rd of May 1917. He is remembered with honour on the Arras Memorial, Bay 8 and also on his parent's grave within the Cudworth Cemetery.

MERRY JACOB. 14/1311 Private 2nd/4th Battalion York and Lancaster Regiment.

Jacob Merry was born in Worsborough Dale in 1897, the son of George and Esther Ann Merry of 23 Starmer Street, Cudworth.

Employed as a miner at Grimethorpe Colliery he enlisted at Barnsley.

He served in "D" Company of the 2nd/4th Battalion which was known, along with the 4th, 1st/4th and 3rd/4th, as the "Hallamshires".

Private Merry was killed in action on Thursday the 28th of March 1918, aged 21, and is remembered on the Arras Memorial, Bay 8.

MILLINGTON RICHARD. SS/112285 Stoker 1st Class HMS "TRIUMPH" Royal Navy.

Richard Millington was born in Carrington in Nottinghamshire. He was the son of Mr. and Mrs. Robert Millington who resided in Pontefract when the Commonwealth War Graves records were compiled. He resided in Cudworth at 12 King's Road.

Stoker Millington was single and age 21 when he was killed in action on Tuesday the 25th of May 1915. He is remembered with honour on Panel 8 of the Portsmouth Naval Memorial.

The Church Magazine for August 1915 refers to him in the Vicar's letters.

MORBY ROBERT ASKEW. G52493 Private 2nd Middlesex Regiment.

Robert Askew Morby was born in North Cave, Yorkshire, and resided in Cudworth. He was the son of Thomas and Emma Morby.

Private Morby enlisted at Pontefract and at the age of 27 he was killed in action on the 27th of March 1918. His place of remembrance is the Pozieres Memorial on the Somme in France, Panels 60 and 61.

MORLEY GEORGE ALFRED. 13/1482 Private 13th (Service) Battalion (1st Barnsley Pals) York and Lancaster Regiment.

George Alfred Morley, single, was the son of Mr C H Morley of 181 Pontefract Road, Cudworth. Prior to enlisting at Barnsley he worked as a miner at Grimethorpe Colliery.

Private Morley died of wounds on Tuesday the 1st of August 1916 and was buried in the St. Pol Communal Cemetery Extension, grave No. B. 21.

NEVILLE WILLIAM. 170318 Private 3rd Reserve Battalion Machine Gun Corps. (Infantry)

William Neville was born in Wombwell, the son of Aaron Burkinshaw Neville and Emma Neville who lived at 219 Barnsley Road, Cudworth. He enlisted at Barnsley.

At the age of 21, Private Neville died of wounds in England on Saturday the 20th of July 1918. He is buried in grave reference 03294 in the Nottingham General Cemetery.

His name is on the Roll of Honour in the Cudworth West End Working Men's Club.

NEWBERRY JOSEPH. 18078 Lance Corporal 8th Battalion King's Own Yorkshire Light Infantry.

Joseph Newberry was born in Wombwell, the son of Joseph and Mary Ann Newberry of 44 Station Lane, Cudworth. Lance Corporal Newberry was the husband of Clara Newberry of Churchfield Avenue, Cudworth. He worked at Grimethorpe Colliery.

The minutes of the Cudworth Council meeting in December 1916 reported, *" Lance Corporal Joseph Newberry of Churchfield Ave was officially reported killed. He was with the 8th K.O.Y.L.I. He went to France in Christmas 1915".*

Lance Corporal Newberry, age 26, was reported as missing on the 1st of July 1916 but he was later known to have been killed on that date. He is remembered with honour on the Thiepval Memorial Pier and Face 11C and 12A.

NICHOLSON ALBERT HENRY. 8348 Bandsman 6th Battalion 6th Dragoons (Inniskilling)

Albert Henry Nicholson was the son of Captain J S Nicholson (Royal Marines) and the grandson of Sgt Major Nicholson of Poplar House, Barnsley Road, Cudworth.

At the age of 23, Bandsman Nicholson was killed in action on Tuesday the 7th of September 1915. He is buried in grave B. 38 at the Authuile Military Cemetery.

OGLEY ARTHUR. 14/1036 Corporal 1st/5th Battalion York and Lancaster Regiment.

Arthur Ogley was born in the Railway Cottages, the son of William and Emma Ogley.

Corporal Ogley enlisted at Barnsley and was killed in action on Monday the 15th of April 1918 at the age of 24. He is remembered with honour on the Tyne Cot Memorial at Zonnebeke, Panels 125 to 128.

His name is on his parents' headstone in the Cudworth Cemetery with the date of his death as the 12th of April 1918 and records that he was serving with the Machine Gun section of the 14th (Service) Battalion (2nd Barnsley Pals) York and Lancaster Regiment.

PEAKER JOSEPH. 12470 Private 7th Battalion York and Lancaster Regiment.

Joseph Peaker was born in Penistone, the son of Walter and Elizabeth Peaker who lived in the shop on Crosby Street, Cudworth. He was married to Lilly Maud and lived at 9 Queen's Road, Cudworth.

Private J Peaker died on Wednesday the 16th of February 1916 and is buried in the Spoilbank Cemetery at Ypres in grave reference I. J. 10.

PEAKER WILLIAM. 42306 Private 1st Battalion Prince of Wales's Own (West Yorkshire Regiment).

Joseph Peaker was born in Penistone, the son of Walter and Elizabeth Peaker who lived in the shop on Crosby Street, Cudworth. He was married to Elsie Midgley and lived at 10 Jackson Street, Cudworth. When the Commonwealth War Graves Commission Records were gathered his wife had remarried becoming Elsie Harte of 1 Back Lane, Glass Houghton, Castleford.

Enlisting at Barnsley, Private W. Peaker died on the 25th of July 1918 and is buried in the Lijssenthoek Military Cemetery at Poperinge in Belgium in grave reference XX. C. 22A.

PEARSON HAROLD. 13176 Private 107th Coy. Machine Corps (Infantry)

Harold Pearson was born in Eckington, Derbyshire. He resided at 9 Albert Street, Cudworth. He enlisted at Doncaster. His brother Mr T Pearson lived at 7 Montague Street.

A shell killed Private Pearson on Tuesday the 5th of June 1917. He was buried in Pond Farm Cemetery at Heuvelland in Belgium. The grave reference is N. 6.

Private Pearson had formerly served as Private 12099 in the King's Own Yorkshire Light Infantry.

PORTER HAROLD. 10627 Private 108th Field Ambulance Royal Army Medical Corps.

Harold Porter was born in Barnsley to William Henry and Suzanna Porter of 50 Lunn Road, Cudworth. He enlisted at Leeds

Aged 28, Private H. Porter was killed in action near Havrincourt on Wednesday the 10th of October 1917 and was buried in grave number F. 2 in the Ruyaulcourt Military Cemetery in France. He is remembered on his parent's gravestone in the Cudworth Cemetery and on the plaque within the Methodist Chapel.

His brother E. Porter had been reported as wounded.

POSKITT WALTER. 14/1174 Lance Corporal "D" Company 14th (Service) Battalion (2nd Barnsley Pals) York and Lancaster Regiment.

Walter Poskitt resided in Cudworth. He was employed as a miner at Monckton Colliery.

Lance Corporal Poskitt died of wounds on Saturday the 2nd of September 1916 and was buried in the Merville Communal Cemetery, in France, grave reference I. A. 7.

POWELL RICHARD HENRY. 49639 Private 54th Field Ambulance Royal Army Medical Corps 18th Division.

Richard Henry Powell was born in Old Mill Lane, Barnsley in 1894 to Frank and Anne (nee Hemmingway) Powell who moved to 233 Barnsley Road, Cudworth. He was a miner at Grimethorpe Colliery and enlisted at Sheffield on the 14th of January 1915.

At the age of 22, Private R H Powell was killed in action on Wednesday the 27th of September 1916. He is remembered with honour on the Thiepval Memorial, Pier and Face 4C.

POWELL THOMAS WILLIAM. 14/1579 Private 14th (Service) Battalion (2nd Barnsley Pals) York and Lancaster Regiment.

Thomas William Powell was born in Swinton. He was married with two children and lived at 16 Church Street, Cudworth.

Private T W Powell enlisted at Barnsley. He was killed in action on Saturday the 1st of July 1916, at the age of 39, and is remembered with honour on the Thiepval Memorial Pier and Face 14A and 14B.

An article in the Barnsley Chronicle reads: -

He was officially reported missing on the 1st July. An officer writing to Mrs Powell, says there is very little hope of Private Powell being again seen alive, "It is difficult to realise in England that our men have died from home and away from their loved ones. If you could see the villages round here- windows and doors blown out, roofs gone, some just heaps of bricks and dust- churches are mere shells of walls. It is then that we realise that we out here are fighting for hearts and home, for the same thing would happen in England if the Germans ever got here."

PRITCHARD STANLEY. 24935 Private "B" Company 8th Battalion King's Own Yorkshire Light Infantry.

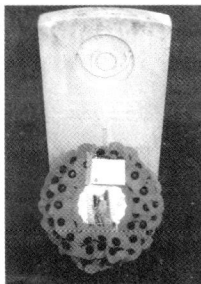

Stanley Pritchard was born in Tankersley, Barnsley, on the 22nd of October 1897. He lived at 48 Manor Road, Cudworth and attended school at Cudworth.

Private S. Pritchard was killed in action on Friday the 3rd of March 1916 at the age of 18 years. He was buried in the Y Farm Military Cemetery at Bois-Grenier, France, in grave reference H. 2. His grave was photographed when his family visited the grave on the 21st of September 2001.

At the Cudworth Council meeting in March 1916 it was reported that - *"Mr. and Mrs. Pritchard received sad news of the death of their son Private Stanley Pritchard who was 18 years, and had been killed in action. Shot through head on sentry duty. Buried in soldiers grave next to trenches".*

His death was published in the Barnsley Chronicle on the 18th of March 1916:

*"ANOTHER CUDWORTH HERO
SHOT DOWN ON SENTRY DUTY."*

Mr. & Mrs. W. Pritchard of 48, Manor Road, Cudworth, have received the sad news that their eighteen year old son, Private Stanley Pritchard, has been killed in action. He was attached to the 8th. K.O.Y.L.I. and went out with his regiment in December last.

The Chaplain, Rev. A.F. M. Hitchcock wrote to the bereaved parents, "I am sorry to inform you of the death of your son Private S. Pritchard, who was shot through the head by a German bullet while on sentry duty in the trenches last night (3rd March). You will like to known that his body was reverently buried this morning in the Soldiers Cemetery close to the trenches where he met his death. May God, who gave His Son for us, grant you strength and comfort in your separation, which is only for a short while."

Sergeant C. H. Martin wrote: "By the time this reaches you, you will have had the sad news of your boy's death. He was killed practically instantaneously, so at least he was spared any suffering. Although I have only recently been placed in charge of the Platoon I had already noticed your son, as being a bright, willing youngster, and it has been a great shock to myself and to the Platoon, amongst whom he was a great favourite. To day I received a parcel, which had been sent by Miss Pritchard. I opened it and divided the contents amongst Stanley's friends. I hope you will approve of my doing so because it is quite possible it would never have reached you had it been sent. Please accept the sincere sympathy of the whole Platoon and myself in your sad bereavement. Although he was a boy in years, he died the death of a hero, and our country has lost a good soldier."

Private E. A. Litton one of the deceased's comrades also sent his sympathy to Mr. & Mrs. Pritchard. "He was unconscious and only lived a few minutes after receiving the wound. I was with him up to the last. We had been together since he joined the Army and I was very fond of him. He was a brave and cheerful little fellow and was well liked by the officers and men of the company amongst whom he will be very much missed. Cudworth should feel proud of him. Although only a boy he died the death of a hero for his country's sake."

REDGATE JOHN WILLIAM. 13/942 Private 13th (Service) Battalion (1st Barnsley Pals) York and Lancaster Regiment.

John William Redgate was born in Barnsley on the 21st of June 1897. He was the son of Charles and Mary Redgate who lived at 86 Barnsley Road, Cudworth. His father was a deputy at Grimethorpe Colliery.

Private Redgate enlisted at Barnsley at the age of 16 years, 3 months. He died of wounds at the age of 19 on Tuesday the 3rd of July 1917 and was buried in grave reference IV. N. 11 at the Dui sans British Cemetery, Return, in France.

REECE JAMES ARTHUR. 34060 Private 7th Battalion South Lancashire Regiment, The Prince of Wales's Volunteers.

James Arthur Reece was born in Sutton-in –Ashfield in Nottinghamshire. He lived with his parents, Arthur and Mary Reece at 31 Charles Street, Cudworth. He enlisted at Barnsley, joining the 15th Battalion of the York and Lancaster Regiment and was later attached to the South Lancashire Regiment.

He was stationed in France from 1915.

Private Reece died shortly after being shot whilst in action against the enemy on Wednesday the 8th of November 1916 and is remembered with honour on the Thiepval Memorial, Pier and Face 7A and 7B. He was 19 years old.

RICHARDS THOMAS. 13/1070 Private 13th (Service) Battalion (1st Barnsley Pals) York and Lancaster Regiment.

Thomas Richards was born in Hucknall Torkhard, Nottinghamshire, in 1882.

Private T Richards was killed in action on Saturday the 22nd of July 1916 and was buried in the Pont-du-Hem Military Cemetery at La Gorgue in grave reference I. E. 19.

His death was reported in the Barnsley Chronicle as follows; -

"CUDWORTH "PALS"
LEAVES WIFE AND THREE LITTLE ONES."

"One of the first Cudworth men to join the Barnsley Battalion was Private Thomas Richards for he joined the ranks in October 1914. News has arrived that he fell in action on July 22nd, leaving a wife and three children, who live at 4, Bow Street, Cudworth. Private Richards, who was better known locally as "Thomas Bates", was 34 years of age and at the time he enlisted he worked at Monckton Colliery.

Details of how Private Richards met his death have been furnished by his namesake, Lance-Corporal Thos Richards, of the same battalion who states that the deceased "was with some more comrades when a rifle grenade came, wounded four and killed poor Tom. I shall miss him very much. I am in charge of a bay, which your husband assisted to hold. I did my best for him, but the case was hopeless. He was struck on the left side just under the arm and only lived a few minutes. He was a good soldier, very well behaved, and never complained when he was told to do anything. He is buried in a hero's grave just behind the firing line with another comrade. I can imagine your feelings when you read this sad news. It is a very severe blow to you and I hope and trust that God will give you strength to bear your great loss".

RICHARDSON CHARLES JOHN. 14/599 Lance Sergeant "C" Company 14th (Service) Battalion (2nd Barnsley Pals) York and Lancaster Regiment.

Charles John Richardson was born in Malpass in Cheshire in 1893. He was married with two children and lived at 28 Church Street, Cudworth and enlisted at Barnsley, Feb. 1915.

He received a wound to the head and died instantly.

The Cudworth Council meeting on the 16th of September 1916 - *"Sgt. Charles Richardson of the 2nd Barnsley Battalion was killed in action on Aug 28. He was aged 23, married with two children and lived at 28, Church St. In peace time he worked at Royston gas Works".*

Lance Sergeant C. J. Richardson was buried at the St. Vaast Post Military Cemetery at Richebourg-L'Avoue in grave reference III. R. 12.

RICKETTS WILLIAM JOHN. 13/1189 Private "B" Company 13th (Service) Battalion (1st Barnsley Pals) York and Lancaster Regiment.

William John Ricketts was born in 1882 at Westbury, Gloucestershire. He was married with one child and lived at 8 Jackson Street, Cudworth. He worked as a miner at Grimethorpe Colliery before enlisting at Barnsley.

He was a member of Cudworth Village Club.

Private Ricketts' death announced at Cudworth Council meeting on the 15th September 1916. He died of wounds on the 10th of April 1916 and was buried in Sucrerie Military Cemetery at Colincamps, grave reference I. H. 67.

ROBERTS ROBERT (Bob). 13/927 Corporal 13th (Service) Battalion (1st Barnsley Pals) York and Lancaster Regiment.

Robert Roberts was born to John and Sarah Roberts in Wigan. He worked as a miner at Grimethorpe Colliery.

Bob Roberts enlisted at Barnsley in September 1914. He commenced training at the Silkstone Army Camp in December 1914 and later transferred to Penkridge Camp at Cannock Chase where the 13th Battalion of the Y & L joined the same Division as the East Lancashire Regiment and the 12th and 14th Battalion of the Y & L Regiments to become the 14th Brigade, 31st Division. (These were all Pals Regiments).

On the 28th of July 1915 they transferred to Ripon for further training and on the 25th September 1915 transferred to Hurdcott in Wiltshire to complete training.

On the 26th of December the Regiments transferred to Devonport ready for embarkation to Egypt.

This is where I am just now.

HURDCOTT

I'm still "on the map" you see!

Hurdcott Camp
25.09.15 to 26.12.15

TSS ANDANIA
29.12.15 to 11.01.16

After a brief stop over in the Grand Harbour at Valletta, Malta on the 6th January, where only officers and sergeants were allowed ashore, the T.S.S. Andania docked in Port Said on the 11th of January, after 13 days at sea. Bob Roberts and his comrades were then based in a rest camp at Port Said until the 20th and were then transferred to El Ferdan on the Suez Canal for four weeks where they strengthened the defences by digging trenches etc.

In March, they were moved back to Port Said and embarked on the R.M.S. Megantic, for Marseilles, in Southern France, on the 15th of March 1916.

Postcard of R.M.S. Megantic.

They arrived at Mailly Maillet 1½ miles behind the front line and moved into the front line trenches opposite the German held village of Serre on the 3rd of April 1916.

The Battle of the Somme began on the 1st July 1916 and 13th/14th Battalions of the York and Lancaster Regiment (Barnsley Pals) went over the top to capture the village of Serre. They made no headway and suffered terrific casualties of around 40%. On the 4th of July the Battalion was withdrawn from the front line and was rested at Louvencourt before the 13th Battalion returned to the front at Neuve Chapelle.

On the 3rd of October 1916 the Battalion returned to Mailly Maillet for another attack on the old front at Serre, where they had been decimated three months earlier, and were engaged in continual fighting until the end of the Battle of the Somme on the 22nd of November 1916.

The 13th Battalion participated in a large-scale attack on the German lines at Herbuterne on the 23rd of December 1916 and was pulled out to rest and train on Christmas Day 1916.

On the 25th of February 1917 the men advanced on Puisieux. March and April saw them training in the Lys Valley near Merville.

The Battalion went back into the trenches at St. Catherine's for the Battle of Arras on the 1st of May 1917, another drawn-out engagement similar to the Battle for the Somme.

Between the 4th and 5th May 1917 the Battalion relieved the remnants of the Bradford Pals near Gavrelle Windmill and saw continuous fighting for 19 days. Once more the Battalion suffered terrible casualties. On the 21st of May the men were pulled back into the support trenches.

The Barnsley Battalions moved back into line for attack on Oppy Wood on the 26th June 1917. The 13th Battalion cleared the German trenches. This action earned the 13th the "Battle Honour of Oppy Wood". On the 30th of June 1917 the Battalion retired to reserve lines in a railway cutting behind Gavrelle Windmill where a stray shell fell killing a number of men, one of whom was number 13/927, Corporal Robert Roberts of the 13th Battalion York and Lancaster Regiment.

The Barnsley Chronicle reported: *"COMRADES IN ARMS" CUDWORTH CORPORAL KILLED. Another gallant Cudworth lad who answered the call soon after the outbreak of hostilities (in September 1914) has made the supreme sacrifice in the person of Corporal Bob Roberts, of the Y and L Regt. In civilian life Corporal Roberts, who was 24 years of age, was employed at the Grimethorpe Colliery, and lived with his parents at 236, Barnsley Rd. Cudworth. A comrade has written to Mr. and Mrs. Roberts from a hospital in France and the following are extracts from the letter: " It is with the deepest and sad regret that I have to write these few lines. You must excuse me for not writing sooner because I have not been able, on account of being in bed, through my wound. I was the last person to speak to your son. He left me for a few minutes, and shortly after I heard the sad news. He was true and noble and I cannot speak too highly of him. I have lost one of my truest and best friends. He had always a warm corner in my heart and his memory I never shall forget. May God comfort you in your sad loss."*

Corporal Roberts was buried at the Albuera Cemetery in grave reference D. 16 on the 30th of June 1917.

Cpl. R Roberts   Albuera Cemetery
Headstone.   N.E. of Arras.

RUCKLEDGE MARK. 23964 Private 10th Battalion Duke of Wellington's (West Riding Regiment).

The 1901 census gives his parents as Mark and Sarah. He was born in Swinton, near Mexborough in South Yorkshire and enlisted at Barnsley.

Private Ruckledge was killed in action on Thursday the 19th of July 1917 and was buried at Larch Wood (Railway Cutting) Cemetery, Ypres in Belgium reference SP. Memorial B. II.

SAYERS CHARLES. 13/841 Sergeant 13th (Service) Battalion (1st Barnsley Pals) York and Lancaster Regiment.

Charles Sayers was born in New Mills in Derbyshire, he was married to Maria Sayers and had a son named Herbert, they lived at 13 Jackson Street, Cudworth. He worked as a miner at Houghton Main Colliery and enlisted at Barnsley.

Sergeant Sayers died of wounds at the age of 42 on the 3rd of July 1916 from injuries received on the 1st of July 1916. He is buried in the Bertrancourt Military Cemetery Plot 1, Row B, Grave 18.

SHEA JOSEPH. 13/853 Private 13th (Service) Battalion (1st Barnsley Pals) York and Lancaster Regiment.

The Church Magazine for February 1915 reports that Private Joseph Shea died of pneumonia whilst in training.

A report in the Barnsley Chronicle in 1914 read as follows: -

"MILITARY FUNERAL AT CUDWORTH. AN IMPRESSIVE SCENE."

"The funeral took place with full military honours at Cudworth cemetery, on Wednesday afternoon, of Joseph Shea, a private in the Barnsley Battalion, whose death occurred on Sunday. Private Shea who lived at 59, Sidcop Lane, Cudworth, was one of the first local men to join the Battalion, volunteering at the first recruiting meeting held in the village. He was 35 years of age and prior to joining the ranks he worked at Grimethorpe Colliery. He leaves a widow and five young children, and the deepest sympathy is felt with the bereaved family.

This was probably the first military funeral that has ever taken place in Cudworth, and despite the bitterly cold weather, the streets on route from Sidcop to the cemetery were lined with spectators, while there was a big crowd outside the cemetery gates.

The men of "C" Company of the Barnsley Battalion of which the deceased was a member were present under Lieutenant Wilkinson (in command), Lieutenant Plumpton, Lieutenant Normansell and Lieutenant Bell, "C" Company paraded at the Camp at Silkstone and marched to the County Borough boundary where they were met by Cooper's Brass and Reed Band, which from this point headed the Company and marched through Barnsley and on to the deceased's residence at Cudworth.

The funeral procession which was most impressive in character, was headed by the men of "C" Company who were followed by the firing party, then came the officers, after them the band, followed by the hearse and mourners. The coffin was covered with the Union Jack, and the soldiers marched slowly in double file to the mournful strains of the Dead March in Saul. Rev. Father O'Shaughnessy of Hemsworth conducted the service. At the conclusion of the service the firing party fired 3 volleys over the grave and the band sounded the Last Post.

Within the cemetery gates a number of men of the 5th Battalion Duke of Wellington's regiment were lined up under Captain Rippon, Lieutenant Jubb and Lieutenant Suttcliffe. The mourners included deceased's wife, 3 children, a number of relations and friends including representatives of the Industrial Club. The bearers were members of "C" Company. There were several floral tributes. Mr. W. Guest was the undertaker. After the interment the men of the Battalion marched back to camp being led as far the Borough Boundary at Dodworth by Cooper's Band under the conductorship of Mr. W. Williams Bandmaster."

The Commonwealth War Graves Commission records his death having occurred on Saturday the 26th of December 1914.

Private Shea is buried in grave reference B. 10. 12 at Cudworth Cemetery.

SIDDALL ROBERT. 14/666 Private "C" Company 2nd Battalion York and Lancaster Regiment.

Robert Siddall was born in Hoyland in 1898, the son of Thomas and Emma Siddall and resided in Cudworth.

Private Siddall joined the 14th Battalion of the York and Lancaster Regiment, (2nd Barnsley Pals), in 1914. He trained at camps in Silkstone, Penkridge Bank at Rugeley, Ripon and Hurdcott on Salisbury Plain.

On Boxing Day 1915 the 13th and 14th Battalions left Hurdcott to board H.M.T. Andania on the 29th of December 1915, and eventually arrived in Port Said in January 1916, they went on to El Ferdan to build defensive trenches along the western bank of the Suez Canal at Abu Aruk.

On the 8th of March 1916, they marched from Kantara to embark on the 10th of March aboard H.M.T. Briton and H.M.T. Megantic to arrive in Marseilles on St. Patrick's Day, the 17th of March 1916. Here they boarded cattle trains for a 50-hour journey north, to Pont Remy on the 19th of March 1916 and begin service on the Western Front.

Private Siddall died of wounds, at home, on Sunday the 7th of July 1918 at the age of 20. He was buried at Hoyland Nether (or Hoyland Law) (St. Peter) Churchyard Extension in grave number E. 345.

The Commonwealth War Graves Commission records his regiment as the 2nd Battalion, another source lists him serving in the 1st/5th Battalion and his number shows that he originally served in the 14th (Service) Battalion (2nd Barnsley Pals) York and Lancaster Regiment.

SIMPSON JOHN JOSEPH. 8394 Lance Corporal 1st Battalion York and Lancaster Regiment.

John Joseph Simpson was born in Cudworth living on Barnsley Road and enlisted at Barnsley.

Lance Corporal Simpson was killed in action on Saturday the 8th of May 1915. He is remembered with honour on Panels 36 to 55 of the Ypres (Menin Gate) Memorial.

SMITH BENJAMIN. 18675 Private 6th Battalion King's Own Yorkshire Light Infantry.

Benjamin Smith was born in Bloxwich, Staffordshire and lived with his wife and two children at 44 Churchfield Terrace, Cudworth. He was employed as a miner at Brierley Colliery until he enlisted at Wakefield in October 1914.

Private Benjamin Smith was killed in action on Wednesday the 16th of June 1915 and is buried in grave B. 50 at the Kemel Chateau Cemetery, Heuivelland, Belgium. The Roll of Honour in the Cudworth West End Working Men's Club bears his name. The Vicar's letter in the August 1915 edition of the Church Magazine names him as one of the fallen Cudworth soldiers.

SMITH PERCY. 1447 Sergeant 5th Battalion York and Lancaster Regiment.

Percy Smith was born in 1894 to Charles and Hannah Smith.

The wounding (December 1915) and subsequent death (January 6th 1915) of Sergeant Smith was reported in the Barnsley Chronicle.

"CUDWORTH SERGEANT'S MISFORTUNE.
WOUNDED BY RIFLE GRENADE."

Mrs. Smith, of 20, Charles St. Cudworth has this week been notified that her husband Sergeant Percy Smith has been wounded and is in hospital in France.

Sergeant Smith is attached to the Barnsley Territorials and prior to the war he worked at Monckton colliery. He was home on furlough a month ago. Mrs. Smith was notified that when admitted into hospital his left ankle was mortifying and that the only chance of saving his life was to amputate the foot. Mrs. Smith received the following letter from Sergeant E. Bull, 10th Platoon C Company, 1st /5th Y. & L. Regiment.

"Dear Mrs. Smith, - I am writing at the request of your husband, and my friend, Sergeant Percy Smith, to tell you that we had a little "business" with the enemy this morning (December 19th) and unfortunately Percy got hit in the left ankle with a piece of rifle grenade. We have made him as comfortable as possible and he will shortly be in the best of hands in hospital, and probably off to England. He asks me to tell you not to worry, but to bear up bravely and he will write to you in the course of a day or two. He is quite as cheerful as he can be under the circumstances and is bearing his wound like a soldier and a man. We are all very sorry this has occurred, and trust he will soon be well on the way to recovery. I assure you of the sympathy all of Percy's friends."

From Ward D, 13 Stationary Hospital, B.E.F., under date December 25th. M.E. Vernon Harcourt, Sister wrote: " Dear Mrs. Smith, I am glad to tell you that your husband is a little better and we are more hopeful about him. He is wonderfully bright and merry. I do hope he will continue to mend now. I will write to you again to let you know how he is getting on; at present there is no sign of blood poisoning spreading. He wishes me to tell you that he has enjoyed his Christmas dinner fine and hopes to be with you soon"

"CUDWORTH SERGEANT'S DEATH.
SUCCUMBS TO RIFLE GRENADE WOUNDS."

A fortnight ago we recorded the fact that Sergeant Percy Smith of the Barnsley Territorials had been badly wounded by rifle grenade at the front. Now the sad tidings have reached his home at 20, Charles St. Cudworth that he has died.

Writing to Mrs. Smith from ward D, 13 Stationary Hospital, B.E.F. France, on January 6th, Sister M.E. Vernon Harcourt says: - "Dear Mrs. Smith, - I am deeply distressed to tell you that your husband got very much worse during the night and died at 6.20 this morning. The Doctor was up with him and did all he could, but he did not rally and passed away peacefully. You were so much in his thoughts. He was always asking me whether I had written to you. Believe me to be, in all sympathy, yours very truly, M.E.V. Harcourt."

At the age of 22, Sergeant Percy Smith was buried in the Boulogne Eastern Cemetery in grave VII. C. 77.

SMITH WILLIS. 241000. Corporal 2nd/4th Battalion York and Lancaster Regiment.

Willis Smith was the son of John Laverick Smith and the late Anne Smith who lived at 19 King's Road, Cudworth. Working at Monckton Colliery, he enlisted in 1915 and went to France two years later.

Corporal Willis Smith was killed in action on the 3rd of May 1917, at the age of 23. He is remembered with honour on Bay 8 of the Arras Memorial.

SNOWDEN FRED. 14/202 Private "A" Company 14th (Service) Battalion (2nd Barnsley Pals) York and Lancaster Regiment.

Fred Snowden was born on the 14th of May 1896 to Tom and Louise Emma Snowden of 39 Market Street, Cudworth. He was baptized on the 30th of November 1896. He was employed as a rope runner at Grimethorpe Colliery and enlisted in the Army at Barnsley.

Private Snowden died of wounds on Sunday the 2nd of July 1916 aged 20. He was buried in the Beauval Communal Cemetery, located on the Somme, in grave number B. 28.

SPENCE GEORGE WILLIAM. 24231 Private "D" Company 1st/5th Battalion York and Lancaster Regiment.

George Spence was born in Goole on the 30th of November 1896 to Wilson and Hannah Spence who lived at 70 Lunn Road, Cudworth.

Private Spence enlisted at Barnsley and died on Monday the 15th of April 1918 at the age 21. He was buried at the Cabaret_Rouge British Cemetery, Souchez, in grave reference II. 1A. 24.

SPENCE WILLIAM ALLAN. 331783 Private 9th Battalion (Glasgow Hds.), Highland Light Infantry.

William Spence's parents, William Booth and Jessie Spence, lived at 51 Exeter Drive, Partick, Glasgow.

At the age of 21, Private Spence was killed on Tuesday the 4th of December 1917 and is buried in Achiet-Le- Grand Communal Cemetery Extension, grave reference II. A24.

This is the only entry for a W.A. Spence in the C.W.W.G. records and we trust that the above information relates to the Soldier named on the original War Memorial.

STAINROD GEORGE STANLEY. 33813 Private 7th Battalion Prince of Wales's North Staffordshire Regiment.

George Stainrod was baptized in Cudworth on the 20th March 1898. His parents were Frank and Arabella Stainrod who lived at 20 Snydale Lane, Cudworth. He enlisted at Barnsley

Private George Stainrod was killed in action in South Russia, on Monday the 26th of August 1918 at the age of 20. He is remembered with honour on the Tehran Memorial in Iran on Panel 4, Column 2. This memorial commemorates some of the men who lost their lives in Iran or South Russia and have no known grave.

STAINROD JOSEPH ARTHUR. 15354 Lance Corporal 1st Battalion Coldstream Guards.

Joseph Stainrod was born in Kimberworth to Frank and Arabella Stainrod who had moved to 20 Snydale Lane, Cudworth. Joseph enlisted at Huddersfield.

Lance Corporal Joseph Stainrod was killed in action on Friday the 15th September 1916 and is remembered with honour on the Thiepval Memorial, Pier and Face 7D and 8D.

STARKEY WILLIAM. 59908 Private 21st Canadian (Eastern Ontario Regiment)

The Barnsley Chronicle reported his death as follows:

"A CUDWORTH VICTIM. CAME OVER WITH THE CANADIANS."

"At the early age of 21 years, Private William Starkey, of the 21st Canadian Regiment, has been killed in action in France. About a year ago, the young fellow emigrated to Canada and not long afterwards he joined the gallant Colonial Regiment. He was killed on October 4th. Prior to going abroad, Private Starkey lived with his Aunt at 3, Victoria St., Cudworth, and worked at Brierley Pit." (A church magazine gives his address as Victoria Terrace).

Private Starkey was killed in action on Monday the 4th of November 1915. He was buried in the St. Quentin Cabaret Military Cemetery at Heuvelleand in Belgium, grave C3.

STRAKER HERBERT. 2nd Lieutenant 6th Battalion Prince of Wales's Own (West Yorkshire Regiment).

Herbert Straker was the eldest son of Charles Herbert and Kate Straker who lived at Claremont, 171 Barnsley Road, Cudworth. He was employed in the Civil Service.

He first served with the London Regiment of Civil Service Rifles and was discharged in January 1916 with trench feet. Re-enlisting in January 1917 he was wounded and then drafted to West Yorkshire Regiment where he took a commission.

2nd Lieutenant Straker died of wounds, at the age of 30, in Rouen Hospital on the 11th of November 1918 and was buried in the St. Sever Cemetery Extension, grave reference S .V. I. 13. He is remembered on the Roll of Honour in the Cudworth West End Working Men's Club.

SWANN THOMAS. 21460 Private Northumberland Fusiliers.

Thomas Swann was born in Barnsley in the second quarter of 1883. He resided at 20 Somerset Street, Cudworth.

Private Thomas Swann died of wounds on the 24th of January 1916, at the age of 20, and was buried in Cudworth Cemetery on the 27th in grave reference B.7.21.

The Barnsley Chronicle reported: -

"MILITARY FUNERAL AT CUDWORTH
FUSILIER DIES OF WOUNDS

On Thursday afternoon at Cudworth, impressive scene marked the interment, with Military Honours, of Private, 21460 Thomas Swann; Northumberland Fusiliers, who earlier in the week had died from wounds received in the Battle of Loos on September 21st last.

Private Swann had been removed from the Base Hospital to London, and he had died in King George's Hospital. The body was subsequently removed to the home of the deceased's parents, 20, Somerset Street, Cudworth, from where the funeral cortege started.

Private Swann was 20 years of age, and prior to enlisting in January 1915, he worked at Grimethorpe Colliery. He went out to France on July 14, 1915."

The original Memorial spelt his name with one N although all records have the spelling Swann. This has been corrected on the refurbished memorial.

SWIFT THOMAS. 2159 Private 7th Battalion Royal Munster Fusiliers.

Thomas Swift was born and lived at 21 Bow Street, Cudworth with his father John Swift.

Private Swift enlisted in the York and Lancaster Regiment at Barnsley and had the service number 14715. He was transferred to the Royal Munster Fusiliers with whom he was serving when killed in action at Gallipoli on the 20th of September 1915 and is remembered with honour on the Helles Memorial in Turkey on Panels 185 to 190.

TAYLOR HAROLD. 152037 Gunner 124th Heavy Battery Royal Garrison Artillery.

Harold Taylor was born in Bradford and resided in Cudworth. He was the son of William R. and Emma Taylor of 2 St. Mary's Road, Lee Brigg, Normanton.

Gunner Taylor enlisted at Barnsley and was killed in action at the age of 20, on Monday the 18th of March 1918. He was buried in the Barlin Communal Cemetery Extension in France. His grave reference is II. E. 32.

TAYLOR WILLIAM. 24356 Lance Sergeant 12th Battalion Northumberland Fusiliers.

William Taylor, the eldest son of Henry and Caroline Taylor who lived at 9 Midland Terrace, Cudworth, was baptized on the 5th of May 1889. He worked as a clerk in the offices at Grimethorpe Colliery. The Barnsley Independent in 1915 states that his previous place of employment was Carlton Main, that he had been a member of the

Church Choir as a boy and man, that he played Sunday Football and was a member of Cudworth Tennis Club.

He died on the 27th of September 1915 at the age of 27. He is remembered with honour on the Loos Memorial, Panels 20 to 22, and the Roll of Honour in Cudworth West End Working Men's Club.

TEAL FRANK. 13603 Private 1st Battalion Scots Guards.

Frank Teal was born in Sharlestone and resided in Cudworth.

Private Teal was killed in action on Wednesday the 13th of September 1916 and is remembered with honour on the Thiepval Memorial Pier and Face 7D.

THOMAS LAWRENCE. 14/209 Acting Corporal "A" Company 14th (Service) Battalion (2nd Barnsley Pals) York and Lancaster Regiment.

Lawrence Thomas was born in Hoyland in the second quarter of 1893, the son of Isaac Thomas 119 Snydale Road, Cudworth. He worked at Woods Glassworks.

At the age of 23, he died on the 1st of July 1916 and is remembered with honour on the Thiepval Memorial, Pier and Face 14A and 14B.

THOMPSON JOHN WILLIAM. 16006 Lance Corporal 9th Battalion King's Own Yorkshire Light Infantry.

John Thompson lived with his parents, George Arthur and Sarah Louise Thompson at 30 Starmer Street, Cudworth.

Lance Corporal Thompson died at the age of 24 on Saturday the 1st of July 1916 and is remembered with honour on the Thiepval Memorial, Pier and Face 11C and 12A.

TIPPING JOHN. G/24247 Private 6th Battalion The Queen's (Royal West Surrey Regiment).

John Tipping was born in Sidcop, Cudworth and later resided and enlisted at Bradford.

Private Tipping was killed in action on Monday the 9th October 1916 and is remembered with honour on the Thiepval Memorial, Pier and Face 5D and 6D.

TUCKWELL HERBERT JAMES. 13/1287 Private 13th (Service) Battalion (2nd Barnsley Pals) York and Lancaster Regiment.

Herbert Tuckwell lived at 44 Manor Road, Cudworth.

Private Tuckwell died on Wednesday the 3rd of March 1915, aged 18 and was buried with Military Honours (according to the Church Magazine) on the 5th of March in the Cudworth Cemetery, grave reference B10. 18.

TURTON F.

The C.W.G.C. has four entries for F. Turton, two serving in the K.O.Y.L.I., one born in Nottingham and enlisted at Doncaster, and one born in Smitniers (Smithies?) and enlisted at Cawthorne.

No information has been found that links any of the four men to Cudworth, further investigation is required.

The 1915 Electoral Roll has a Walter Turton living at 43 Albert Street.

WADDINGTON WILLIAM. 13/692 Private 13th (Service) Battalion (1st Barnsley Pals) York and Lancaster Regiment.

William Waddington was born in Castleford and resided at Cudworth.

He died on Friday the 28th of June 1918 and is remembered with honour on the Ploegsteert Memorial, Panel 8, at Comines-Warneton, Hainaut, Belgium.

WARD WALTER. 282423 Gunner 120th Heavy Battery Royal Garrison Artillery.

Walter Ward lived at 48 Darfield Road, Cudworth.

Gunner Ward died of wounds on Friday the 9th of August 1918 and was buried at the Crouy British Cemetery on the Somme in grave reference IV. E. 21.

WASSELL CHARLES EDWARD. CH19317 Private 1st Royal Marine Battalion 2nd Brigade Royal Navy Division.

Charles Wassell was born in Allerton Bywater, near Pontefract on the 11th of July 1896. He lived with his mother Elizabeth, who died in 1945, at 18 Charles Street, Cudworth. Private John Hann who had married Wassell's sister, Eliza Ann, lived with them at this address.

Before joining the Marines Charles Wassell worked as a Coal miner.

On the 20th of October 1914, at the age of 18, he enlisted at York, where his height was recorded as 5 ft 61/4". He was stationed at Deal in Kent until the 24th of March 1915 and then embarked on H.M.S. Victory on the 24th of June 1915.

Private Charles Wassell was serving in Gallipoli where he died of wounds on Saturday the 4th of September 1915 (Bullet wounds to the skull, at Cape Helles on the 3rd of September 1915). He was 19 years of age. His grave is in the Skew Bridge Cemetery Special Memorial B. 62, Turkey.

He had played the side drums for the Cudworth Boys Life Brigade. A memorial service was held for him at St. John's Church Cudworth attended by members of the Life Brigade.

WASSELL SAMUEL JAMES. 1216 Private 5th Battalion York and Lancaster Regiment.

Samuel James Wassell was born in Allerton, near Pontefract. He was the elder son of Elizabeth and James Samuel Wassell of 18 Charles Street, Cudworth. He was married with three children.

He worked at Brierley Colliery and was in the Territorials, enlisting at Barnsley.

Private Samuel Wassell died of wounds on Tuesday the 13th of March 1917, aged 26, whilst serving in France. He was buried at Merville Communal Cemetery Extension in grave reference I. B. 20.

WATERFIELD GEORGE HENRY. 16093 Lance Corporal 9th King's Own Yorkshire Light Infantry.

George Waterfield was born in Sutton In Ashfield, Nottinghamshire, and resided at Bleachcroft, Cudworth. Before enlisting at Barnsley he worked at Wharncliffe Woodmoor Colliery.

Lance Corporal Waterfield was killed in action on the 1st of July 1916 and is remembered with honour on the Thiepval Memorial Pier and Face 11C and 12A.

WATSON CHARLES GEORGE. 19774 Private 15th Battalion Cheshire Regiment.

Charles Watson was born in Surrey to Charles and Mary Watson of Witchford. He lived with his wife, Hephizibah Watson and four children at 11 Market Street, Cudworth. Employed at Grimethorpe Colliery, he enlisted at Barnsley.

Private Watson was killed in action on Thursday the 2nd of November 1916 at the age of 41. He was buried at the Faubourg d'Amiens Cemetery at Arras in grave reference I. H. 33.

WEALTHALL RICHARD WARD. 35400 Private 2nd Battalion Duke of Wellington's (West Riding Regiment)

Richard Wealthall was born in Cudworth to James and Kate Wealthall of 236 Pontefract Road, Cudworth. He worked at Monk Bretton Colliery.

On the 24th of October 1918 he was killed in action at the age of 23 and was buried at Verchain British Cemetery, Verchain-Maugre in grave reference B. 11.

WEST EDGAR. J/78232 Ordinary Seaman.. H.M.S. ENDYMION Royal Navy.

Born in Cudworth, Edgar West lived with his father William West, at 54 Manor Road, Cudworth. Before joining the Navy he was employed at Grimethorpe Colliery.

At the age of 20 he was killed in action in the region of Salonika on Friday the 30th of August 1918 and is buried at the Mikra British Cemetery in Grave reference 1784, Kalamaria. Greece.

The Roll of Honour located in the Cudworth West End Working Men's Club bears his name.

WESTBURY R.WALTER. 11720 Private 1st Battalion Gloucester Regiment.

Walter Westbury was a native of Tupton near. Chesterfield. He worked as a number taker at Midland Railways, Carlton Exchange sidings and lodged with Mrs. Reeves in Prospect Street, Cudworth.

Enlisting in October 1914 he trained with the Gloucestershire Regt. At Easter 1915 he was wounded in the head and was admitted to the A1 Division No. 9 Ward, 16th General Hospital (Surgical) France.

Private Westbury had to go to the trenches again after recovering from his wounds and he was killed in action on Friday the 9th of October 1915 by a bursting shell in the dugout. He died at the age of 20.

He is remembered with honour on the Loos Memorial on Panels 60 to 64.

WESTMORELAND BENJAMIN. 27549 Lance Bombardier "D" Battery Royal Field Artillery 155th Brigade.

Benjamin Westmoreland was born in Cudworth in 1895 to George and Elizabeth Westmoreland of 60 Whitecross Road, Lower Cudworth. He enlisted in the Army at Rotherham.

Lance Bombardier Westmoreland died of wounds on Saturday the 8th of June 1918 at the age of 22. He is buried at the Douilens Communal Cemetery Extension No. 2 in grave D. 8.

He is remembered on the Cudworth West End Working Men's Club Roll of Honour.

WHITE HARRY. 201577 Private 1st/4th Battalion King's Own Yorkshire Infantry.

Harry White was the brother of Herbert White who lived at 17 Saville Street, Cudworth. He was born in Barnsley in the 1st Quarter of 1895.

At the age of 25, he was killed in action on the 23rd April 1918 and was buried at the Etaples Military Cemetery in grave XXXII. C. 5.

WILDE JOSEPH. 6412 Private 8th Battalion King's Own (Royal Lancaster Regiment).

The Barnsley Chronicle reported: -

"CUDWORTH RESERVIST FALLS. MARRIED ONLY EIGHT MONTHS AGO."

"Deep sorrow is felt at Cudworth at the death in action of Private Joseph Wilde, 1st King's Own Loyal Lancaster Regiment, whose home was at 5, Saville Street.

The deceased, who was 33 years of age, was a reservist, and joined at the outbreak of war. At the time he was working at Grimethorpe Colliery.

He was gassed in France, and during convalescence he was married, subsequently again going to the front.

Second-Lieutenant J. A. Barraclough, whose orderly the deceased was, has written to the bereaved widow: 27th March 1916, -

"Dear Mrs. Wilde, - I very much regret to have to inform you that your husband, Private J. Wilde, was killed in action on March 2nd. As you probably know, he was my servant. He was an excellent man in every way - brave as a lion, trustworthy to a degree. I am genuinely sorry to have lost him. He died doing his duty to the full, and you have every reason to be proud of him. He was killed instantly and suffered no pain.""

Joseph Wilde's wife was Mary Anne Wilde who had moved to 9 George Street, Dukinfield, Cheshire by the time the C.W.G.C. records were compiled.

Private Joseph Wilde was killed in action on Thursday the 2nd of March 1916 and he is commemorated on the Ypres Memorial Panel 12.

WILLIAMS ERNEST. Bosun. Steam Trawler "Shakespeare".

Ernest Williams was born in Cudworth, the son of Jane Williams and the late Walter Samuel Williams. His wife, Ethel May Williams, nee Pearson, of 103 Snydale Road, Cudworth lived at 2 Princess Avenue, West Dock, Hull at the time the C.W.G.C. records were gathered.

Bosun Williams lost his life at sea on Wednesday the 7th of February 1917 at the age of 32. He is remembered with honour on the Tower Hill Memorial, London.

WILLIAMS H.

WILLIAMS T.

WILLIAMSON HARRY. KP/224 Able Seaman (R.N.V.R.) RN Division Royal Navy.

Harry Williamson was the son of Abner and Ruth Williamson 1A Bow Street, Cudworth.

The Barnsley Chronicle reported on the 22nd of March 1919: -

"DIED AFTER DEMOBILISATION."

"The death occurred on Saturday morning of Harry Williamson (21), of 3, Bow Street, Cudworth. The deceased, who was a demobilised soldier, enlisted on September 10th, 1914, in the Royal Naval Division.

In March 1915, he took part in the landing of British troops in the Dardanelles, and a few days later was blown up by a shell and buried, not, however, being seriously hurt. Deceased continued with his duties and a month or two afterwards was taken ill with enteric fever and invalided home. He was admitted to the "Dreadnought" Hospital, Greenwich, and in October 1916, went to France where he remained until August 1918. Receiving shrapnel wounds in the left arm and shoulder he came to England and received treatment in hospitals in Cardiff and Swansea. The deceased was demobilised on February 13th and returned home.

Every night he complained of severe pains in the head and said that whilst in France he fell off a plank in the trenches, a distance of 15 feet. Dr. Eliott, of Cudworth, attended him, and on March 3rd he was removed to Beckett Hospital. Deceased, however, returned to his home on Friday last. He again complained of pains in his head and died on Saturday. An inquest was held on Tuesday, when, as the result of a post-mortem examination the following verdict was returned, "Died from cystic tumour of the brain consequent upon injuries received whilst he was taking part in operations of war.""

Able Seaman Williamson was buried in Cudworth Cemetery on the 19th of March 1919 in grave reference B. 3. 38.

WILMOTT ERNEST. 13/751 Private 13th (Service) Battalion (1st Barnsley Pals) York and Lancaster Regiment.

Ernest Wilmott was born on the 16th July 1886 and baptized at Cudworth on the 30th October 1887. His parents were Henry (a miner) and Mary Ann Wilmott who lived in the Sidcop area of Cudworth.

Private Ernest Wilmott enlisted at Barnsley and was killed in action on Sunday the 9th April 1916. He was buried in the Sucrerie Military Cemetery at Colincamps, Somme. His grave reference is I. H. 65.

WINTER HERBERT WILLIAM. 13/750 Private 13th (Service) Battalion (1st Barnsley Pals) York and Lancaster Regiment.

Herbert Winter was born in Nottingham the son of Charles Edwin Winter a joiner/grocer of 9 Kings Road, Cudworth and had a shop on Pontefract Road. Herbert's wife Alice lived at Montague House, Cudworth.

He enlisted in the Army at Houghton. His death was announced at the Cudworth Council Meeting on the 22nd of April 1916.

Private Winter died on the 9th April 1916 and he was buried in the Sucrerie Military Cemetery at Colincamps, Somme, at the age of 25. His grave reference is I. H. 68.

WRIGHT EDMUND (NED). 242349 Sergeant "Z" Company 1st/4th Battalion King's Own Yorkshire Light Infantry.

Edmund Wright was born in Belle Green, Cudworth to Henry and Agnes Wright and baptized in October 1893. At the time of his death the family resided at 31 Albert Street, Cudworth.

Prior to enlisting at Barnsley, he worked as a steam wagon driver at Kinsley Gasworks near Hemsworth.

Sergeant Edmund Wright died at 24 years of age on the 29th of April 1918 and is buried at the Esquelbecq Military Cemetery Nord in grave number I. B. 15.

He is remembered on the Roll of Honour in the Cudworth West End Working Men's Club.

WRIGHT ELIJAH. 14/1545 Private "C" Company 1st/4th Battalion York and Lancaster Regiment.

Elijah Wright was the son of Hannah Wright who lived at 50 Bow Street, Cudworth and had been employed at Grimethorpe Colliery as a miner before enlisting.

Private Elijah Wright was wounded in April 1916 and sent home as an invalid. He returned to the front line in September 1916 and died of fever on Tuesday the 26th of February 1917 at the age of 19.

He was laid to rest in the Longuenesse (St. Omer) Souvenir Cemetery in grave reference IV. F. 57.

WRIGHT FRED DEARDEN. 10/88 Lance Corporal "A" Company 1st Battalion York and Lancaster Regiment.

Fred Wright was the son of Henry and Agnes Wright who were residing at 86 The Avenue, Newtown, Cudworth. (The same parents as Edmund Wright but a different address (31 Albert Street) at the time of the compilation of the C.W.G.C. records).

Lance Corporal Fred Wright was killed in action on the 8th of May 1915, age 23, and is commemorated on the Ypres (Menin Gate) Memorial Panels 36 and 55.

WRIGHT WILLIAM HENRY. 45853 Private 9th Battalion Leicestershire Regiment.

William Wright was born in, and resided at, Cudworth. At the time the Commonwealth War Graves Commission records were gathered his wife, Edith H. Wright lived at 17 Fish Dam Lane, Monk Bretton.

He enlisted in the York and Lancaster Regiment (43533) at Barnsley and later transferred to the Leicestershire Regiment.

Private William Wright was killed in action at the age of 31 on Tuesday the 30th of October 1917 and is remembered with honour on the Tyne Cot Memorial at Zonnebeke, Belgium, Panels 50 to 51.

YARROW ERNEST. 267976 Gunner 6th Signal Company Royal Engineers.

Ernest Yarrow was born at Snydale Road, Cudworth to Mark and Charlotte Yarrow. He was baptized at Cudworth on the 6th of November 1898. Before enlisting at Barnsley he had been employed on the Hull and Barnsley Railway as a clerk.

Gunner Yarrow, age 19, was killed in action on Thursday the 21st of March 1918 and is commemorated on Bay 1 of the Arras Memorial in the Faubourg d'Amiens Cemetery.

CHAPTER 4.

CHRONOLOGY

OF

WORLD WAR TWO.

World War 2 Calendar

1939   **Sept:** German invasion of Poland; Britain and France declared war on Germany; the USSR invaded Poland; fall of Warsaw (Poland divided between Germany and the USSR)

      Nov: The USSR invaded Finland.

1940   **March:** Soviet peace treaty in Finland.

      April: Germany occupied Denmark, Norway, the Netherlands, Belgium and Luxemburg. In Britain a coalition government was formed under Churchill.

      May: Germany outflanked the defensive French Maginot line.

      May-June: Evacuation of 337,131 Allied troops from Dunkirk, across the channel to England.

      June: Italy declared war on Britain and France; the Germans entered Paris; the French Prime Minister Petain signed an armistice with Germany and moved the seat of government to Vichy.

      July-Oct: Battle of Britain between British and German air forces.

      Sept: Japanese invasion of French Indochina.

      Oct: Abortive Italian invasion of Greece.

1941   **April:** Germany occupied Greece and Yugoslavia.

      June: Germany invaded the USSR; Finland declared war on the USSR.

      July: The Germans entered Smolensk, USSR.

      Dec: The Germans came within 40 kilometres (25 miles) of Moscow, with Leningrad (now St. Petersburg) under siege. First Soviet counter offensive. Japan bombed Pearl Harbour, Hawaii and declared war on the USA and Britain. Germany and Italy declared war on the USA.

1942   Japanese conquest of the Philippines.

      June: Naval battle of the Midway, the turning point of the Pacific war.

      Aug: German attack on Stalingrad (now Volgograd), USSR.

      Oct -Nov: Battle of El Alamein in North Africa turns the tide for the Western Allies.

      Nov: Soviet counter-offensive in Stalingrad.

1943   **Jan:** The Casablanca Conference issued the Allied demands of unconditional surrender. The Germans retreated from Stalingrad.

      March: The USSR drove the Germans back from the River Donetz.

      May: End of the Axis resistance in North Africa.

      July: A coup by King Victor Emmanuel and Marshal Badogio forced Mussolini to resign.

Aug: Beginning of the campaign against the Japanese in Burma (now Myanmar). US Marines landed at Guadalcanal, in the Solomon Islands.

Sept: Italy surrendered to the Allies; the Germans rescued Mussolini who set up a republican Fascist Government in Northern Italy. Allied landings in Salerno. The USSR retook Smolensk.

Oct: Italy declared war on Germany.

Nov: The US Navy defeated in the Battle of Guadalcanal.

Nov-Dec: The allied leaders met at the Tehran Conference.

1944   **Jan:** Allied landing in Nazi-occupied Italy: Battle of Anzio.

March: End of the German U-boat campaign in the Atlantic.

May: Fall of Monte Casino in Southern Italy.

6th**June:** D-day landing in Nazi-occupied and heavily defended Normandy

July: The bomb plot by German Generals against Hitler failed.

Aug: Romania joined the Allies.

Sept: Battle of Arnhem on the Rhine: Soviet armistice with Finland.

Oct: The Yugoslav guerrilla leader Tito and Soviets entered Belgrade.

Dec: Germans counter-offensive at the Battle of the Bulge in Belgium.

1945   **Feb:** The Soviets reached the German border. Yalto conference. Allied bombing campaign over Germany (Dresden destroyed). The US re-conquest of the Philippines was completed. The Americans landed on Iwo Jima, south of Japan.

April: Hitler committed suicide: Mussolini was captured by Italian partisans and shot.

May: Germans surrender to the Allies

June: US troops completed the conquest of Okinawa (one of the Japanese Ryukyu Islands).

July: The Potsdam Conference issued an allied ultimatum to Japan. Atom bombs were dropped by the USA on Hiroshima and Nagasaki: Japan surrendered.

CHAPTER 5.

WORLD WAR TWO

CASUALTIES.

THE MEN WHO MADE THE SUPREME SACRIFICE
IN THE SECOND WORLD WAR.

ALLSEBROOK ARTHUR. 2657084 Guardsman Lance Corporal 3rd Battalion Coldstream Guards.

The War Memorial listed the name W. Allsebrook but no records have been found with this initial.

Arthur Allsebrook was baptised on the 17th March 1915. His parents John William and Anne Allsebrook lived at 6 The Avenue Cudworth.

Addresses, 121 Darfield Road, Cudworth and 14 Highroyd, for Allsebrook, have been found in the electoral roll 1915.

ATTER E.C.

While discussing E.C. Atter with residents of Cudworth it was stated that he had a brother named George and a sister named Nellie.

An extract from a letter from Pat & Trevor Tillotson states that,

"Eric Charles Atter was killed in action in Burma at the end of WW2.
He was 'adopted' possibly from Dr Barnados by Margaret's grandma, who lived at 2 Quarry Vale, (A house owned by Harrison the Chemist) and at 18 Stanley Street.
A very blonde haired boy called 'Snowball' at school. He went in search of his birth parents probably named Smith.
He joined up for the war effort. Grandma wrote to him as Captain Eric Charles Atter, but her letter was returned to her. The Atter family lived next to the Police Station at 52 Manor Road.
Thomas married Margaret Smart and lived 18 Stanley Street in 1945".

The Commonwealth War Graves Commission records lists four men named Atter but none with the initials E.C. or who lived in the Barnsley area.

A John Atter was listed in the Barnsley Chronicle as a Leading Seaman R.N., serving overseas, who lived at 78 York Street, Cudworth.

BARRACLOUGH CYRIL. 1029627 Sergeant Royal Air Force Volunteer Reserve.

Cyril Barraclough was born in Cudworth the son of Seth Tom and Maggie Barraclough of 310 Barnsley Road, Cudworth.

He was educated at Pontefract Road school and then attended classes at Barnsley Mining and Technical College where he gained a 1st Class Certificate on each occasion.

His working life, before joining the R.A.F. was spent in the Colliery offices on the staff of Carlton Main Colliery at Grimethorpe.

Before he left for the R.A.F. he had served with the local Home Guard for approximately 18 months.

The Barnsley Chronicle for the 12th of November 1943 reported: - *"Cudworth Airman Missing. Official information has been received by the parents that their only son, Sgt. Cyril Barraclough (age 23), a Wireless Operator/Air Gunner, of 310 Barnsley Road,*

Cudworth is missing during the recent operations with Coastal Command. He was well known in Cudworth. He had joined R.A.F. two and a half years ago."

Sergeant Barraclough was one of the Wireless Operators/Air Gunners on Catalina Mark 1B serial number FP120 that went missing whilst on a non-operational training flight on the 2nd of November 1943. Sgt. Barraclough was attached to No. 131 Operational Training Unit for the purpose of his training, having served with No. 201 Squadron RAF. Catalina FP 120 was detailed to carry out an early morning navigational flight exercise from its base at RAF Killadeas, Northern Ireland, to a point off the West Coast of Scotland. Approximately one hour after take off it signalled its position to base. The next message was due an hour later.

The weather, which had been favourable at the start of the flight, deteriorated later and it was decided to recall the aircraft. A signal was sent to this effect, but as no answer was received the message was broadcast repeatedly but nothing further was heard from the aircraft. Two more broadcasts were then made within a half-hour of each other giving instructions to land immediately at the nearest RAF Station, but no answering signals were received. A search was made by other aircraft but failed to reveal any trace of Catalina FP120, and it had to be assumed that it was lost without trace over the sea together with all of its crew. The details of the other crewmembers are as follows.

J8372	Flying Officer Edward Earle Muffitt RCAF – Pilot
J14405	Pilot Officer Douglas Haig Disney RCAF – 2nd Pilot
127286	Flying Officer Kenneth Hipwell – Navigator
970123	Sergeant James Male – Flight Engineer/Air Gunner
1456621	Sergeant Albert Upton – Flight Mechanic/Air Gunner
1392444	Sergeant Charles Edward Poots – Air Gunner
1216706	Sergeant Peter Philip Bacon – Wireless Operator/Air Gunner
576483	Sergeant Harold Edwin Scarman – Wireless Mechanic/Air Gunner

Sergeant Cyril Barraclough and his fellow crewmembers are commemorated on the Air Forces Memorial at Runnymede. The Memorial is situated off a spur on Coopers Hill, overlooking the River Thames. It commemorates those airmen who lost their lives in North West Europe and the adjacent seas and have no known grave. The name of Sgt. Barraclough is inscribed on panel 41.

**Cyril Barraclough Memorial Window.
(Cudworth Parish Church)**

At the Parochial Church Council meeting on the 7th of December 1948 the Vicar said that Mr. & Mrs. Barraclough had expressed the wish to have a stained glass window installed in the sanctuary in memory of their son Cyril. On the 6th of June 1949 the design for the window was presented to the meeting and a vote for the installation was carried.

The stained glass window depicting St. Michael and St. George was unveiled and dedicated by the Reverend G H Stanney on the 23rd April 1950.

BAUGH ISAIAH. 4537893 Corporal 2nd Battalion Prince of Wales's Own (West Yorkshire Regiment).

This report appeared in the Barnsley Chronicle on the 24th of February 1945 that: -

"DIED OF WOUNDS.

Cudworth Corporal's Fate in Far East.

Many months ago Mr. And Mrs. I. Baugh, 14, Park Avenue, Cudworth, received notification that their eldest son, Cpl. Isaiah Baugh (24), West Yorkshire Regt. had died of wounds in the Far East in February 1944. They never gave up hope however that he might have survived, but now that hope has been dispelled with the receipt of a number belonging to their son. Cpl. Baugh joined the Army in 1937 and went overseas to Palestine the following year. After seeing service in Persia and Iraq he was drafted to the Far East. Before enlisting he was employed as a haulage hand at Wharncliffe Woodmoor Colliery. He attended Pontefract Road School, Cudworth, and was a member of the Cudworth Troop of Boy Scouts."

The Commonwealth War Graves Commission give his mother and father's names as Isaiah and Ellen Baugh and Corporal Baugh's age at the time of his death as 25. He died on Thursday the 24th of February 1944. He was buried in the Taukkyan War Cemetery, Myanmar (formerly Burma) in grave reference 10. A. 15.

BOLTON GEORGE ARTHUR. 4691012 Private 1st Battalion King's Own Yorkshire Light Infantry.

George Arthur Bolton lived at 12 Stanley Street, Darfield Road, Cudworth.

Private Bolton was 25 years of age when he died on Tuesday the 25th of January 1944. He was laid to rest in the Minturno War Cemetery, South of Naples, Italy in grave reference I. D. 23. The adjacent picture shows the grave before the C.W.G.C. took charge of the Cemetery and replaced the crosses with headstones.

Memories of Private George Arthur Bolton. Killed in Action 25th January 1944.

By Haydn Buckley. (Cousin).

George must have been 4 or 5 years older than me. He joined the King's Own Yorkshire Light Infantry at the start of WW2, although miners were exempt from call up. I was very proud of him, especially when he had a spell in the Maginot Line. I was collecting stamps at the time and asked him to bring some back next time he went to France. He was sent to Norway when the country was invaded, and they had quite a hard time fighting their way back to Narvik, with paratroops being dropped behind them. They were short of ammunition, and he told us that they had to use bayonets whenever possible. We went over to Cudworth when he was sent home on leave as soon as they landed back in this country. He was sleeping off his tiredness when we arrived there. He had brought me two Norwegian stamps back, and I wish I had kept them when I gave away my album. He missed the Dunkirk evacuation; I imagine the battalion was retraining. There was a story that he ran a troop carrier into a tree whilst training in Northern Ireland and was in trouble. He was involved in the Sicily invasion and I saw a newspaper cutting at Cudworth in which he was driving a jeep up a muddy gully in Italy. He took part in the Anzio landing and was killed there.

He was buried at the Minturno War Cemetery with over 2000 other soldiers from the Second World War.

The following personal letter to his parents shows how soldiers thought of those at home. It is very moving when relatives are willing to share private information with you. A name becomes a person. Thank you to the family.

BOWEN CHARLES WILLIAM. 4613203 Lance Sergeant 2nd. Battalion Duke of Wellington's (West Riding Regiment)

Charles William Bowen resided at 1 Church Street, Cudworth according to the 1937 to 1939 Absent Voters Register.

At the age of 28, Lance Sergeant Bowen died on Monday the 30th of September 1942 and is commemorated on the Rangoon Memorial in the Taukkayan War Cemetery in Myanmar (Burma) on face 13.

BRADSHAW ARTHUR. 5382370 Corporal 2nd. Airborne Battalion Oxford and Bucks Light Infantry.

Arthur Bradshaw, the husband of Edith Bradshaw, resided at 113 Snydale Road, Cudworth.

Corporal Bradshaw died at the age of 25 on Friday the 27th of November 1942 and was buried in Cudworth Cemetery on the 2nd of December in grave reference section D south, row 4, grave 10.

CALVERLEY IVOR JOHN. 1814318 Sergeant 100 Squadron Royal Air Force Volunteer Reserve.

Ivor Calverley was the son of John W and Lillie Calverley who lived in the Pinfold area of Darfield Road in the houses that were later demolished for subsidence.

Ivor Calverley was educated at Cudworth Secondary Modern School. A member of Cudworth Youth Club, he enlisted in the Barnsley Squadron of the Air Defence Corps (later to become the Air Training Corps) in 1940. In 1941 he transferred to Cudworth A.T.C. and became a Flight Sergeant.

At the age of 20, Sergeant Calverley was on a training flight on Monday the 21st of May 1945 in Lancaster 1, number LL 952 HW-W2 when it ditched 5 miles east of the Donna Nook ranges during air firing practice.

"Fellow crewmembers" Flight Sergeant Chalmers of the RAAF was buried in the Cambridge City Cemetery, and Sergeant Padmore was buried in the Abertillery Cemetery.

All the others are commemorated on the Runnymede Memorial in Surrey along with Sergeant Ivor John Calverley whose name is located on Panel 274.

CHAMBERLAIN CHARLES ERNEST. 4748983 Private 5th Battalion Queen's Own Cameron Highlanders.

Charles Ernest Chamberlain was born in Grimethorpe and went to live in Cudworth after his marriage.

The Barnsley Chronicle reported on the 11th of November 1944: -

"CUDWORTH SOLDIER KILLED IN NORTH WEST EUROPE.

News has been received by Mrs. C.E. Chamberlain, 102, Newtown Avenue, Cudworth, that her husband, Pte. Charles Ernest Chamberlain (27) was killed in action on service in North West Europe during October.

Pte. Chamberlain returned from the Middle East 12 months ago after serving in that theatre of war three years and 10 months, and went out to France a week after D-day. He is a native of Grimethorpe, but following marriage in January 1940, had resided at Cudworth. Before joining the Forces Pte. Chamberlain worked at Grimethorpe Colliery."

Private Chamberlain was killed in action on Wednesday the 4th of October 1944 and was buried in the Valkenswaard War Cemetery, Noord-Brabant in the Netherlands in grave reference I. D. 19.

COLWOOD ALBERT. 1838799 Gunner 118 H.A.A. Regiment Royal Artillery.

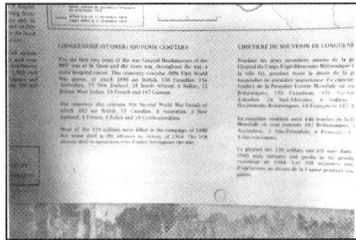

Albert Colwood was born at Pontefract Road, Cudworth to Herbert and Emma Colwood, later of Churchfield Avenue.

Enlisting in London, Gunner Colwood died at the age of 25 on Sunday the 20th of May 1945. He is buried in the Longuenesse (St. Omer) Souvenir Cemetery in grave number 32, row AA, Plot IV.

CONWAY STANLEY. 1520665 Gunner 2nd Bty. 1 Searchlight Regiment Royal Artillery.

Stanley Conway was the youngest son of George Patrick and Elizabeth Conway of 64 Lunn Road, Cudworth. He was known locally as "Tom" or "Tim".

Gunner Conway was taken prisoner at Dunkirk in April 1940 and was held in Stalag VIII. When repatriated at the end of 1943/ beginning of 1944, a German Doctor gave him a pint of his own blood and accompanied him to the boat for England so that he could get home to see his mother before he died.

A Cudworth Variety Concert was held at the Catholic Club in aid of Norman Stacey and Stanley Conway, repatriated prisoners of war. After the concert was originally planned Stanley Conway died in Hospital, but it was agreed that the project should be carried through, his mother to receive his share. There was a good company of talented artistes, all of whom gave their services free.

Gunner Conway died on Tuesday the 18th of January 1944 and is buried in the Dearne (Thurnscoe) Cemetery in section E. 1. R.C. grave 43. He was 24 years old.

His brother Driver J. Conway R.A. also of 64, Lunn Rd. was a Dunkirk evacuee.

COOPER LAWRENCE. 870086 Gunner 5/3 Maritime Regiment Royal Artillery.

Lawrence Cooper was born in Barnsley and died at sea at the age of 22. He was killed on Tuesday the 22nd September 1942 and is commemorated on the Chatham Naval Memorial Panel number 67.1.

COTTAM RONALD. 14449256 Lance Corporal 4th Battalion Northamptonshire Regiment.

Ronald Cottam was the son of Thomas and Nellie Cottam of Cudworth.

Lance Corporal Cottam died at the age of 19 on Thursday the 20th of September 1945 and was buried in the Reichswald Forest War Cemetery in Germany. His grave reference is 56. H. 8.

CROSSLAND A.

A search of the Commonwealth War Graves Commission records for "Crossland A. for WW2, Force unknown, Date unknown and nationality unknown" revealed four men who could not be connected to Cudworth without further information.

Crossland Alfred.	Parents Bradford.	K.O.Y.L.I.
Crossland Albert Alfred Elliss.		R.A.F.
Crossland Alfred Harold.	Parents Hull.	R.N. Patrol Service.
Crossland Albert Oliver.	Parents Job and Priscilla.	R.A.S.C.

Research was carried out using other sources but no information was found.

DAY LESLIE. 2120630 Sapper 10 Field Squadron Royal Engineers.

Leslie Day, the son of Charles and Florence Day of 119 Darfield Road, Cudworth. He and his wife Betty lived at 44 Ladywood Avenue, Grimethorpe.

Sapper Day was killed in a road accident during military action on Tuesday the 13th of January 1942 and was brought home to Cudworth for burial in the churchyard in grave reference section D south, row 5, grave 3. He was 25 years old.

DICKENS RICHARD GEORGE. 1515122 Leading Aircraftman Royal Air Force Volunteer Reserve.

A search of the Commonwealth War Graves Commission records for "Dickens R. for WW2, Force unknown, Date unknown and nationality unknown" revealed one man. However nothing connects him to Cudworth without further information.

Leading Aircraftman Dickens died on Monday the 11th of February 1946 and was buried in the Heath Town (Holy Trinity) Churchyard in Staffordshire. The grave reference is Old Ground, Row 36. Grave 38 1/2.

DUCKWORTH CHARLES. 1691341 Private 1st/4th King's Own Yorkshire Light Infantry.

Charles Duckworth was born in *'Barnsley'*. His parents, Charles Wetton and Emily Duckworth resided in Leeds when the C.W.G.C. records were compiled. The 1918 Electoral Roll for Cudworth shows Charles Wetton and Emily living at Low Cudworth. The 1919 Electoral Roll shows them residing at 219 Barnsley Road.

Aged 23, Private Duckworth was killed in action on Saturday the 1st of July 1944 and is buried in the Fontenay-Le-Pesnel War Cemetery at Tessel in the Calvados Region of France. His grave reference is IV. C. 12.

DUNHILL CLIFFORD. 4749674 Lance Corporal 6th Battalion York and Lancaster Regiment.

Lance Corporal Dunhill's death was reported in the Barnsley Chronicle:

"Cudworth Lance-Corporal Killed in Action.

Mr. And Mrs. Walter Dunhill, 34, Moorland Terrace, Darfield road, Cudworth, have received an official notification that their son, Lance-Corporal Clifford Dunhill (25), York and Lancaster Regiment, was killed in action during January while serving with the Central Mediterranean Forces.

L./Cpl. Dunhill, who joined the Forces in January 1940, and had been overseas two years, had served in India, Persia and Iraq and before taking part in the fighting in Italy was in Sicily.

An ex-Pontefract Road, Cudworth, scholar, L./Cpl. Dunhill worked as a haulage hand at Brierley Colliery. A brother Walter is a gunner in the R.A".

Clifford Dunhill also had two sisters, Edith and Phyllis.

Lance Corporal Dunhill died on Saturday the 29th of January 1944 and was buried in the Minturno War Cemetery in Italy, grave reference V. L. 17.

EDWARDS A.E.

A search of the Commonwealth War Graves Commission records for "Edwards A.E. for WW2, Force unknown, Date unknown and nationality unknown" revealed 16 men who could not be connected to Cudworth without further information.

Three are Civilian War Dead and two in the RAF. Two with the initials A.E. have no place of residence, (one of these is Australian) and three men have a third initial. Of the three civilians one has a Portsmouth address and the other two London addresses.   ·

EVERETT WILLIAM. 1658664 Gunner 148 Battery 11A.A. "Z" Regiment Royal Artillery.

William Everett the son of Hector Samuel and Celine Lewis Everett of 13 Pindar Street, Barnsley. The Electoral Roll of 1918 shows his parents living at 6 Bow Street, Cudworth.

He died while on sentry duty at Hull Docks on Thursday the 17th April 1941 at the age of 28. He was buried a month later in Cudworth Churchyard, section C south, row 10, grave 39.

EVERSEDGE WILFRED. 1898642 Sapper 192 Railway Operating Coy. Royal Engineers.

Sapper Wilfred Eversedge's death was reported in the Barnsley Chronicle on the 20th of May 1944:

"Cudworth Sapper's Death From Wounds.
The death from wounds in hospital, received through an accident while with the C.M.F. during May, is announced of Sapper Wilfred Eversedge (25) R.E., son of Mr. And Mrs. Eversedge, of 10, Kings Rd., Cudworth.

The news of their son's injury was first received by the parents in an official letter, which stated that he had been admitted to a hospital. This was followed by an air letter from the Matron of the General Hospital, who said that though Sapper Eversedge was conscious and knew she was writing the letter, he had severe chest complications, and was very seriously ill. A further official communication stated that he was "wounded in the neck through an accident in the battle area," and the news of his death was conveyed in a letter from the war office on Monday. Sapper Eversedge, who joined the forces in November 1939, was among the troops who were landed in Norway in 1940, but after an hour was evacuated. He was sent to Persia and Iraq, and was there until the Italian fighting commenced. The last air-graph received from him was dated April 28th, when he was quite fit and well.

He formerly worked as a cleaner and fireman in the L.M.S. Railway shed at Royston, and attended Pontefract Rd. Boys School, Cudworth. A brother, Eric, is in the R.A.F."

The following is a summary of a conversation with a relative and the words are reported 'SIC'. *"Father wrote to the War Office, and they replied by letter that has been lost! A group of mates went into a cafe, a local 'wog' set about Wilf's mate. Wilf intervened and got knifed through the heart by a turban clad 'wog'.*

Belongings sent home included a rosary, (but he was not religious) and a photograph of a young 10 years old girl. The family like to think that he befriended a family and these were the good luck tokens."

Sapper Eversedge was killed on Thursday the 5th of May 1944 and was buried at the Bari War Cemetery in the Carbonara Region of Italy, grave reference VI. C. 8.

His mother and father's Christian names were Elizabeth and John.
He is commemorated on his mother's gravestone in the Cudworth Churchyard.

FENTON KENNETH. LT/JX 232918 Seaman RN. Patrol Service HM Trawler 'Stella Capella'.

Kenneth Fenton was the son of Walter Fenton, a Cudworth butcher who died in March 1944 at the age of 60. They resided at 234 Barnsley Road, Cudworth.

Seaman Fenton was posted missing presumed dead on the 11th of March 1942 and is remembered on the Lowestoft Naval Memorial Panel 8, Column 3.

The Lowestoft Memorial is to commemorate officers & men of the Royal Naval Patrol Service who lost their lives and have no other grave than the sea.

The STELLA CAPELLA was an A/S type trawler of 440 tons gross, built in 1937, and requisitioned by the Admiralty in September 1939 for anti-submarine duties.

German documents show that the STELLA CAPELLA was probably torpedoed by U 701 at 0212 on 11 March 1942 in the approximate position 64 deg. 52 min. North, 13 deg. 18 min. West or 64 deg. 48 min. North, 13 deg. 20 min. West. There were no survivors.

The log of the ship's movements between 1939 and 1942 show that its last port of call was Seidisfjord where it was due to arrive on the 7th of March and depart on the 10th. At the side of this entry it says ' SUNK Overdue off Iceland 19.3.1942.

U-701 was a type VIIC submarine built at the H C Stülcken Sohn Construction Yard, Hamburg, and commissioned in July 1941. Her commander was KL Horst Degen under whom she was responsible for the sinking of 14 ships on 4 active patrols. The Stella Capella was the last ship sunk on her 2nd patrol that lasted from the 26th of February 1942 to the 1st of April 1942.

U-boat U-701 was depth-charged and sunk by United States Army Air Force aircraft of 396 Squadron off Cape Hatteras, North Carolina on 7th July 1942.

A full crew list of the STELLA CAPELLA is available.

GASKELL OLIVER. 964506 Bombardier Royal Artillery.

Oliver Gaskell was the son of Oliver and Polly Gaskell of West Derby, Liverpool and the husband of Alice M. Gaskell, nee Geeson who later remarried and became Mrs Alice Underwood. The C.W.G.C. record says after Alice M. Gaskell "of Cudworth".

Bombardier Gaskell was 25 years old when he died on Friday the 10th of August 1945. He was laid to rest in the Liverpool (West Derby) Cemetery reference E. Grave 699.

GILLESPIE Leslie. P/JX 275191 Able Seaman H.M. Submarine 'Splendid'.

Leslie Gillespie was the son of Joe and Alice Gillespie of 30 Charles Street, Cudworth. His father was employed by Mason Bros. who were haulage contractors in Cudworth.

Able Seaman Gillespie was 23 years of age when he died on Sunday the 2nd of May 1943. He is commemorated on the Portsmouth Naval Memorial at Southsea Common on Panel 74, Column 3.

H.M. Submarine 'Splendid' was built in the Chatham Dockyards in 1941 and launched in 1942. Based in Gibraltar she sank seven enemy ships including the Italian destroyer 'Aviere', the cargo ships 'St. Antioco' and 'Emma' and the tankers 'Devoli' and 'Giorgio'. During January 1943 she landed agents on the island of Corsica.

On the 21st April 1943 the submarine was on patrol in the Southern Tyrrhenian Sea when the German Destroyer 'Hermes', a captured Greek vessel, spotted her. Hermes attacked using depth charges and by gunfire when the 'Splendid' surfaced. The hull of the submarine was so badly damaged that the crew scuttled the vessel South to Capri at 40°30'N, 14°15'E.

30 members of the crew were rescued by the 'Hermes' with 18 dead or missing.

GREEN FRANK. 402745 Sergeant The Royal Scot Greys (2nd Dragoons).

Frank Green was born at Dinnington in 1911, the son of John and Hannah Green.

The Barnsley Chronicle reported on the 26th of August 1944:

" Cudworth Soldier Killed in France.

Shook Hands with Prime Minister.

Information has reached the relatives at 193, Birkwood Ave., Cudworth, that Sgt. Frank Green (33) has been killed in action in France during July. He had served in many parts overseas and went out to France on D-day. His chaplain in a letter of condolence states that, Sgt. Green was buried in a little village near Caen.

A native of Dinnington, Sgt. Green came to Cudworth when a boy and attended Pontefract Road School. Later he was employed at Monckton Colliery, joined the army when seventeen, and went to the Middle East in 1938. After serving in Palestine, Syria and Iraq he was with the 8th Army in the glorious North African advance. He went to Italy, and was wounded at Cassino. He returned from Italy in February.

In August 1942, on the occasion of the visit to the Middle East of Mr. Winston Churchill, Sgt. Green was among those chosen to represent his regiment. Mr. Churchill shook hands with him and asked him how he was progressing. An all-round sportsman, Sgt. Green at the age of 19 won the welter-weight boxing championship for the Army."

An earlier article on soldiers serving overseas had given his address as 171 Birkwood Avenue.

Sergeant Frank Green was killed in action on Sunday the 30th of July 1944 and is buried at the Ranville War Cemetery in the Calvados region of France in grave reference III. D. 18.

GROCOTT WILLIAM HENRY. 1061174 Private Royal Army Service Corps.

Private William Henry Grocott is buried in Section C south, Row 6, Grave 14 of Cudworth Cemetery. An address of South Moor House, Hemsworth is given in the burial records.

He was 41 years old when he died on the 17th of January 1944. The details of his death have not been found in the C.W.G.C. records using a "search with no initials, year, force and nationality all unknown".

HASKEY LESLIE. D/KX80856 Petty Officer H.M.S. HURWORTH Royal Navy.

Leslie Haskey was the husband of Lilly Haskey of Garden Cottages, Cudworth and the son of Harold and Agnes Haskey of 2 Royd Avenue, Cudworth.

On Friday the 22nd of October 1943 Petty Officer Haskey was killed in action at the age of 31. He is commemorated on the Plymouth Naval Memorial sited on Plymouth Hoe on Panel 81, Column 3.

H.M.S. Hurworth was an Escort destroyer of the Hunt (Type II) class with the penant L28. Vickers Armstrong of Newcastle-on-Tyne and Parsons built her. Laid down on the 10th of April 1940 and launched on the 10th of April the following year, she was commissioned on the 5th of October 1941.

Emblem of Current Vessel

A German mine sank H.M.S. Hurworth on the 22nd of October 1943 off east of Kalymnos, Dodecanese.

HEATH HERBERT. 4607368 Private 1st Battalion Duke of Wellington's (West Riding Regiment).

Private Heath lived at 44 Kings Road, Cudworth.

He was 35 years old when he was killed in action on Friday the 31st of May 1940 and was buried in the Les Moeres Communal Cemetery, Nord, in France. His grave reference is Row B, Grave 43.

HEATON JOHN. 815606 Corporal 7 Bty. 1 Searchlight Regiment Royal Artillery.

John Heaton was 31 years old, the husband of Mary Heaton (nee Burke) of Cudworth. She remarried and became Mrs Mary Clay.

He was the son of Private George Heaton who died on active service in the 1st World War and Mary Heaton.

Corporal Heaton died on the 27th of February 1945. As can be seen from the Dual Regimental Crests on the headstone in Cudworth

Cemetery, father and son are buried together. However the C.W.G.C. gives the grave reference for George Heaton (Father) as B. 10. 16 and reference B. 9. 10 for John Heaton (Son).

HIRST DOROTHY. Civilian Staff Nurse.

Dorothy Hirst was the daughter of the late Mr and Mrs J. Lister Hirst of 14 Newtown Avenue, Cudworth.

Aged 45, Dorothy was working as a Staff Nurse with the Malayan Nursing Service when she was killed as the result of enemy action on Saturday the 14th of February 1942. She is remembered in the S.S. 'KUALA' section of the Civilian War dead register.

The S.S. 'KUALA' was purchased by the Straits Steamship Company form the Caledon S.B. & E. Co. in 1911. She had a gross displacement of 954 tons and 132 n.h.p. Triple expansion engines.

At the outbreak of War the Straits Steamship Co. had 51 vessels, some of the smaller we requisitioned into service by the Navy for use as minesweepers and patrol boats.

Before the surrender of Singapore, vessels from the Straits Steamship Co. along with those from other companies found themselves split into four groups. The first group included six ships from the company including H.M.S. Kuala.

H.M.S. Kuala survived a bombing attack on the 12th of February 1942 and arrived safely at Singapore. On the 13th orders were received to assist in the evacuation of the city. Under command of the Captain, Lieutenant F. Caithness, she embarked 500 civilians including 250 women and children and set sail for South Java via the straits of Rhio, Barbala and Banka.

The following morning, the 14th of February 1942, she sought refuge along with other vessels close to the island Pom Pom. They were soon spotted by a large formation of Japanese aircraft heading for Java. Approximately forty planes were detached to attack the lightly defended Ships. H.M.S. Kuala received a direct hit on the bridge and caught fire. Although badly wounded the Captain, Lt. Caithness was the last man to leave the ship accompanied by Lt. George. Eleven ships were sunk on that Saturday morning with a great loss of life, the planes fired at those in the water and those had managed to gain land. Because of the date of death recorded for Dorothy Hirst it is believed that she was killed during this attack.

On the 16th of February the Heap Eng Moh Steamship vessel, Tanjong Pinang, lifted approximately 130 women and children from the vessels sunk on the 14th, off the island. Their relief was short-lived when the small vessel itself was bombed claiming all except three or four lives.

Lieutenant Caithness was taken off the island on the 17th, along with seventy walking wounded, by an ex-Japanese fishing craft commanded by an Australian, Bill Reynolds formerly of the Johore Government Service. The rescue vessel, named the Krait, was later to distinguish herself in an attack on Japanese shipping in Singapore Harbour.

At a ceremony after the War the Red Ensign was placed in Singapore Cathedral on the 22nd of May 1946 by members of the British Coastal Shipping Community as a memorial to those of their community who lost their lives afloat or on shore during the War. Captain F. Caithness a survivor of the Kuala carried the Ensign into the Cathedral.

The Singapore Straits Co. Ltd. lost 30 vessels, the Sarawak Steamship Co. Ltd. lost 6 vessels, the Hua Khiow Steamship Co. Ltd. and the Kheng Seng Steamship Co. Ltd. each lost one vessel.

HUDSTON MAURICE GREGORY. 1540155 Sergeant Royal Air Force Volunteer Reserve.

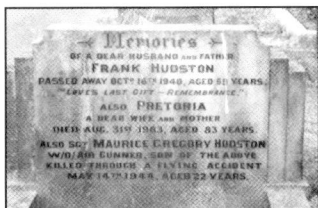

Maurice Hudston was the 22-year-old son of Frank (a railway controller) and Pretoria Hudston who lived at 251 Barnsley Road, Cudworth.

Sergeant Hudston was a Wireless Operator/Air Gunner and killed in a flying accident on Sunday the 14th of May 1944.

He was buried in Cudworth Cemetery on the 19th of May 1944 in Section C south, Row 8, Grave 37.

HYDE JOSEPH EDWARD. 1863568 Aircraftman 1st Class Royal Air Force Volunteer Reserve.

Joseph Edward Hyde was the husband of Violet Hyde of 33 School Hill, Cudworth.

Aircraftman Hyde died on Monday the 20th of December 1943 at the age of 42. He was buried on the 23rd in Cudworth Cemetery, grave reference Section D south, Row 9, Grave 77.

HYMAN WILLIAM. 798730 Gunner 27 Field Regiment Royal Artillery.

William Hyman was the second son of Charles and Florence Hyman of Victoria Street, Cudworth. He was married to Ellen Hyman and had one son, aged 5, named David.

William Hyman was the uncle of Cudworth's highly successful Olympic Athlete Dorothy Hyman.

Gunner Hyman joined the Royal Artillery at Aldershot sometime before WW2 when no work was available. He signed for 3 years on 3 years off in the reserves. Re-called up immediately in August 1939.

Reported missing, he had been wounded and taken prisoner.

At the age of 34, he died during an operation to amputate his arm on Saturday the 7th of December 1940 and was buried in the Berlin 1939-1945 War Cemetery, Brandenburg, Germany. His grave reference is 9. A. 27.

JACKSON HENRY. 2653758 Lance Corporal 1st Battalion Hampshire Regiment.

Henry Jackson the son of Peter and Pru Jackson and was educated at Cudworth Roman Catholic School. He was married to Annie Eliza Jackson, had two daughters and lived at 116 Barnsley Road, Cudworth.

He formerly worked at a Carlton Pit

The Barnsley Chronicle reported on the 19th Aug 44:

"Mrs. A.E. Jackson has just received official information that her husband has been killed in action in France during July.

L/Cpl. Jackson was a reservist in the Coldstream Guards and joined the Army 18 months before the outbreak of war. He returned to this country in 1942 after serving four years with the North West Frontier Force. He had served in North Africa, Sicily and Italy.

Only a few weeks before this news there appeared in the "Barnsley Chronicle" a thrilling account of Cpl. Jackson's experiences on a night patrol in Normandy."

Lance Corporal Henry Jackson was killed in action on Tuesday the 11th of July 1944 and was buried in the Hottot-Les Bagues war Cemetery in the Calvados Region of France in grave reference VIII. F. 10. He was 35 years old.

JAQUES WILLIAM. 1554368 Gunner 5 Searchlight Regiment Royal Artillery.

William Jaques was the son of George and the late Ada Jaques living on Lunn Road, Cudworth.

Gunner Jaques died on Friday the 25th of June 1943 at the age of 26. He was buried in the Kanchanaburi War Cemetery in Thailand in grave reference 8. L. 37.

KIRK ERNEST. 1650465 Gunner 412 Bty. 54(1st/5th Battalion The Durham Light Infantry) Searchlight Regiment Royal Artillery.

Ernest Kirk, the husband of Phyllis Jemima Kirk of Barnsley, was the son of Fred and Florence Kirk of 40 Market Street, Cudworth.

Gunner Kirk was 31 years old when he died of wounds on Saturday the 20th May 1944. He was buried on the 24th of May in Cudworth Cemetery in grave reference Section D south, Row 9, Grave 10.

LAKE WILLIAM. 4546462 Trooper Reconnaissance Corps Royal Armoured Corps.

William Lake was born in Lancashire, the son of Clifford and Martha Alice Lake who later moved to Ingrow, near Keighley.

The Barnsley Chronicle reported his death on the 14th of October 1944:

"CUDWORTH TROOPER KILLED IN ACTION.

The death in action is reported, on the North West Front, during September, of Trooper William Lake (23), of the Recce. Corps., whose parents reside at the Police Station, Cudworth. He volunteered for the Army in January 1941, leaving his employment as assistant storekeeper at Grimethorpe colliery, where he was well known and respected. He had resided in Todmorden and Goole before coming to Cudworth with his parents; he was known in Goole as a member of the Cycling Club, where he won many events. His father, Police Sergeant Lake served in the last war and was wounded three times."

Trooper Lake was killed in action on the 25th of September 1944 during the Western Europe Campaign of 1944/45. He was buried in the Uden War Cemetery, Noord-Brabant between Eindhoven and Nijmegen in grave reference 4. D. 1.

LEADBEATER ERIC. 4397480 Private 4th Battalion The Buffs (Royal East Kent Regiment)

Eric Leadbeater was the husband of Eva Leadbeater of Grimethorpe and the son of Charles and Annie Leadbeater.

At the age of 27, Private Leadbeater was killed in action on Saturday the 23rd of October 1943. He was buried at sea and commemorated on the Athens Memorial in Greece on Face 5.

MELLOR H.

A search of the Commonwealth War Graves Commission records for "Mellor H. for WW2, Force unknown, Date unknown and nationality unknown" revealed nine men who could not be connected to Cudworth without further information.

MIDGLEY HAROLD. Sailor M.V. 'Abosso' (Liverpool), Merchant Navy.

Harold Midgley lived with his wife Muriel at Newtown, Cudworth. He was the son of Mr and Mrs H Midgley of Grimethorpe.

He was killed in action on Thursday the 29th of October 1942, aged 37, and is commemorated on the Tower Hill Memorial in London, Panel 2 and the Roll of Honour in the West End Working Men's Club, Cudworth.

The MV Abosso was the second ship of that name and was owned by the Elder Dempster Line Ltd. (Blue Funnel Line) of Liverpool she plied the West and South Africa Services. She was built in 1935, with a displacement of 11350t.

On the 8th/9th of October 1942 the MV Abosso departed Cape Town during the night bound for England. She had a crew of 182 and 189 passengers including the crew of a Dutch submarine lost when the Dutch East Indies fell to the Japanese who were returning to England to pick up a new submarine. Reports differ as to the number of people on board, some state 2000, but 400 seems to be the generally agreed figure.

On the 29th of October 1942 'U' Boat U575 homeward bound to France spotted the Abosso to the west of Ireland, approximately three days sailing from Liverpool. The submarine approached the Abosso and surfaced at full speed. At 19:42 hours the U-boat fired 4 torpedoes. At 20:15 GMT, the Abosso was hit on the portside by one torpedo and after approximately 25 minutes a torpedo from a second salvo hit her on the starboard side. Within 10/15 minutes the Abosso sank vertically at position 48° 30'N - 28°50'W.

The English Sloop 'Bideford' picked up thirty-one survivors, including five Dutch survivors, of whom four were submariners.

MIDGLEY RONALD. C/JX 234836 Able Seaman H.M.S. President III. Royal Navy.

Ronald Midgley of 53 Albert Street, Cudworth died at the age of 22 on the 25th of March 1942 and was buried in grave reference Section B north, Row 8, Grave 34 in the Cudworth Cemetery.

HMS 'President III' was not a ship but one of three Royal Naval training bases for gunners to man Merchant ships, known as Defensive Equipped Merchant Ships or D.E.M.S. for short. During the war 24,000 RN gunners were trained plus 14,000 from the Army and 150,000 Merchant seamen. On being assigned to a ship they had to sign the ships articles and come under the command of the Merchant Ship's Captain. During the war D.E.M.S. gunners were not given the credit they deserved.

Royal Navy DEMS records are held at HMS Centurion naval base. Information will only be given to next of kin and may take some time to obtain.

As part of the complement to HMS 'President' a number of accounts and administration establishments bore the same name, for example Debworth Manor, Hodgson House in Eton and Chelsea Court in London. Wrens mainly staffed these but they had a regular naval officer in charge. Survivors from Naval vessels sometimes joined these establishments as recorded by a Chief Petty Officer who joined in 1942 as a survivor from HMS 'Ark Royal'.

MILLWARD ALBERT. 4457672 Corporal 5th Battalion Highland Light Infantry.

(City of Glasgow Regiment)

Albert Millward was born on the 19th of December 1919 and lived at 39, Barnsley Rd., Brierley with his parents James Osmand and Eva Millward.

On the 28th of April 1945 the Barnsley Chronicle reported:

"CUDWORTH CORPORAL DIES OF WOUNDS,

WHILE SERVING WITH THE B.L.A.

Mrs Doreen Millward, 45, Lunn road, Cudworth, received news on Monday, 16th April, that her husband, Cpl. Albert Millward, had been seriously wounded while serving with the B.L.A., and this was followed on Tuesday 17th, that he had died of wounds in Western Europe. Cpl. Millward was called up in October, 1939, and had previously been a Sergeant for four years, and served with the Durham Light Infantry in the rear guard action in the Dunkirk evacuation, and also served in Iceland for 15 months. He landed in Normandy four days after D-day and recently was transferred to the Highland Light Infantry.

Previous to serving with the Forces he was employed by the L.N.E.R. Co. He married Miss Doreen Race in June 1940 and leaves a wife and seven months old baby daughter." (Named Carol)

His wife' maiden name was Doreen Muriel Race and after his death she remarried and became Grayson.

The Commonwealth War Graves Commission records Corporal Millward as having died of wounds on Monday the 9th of April 1945 and his burial in the Reichswald Forest War Cemetery, Kleve in grave reference 61. B. 2.

According to a family member he was injured on the 7th by standing on a landmine and died afterwards.

Corporal Millward is also commemorated on the Brierley War Memorial.

MYATT FRANK. 14315431 Driver Royal Corps of Signals.

Frank Myatt was the son of Harry and Harriet Myatt (nee Bowen) of 332 Barnsley Road, Cudworth.

Driver Myatt died at the age of 19 on Thursday the 29th of April 1943 and is commemorated on the Medejez-El-Bab in Tunisia on Face 11.

Frank Myatt Memorial Window. (Cudworth Parish Church)

At the Parochial Parish Council meeting on the 9th of September 1950 it was reported that Mrs Harriet Myatt was desirous of installing a Memorial Window for her son in the right hand window adjacent to the Font. The design would be submitted to the council prior to the application being made to the church faculty.

The design was submitted to the council on the 26th of November 1950.

In was agreed at a meeting on August the 7th 1951 that the Frank Myatt Memorial Window would be dedicated with a service with Mrs Myatt, the family and other donors attending.

The window was dedicated on the 9th of September 1951.

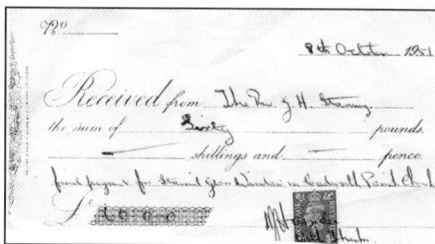

NAYLOR WILLIAM EDWARD. 4698620 Private 1st Battalion Green Howards (Yorkshire Regiment)

William Naylor was the son of Edward and Rose Naylor who lived at 43 Lunn Road, Cudworth. He was known locally as Teddy.

Private Naylor, aged 20, died on Tuesday the 1st of August 1944 and was buried in the Ramieh War Cemetery in Israel in grave 5. F. 8.

Reported in the Barnsley Chronicle for the 2nd of September 1944 *"that Mrs and Mrs Naylor of Lunn Road, Cudworth, has been informed that their only son William Edward had been drowned."*

NOON JOHN PATRICK. C/JX 353207 Ordinary Seaman H.M.S. 'Achates' Royal Navy.

Ordinary Seaman John Noon who lived on Snydale Road, Cudworth was killed on Thursday the 31st of December 1942 and is commemorated on the Chatham Naval Memorial Panel 58.Column 1.

PARKINSON STANLEY. 4689734 Private 2nd Battalion King's Own Yorkshire Light Infantry.

Stanley Parkinson was born on August the 18th in 1917, the son of John (a Miner) and Sarah Parkinson, and baptised on the 2nd of September 1917. Their address was given in the birth/baptism register as 8 Victoria Road. Victoria Road did not exist but the 1918 Electoral Roll lists a John and Sarah Ann Parkinson living at 8 Victoria Street.

Private Parkinson was killed in action on Monday the 30th of March 1942 and is commemorated on Face 16 of the Rangoon Memorial in the Taukkyan War Cemetery in Myanmar (Burma). He was 24 years old.

PEARY JAMES WILLIAM. 929657 Gunner 13 Bty. Super-Heavy Regiment Royal Artillery.

James William Peary was born in Skinningrove, North Yorkshire the son of Mr and Mrs John Thomas Peary of 15 Belmont, Cudworth.

He was one of nine children including Lily, John, Joyce, Doris, Ronald, Arthur and James William.

An iron miner in the North East, he moved to the coalmines in Yorkshire and found employment at Brierley Colliery.

Gunner Peary was called up and stationed at Canterbury, in Kent. He had lived with his wife's parents. He married Margaret (Peggy) Ada six months before he died.

On returning from Dunkirk, James Peary died of wounds on the 2nd of January 1943. He was buried in Elham Burial Ground in Kent in grave reference Line F, grave 4 at the age of 23.

Margaret Tillotson was a bridesmaid at his wedding.

PIPE JACK. 2764455 Private 70th Battalion Black Watch (Royal Highlanders).

Jack Pipe was the son of William George and Margaret Pipe of 5 Emsley Avenue, Darfield, Cudworth.

He was employed as a coal cutter at Royston and had served as a member of the Home Guard.

Attached to the R.N.A.S., he was killed in action, at the age of 18, on Sunday the 6th of July 1941 and is laid to rest in Barnsley Cemetery in grave reference Section 10, Grave 316.

PLATT GEORGE. Captain 14th Canadian Hussars R.C.A.C. 8th Reconnaissance Regiment.

George Platt was married with one child.

Captain Platt died on the 17th of June 1945 and was buried at the Holten Canadian War Cemetery in Holland in grave reference XI. G. 16.

PYGOTT WILLIAM EDMUND. 4695385..Gunner 4/2 Maritime Regiment Royal Artillery.

William Pygott lived with his wife Sarah Emma Pygott at 43 Albert Street, Cudworth. He was the son of Roger Gardam and Frances Pygott of 3 Queens Road, Cudworth.

Gunner Pygott was awarded the following medals 1939/45 Star, Atlantic Star, Pacific Star, War Medal. He was stationed at the Queen Elizabeth Barracks, Strensall, York, Cape Town, South Africa and Bermuda. Aged 27, he was killed in action on the S.S. 'ARABISTAN' in the Atlantic Ocean on Friday the 14th of August 1942. He is commemorated on the Portsmouth Naval Memorial Panel 72, Column 2.

On or about the 11th of August 1942, the S.S. Arabistan was shelled by the German auxiliary cruiser 'Michel'. She sank at the position 11°30'S. 26°00'W. with a loss of 65 lives. The only two survivors were taken prisoner.

RACE ERNEST.   Fusilier

Ernest Race was the son of Fred and Eliza Race of St John's Cottages, Cudworth.

The report in the Barnsley Chronicle in July 1944 states;

" The parents of Fusilier Ernest Race (29) of St John's Cottages, Cudworth have been officially informed that he has been killed in action in Normandy. Two other brothers are also serving Rifleman. Harold and Driver Edwin."

Ernest Race was killed in action at the age of 28 on the 27th of July 1944 and was buried in Cudworth Cemetery in grave reference Section C south, Row 10, Grave 3

RACE HAROLD. 3248601 Lance Corporal 2nd Battalion Cameronians (Scottish Rifles).

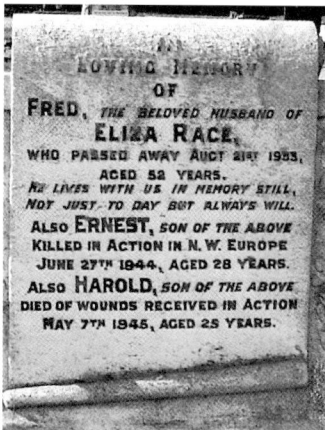

Harold Race was the son of Fred and Eliza Race of St John's Cottages, Cudworth.

Lance Corporal Race died of wounds received in action on the 7th of May 1945 at the age of 25 and was buried in Cudworth Cemetery in grave reference Section C south, Row 10, Grave 3.

RANDLE JAMES. 4689394 Private 7th Battalion Parachute Regiment A.A.C.

James Randle lived at 19 Bow Street, Cudworth (Guests Yard from family member). He worked at New Carlton, joining the 1st Battalion of the King's Own Yorkshire Light Infantry prior to the war starting.

Private Randle died at the age of 32 on Tuesday the 9th of January 1945. At the time of his death he was serving with the Army Air Corps (Parachute Regiment).

A letter to his family from the Reverend W.H.C. Hyde C.F., Chaplain of the 7th Battalion, Light Infantry, the Parachute Regiment reads as follows:

"Dear Mr Randle

May I first express to you my very deep sympathy in the sad loss of your son during the early part of the campaign in Belgium.

I believe you have already received a letter from the Commanding Officer giving details of his injuries and death. I am indeed sorry that you have not heard from me earlier – unhappily my previous letter, together with some others, went astray.

Your son's Company was in a forward position on some high thickly wooded ground east of the river HOMME when the tragedy occurred. He received a severe bullet wound in the left thigh and although medical attention was immediately available he did not recover from the effects of the initial shock. The medical Officer was sent for at once and I accompanied him up the hill to the Company position. Your son had been given some morphine and appeared to be in no pain whatsoever which was a great blessing. We then carried him down on a stretcher to a waiting ambulance in which he was taken to the nearest c.c.s. and given a blood transfusion.

Everything possible was done for him our prayers and our labours were unable to save him and he died shortly afterwards. None could have borne his pain and suffering so bravely or so silently. He was a proud example to all of us.

I know his loss will be a very heavy burden for yourself and your loved ones and I pray that God will give you strength to bear it and also courage to go forward into the future until the glad day of re-union.

May God's blessing be with you
Yours very sincerely
W.H.C. Hyde
Chaplain

P.S. Your son was buried by the Field Ambulance Chaplain in a little Cemetery N.W. of ROCHEFORT. I have visited the grave and placed a cross upon it.

He is buried in the Rochefort Communal Cemetery near Namur, in Belgium.

The Under-Secretary of State for War presents his compliments and by Command of the Army Council has the honour to transmit the enclosed Awards granted for service in the war of 1939-45.

The Council share your sorrow that

PTE J. RANDLE

in respect of whose service these Awards are granted did not live to receive them.

Campaign Stars, Clasps and Medals
instituted in recognition of service in the war of 1939-45

NUMBER OF STARS, MEDALS, CLASPS or EMBLEMS ENCLOSED 5

Order in which the awards should be set up, e.g., for framing	Description of Ribbon	Clasp or Emblem (if awarded)
1 1939-45 Star	Dark blue, red and light blue in three equal vertical stripes. This ribbon is worn with the dark blue stripe furthest from the left shoulder.	Battle of Britain
2 Atlantic Star	Blue, white and sea green shaded and watered. This ribbon is worn with the blue edge furthest from the left shoulder.	Air Crew Europe or France and Germany
3 Air Crew Europe Star	Light blue with black edges and in addition a narrow yellow stripe on either side.	Atlantic or France and Germany
4 Africa Star	Pale buff, with a central vertical red stripe and two narrower stripes, one dark blue, and the other light blue. This ribbon is worn with the dark blue stripe furthest from the left shoulder.	8th Army or 1st Army or North Africa 1942-43
5 Pacific Star	Dark green with red edges, a central yellow stripe, and two narrow stripes, one dark blue and the other light blue. This ribbon is worn with the dark blue stripe furthest from the left shoulder.	Burma
6 Burma Star	Dark blue with a central red stripe and in addition two orange stripes.	Pacific
7 Italy Star	Five vertical stripes of equal width, one in red at either edge and one in green at the centre, the two intervening stripes being in white.	
8 France and Germany Star	Five vertical stripes of equal width, one in blue at either edge and one in red at the centre, the two intervening stripes being in white.	Atlantic
9 Defence Medal	Flame coloured with green edges, upon each of which is a narrow black stripe.	Silver laurel leaves (King's Commendation for brave conduct. Civil)
10 War Medal 1939-45	A narrow central red stripe with a narrow white stripe on either side. A broad red stripe at either edge, and two intervening stripes in blue.	Oak leaf

Private James Randle was awarded a total of five medals including the Burma Star.

RICHARDS JOHN. 7911392 Corporal Royal Armoured Corps.

John Richards was born in Barnsley to William and Sarah Ellen Richards and was married to Ivy Richards of Darfield.

Corporal Richards was killed in action on Wednesday the 5th of August 1942, at the age of 27. He was buried at the Heliopolis War Cemetery in Egypt, grave reference 2. B. 11.

SIDDALL DENNIS. 7521896 Private 32 Company Royal Army Medical Corps.

Dennis Siddall was the son of Joseph and Annie Siddall of Birkwood Avenue, Cudworth. He was born on the 6th of October 1919.

Dennis worked in the surveyors' office for Cudworth council.

Within 6 weeks of joining the Army, in 1939, he was posted to Singapore.

On the fatal night between the 13th and 14th of February 1942 the

Japanese burst into the Alexandra Hospital where he worked as Sanitary Inspector. They killed most of the first floor people, patients included. The Nurses were locked in a room before being killed.

Dennis, along with others, were fastened back to back in three's in another room for the night, and then taken out the next day to be put to death and placed in a pit. His grave is unknown.

At the age of 22, Private Siddall died on Saturday the 14th of February 1942. He is commemorated on the Singapore Memorial in the Krangi War Cemetery, on Column 106.

THOMAS LEONARD. 4744281 Private Attached Auxiliary Military Pioneer Corps.

Leonard Thomas was the son of John and Elizabeth Thomas of 8 Guest's Yard, Cudworth. Leonard was listed in the absent voters register as living there in 1937. He was married to Ivy Thomas who was living in Barnsley when the Commonwealth War Graves records were gathered or Barnsley was taken as the postal address.

Private Thomas died at the age of 33 on Monday the 17th of June 1940. He is remembered with honour on the Dunkirk Memorial, column 121 at Nord in France.

TILLOTSON HARRY. 2654642 Guardsman 2nd Battalion Coldstream Guards.

Harry Tillotson was born on the 4th of March 1908 to Ben Smith and Mary Ann Tillotson who had five children. He worked at Woodcock's garage as a boilersmith. His father was employed as an engine driver on the Hull and Barnsley Railway and then the L.N.E.R. and moved to Hull.

He married Elsie Proctor and lived on Stanley Street where their only child Margaret was born. Margaret was 5 years old when her father died.

Guardsman Tillotson was an Army Reservist having originally served with the Horse Guards, 3 years with the colours and 9 years in reserve. He died on Sunday the 2nd of June 1940, aged 32, and is commemorated on the Dunkirk Memorial, column 34, at Nord, in France.

Harry Tillotson was the first man from Cudworth to be killed in the rear guard action at Dunkirk.

WALLACE JOHN HENRY. 3247266 Rifleman 1st Battalion Cameronians (Scottish Rifles).

John Wallace was the son of Harry and Emily Jane Wallace of The Grove, Cudworth

Private Wallace was 21 years old when he was killed in action on Sunday the 19th of April 1942 and is remembered on the Rangoon Memorial, Taukkyan War Cemetery in Myanmar (Burma), Face 10.

WHITELEY GEORGE EDMUND. 806952 Gunner 1ˢᵗ Regiment Royal Horse Artillery.

George Whiteley was born in Wakefield. He married Sarah Ann Whiteley (nee Baker) and lived at 179 Barnsley Road, Cudworth.

The C.W.G.C. records show his wife residing at Hood Green.

Gunner Whiteley was 32 years of age when he died on Sunday the 14th of December 1941. He is commemorated on column 11 of the Alamein Memorial in Egypt.

WIGGLESWORTH BERNARD. 1606091 Bombardier 171 Battery, 57 Lt. A.A. Regiment Royal Artillery.

Bernard Wigglesworth lived at 223 Barnsley Road, Cudworth the son of Ernest Wigglesworth.

Bombardier Wigglesworth died on Sunday the 7th of March 1943 at the age of 32. He was buried at the Tripoli War Cemetery in Libya, grave reference 5. G. 17.

WILBY GEORGE ARTHUR. 1590994 Flight Sergeant Air Gunner 156 Squadron Royal Air Force Volunteer Reserve.

Flight Sergeant Wilby died on Saturday the 24th of June 1944 and is buried in Zuytpeene Churchyard Nord, France, Row C, Grave 3.

WILBY JACK MADELEY. 1595172 Sergeant 102 Squadron Royal Force Volunteer Reserves.

Jack Wilby was the 19-year-old son of William Henry and Ethel Mary Wilby of 254 Barnsley Road, Cudworth.

Sergeant Wilby died on Sunday the 5th of November 1944 as a member of a Halifax III bomber, which took off from Pocklington and crashed in Laurensberg a village near Aachen in Germany.

Six of the crew were taken into Belgium and laid to rest at Henry-Chapelle, their remains were later removed to the Hotton War Cemetery and Sergeant Swart rests in Holland in Overloon War Cemetery.

Sgt. Wilby's grave reference at the Hotton War Cemetery is V. A. 2.

Crew of 102 Sqn. Halifax III.

F/O	A C Cameron	R.A.A.F.	Sgt	T Jones
F/O	R F Hudson		F/O	M P Frobisher
F/O	E Bolton		Sgt	J M Wilby
Sgt	E C Swart			

WOOTTON JOSEPH HENRY. C/J 107299 Leading Seaman H.M. Trawler "Stella Sirius".

Joseph Wootton was born in Staincross the son of Charles and Lilly Wootton. He, his wife Edith (nee Smith of Barnsley) and their eleven-year-old daughter, Doreen, lived at 14, Saxon Street, Cudworth.

Formerly a postman and the secretary of the local British Legion, he was a reservist seaman and was called up when the Navy mobilised in 1939.

Leading Seaman Wootton, aged 42, was killed in action at Gibraltar on Wednesday the 25th of September 1940. He was commemorated on the Chatham War Memorial 35,1 and the Cudworth West End Working Men's Club Memorial Plaque.

H.M.S. "Stella Sirius" was a 404-ton fishing trawler, built in 1934. As World War 2 became imminent she was requisitioned by the Navy in 1939 and converted for anti-submarine duties. Assigned to the 7th Anti-Submarine group in Gibraltar she was sunk during an air attack on the Rock on the 25th of September 1940.

The Board of Inquiry report into the sinking (ADM 1/10776) gave the following information: -

In retaliation for a Royal Navy attack on the interned French fleet in Dakar, the Vichy French Air Force carried out raids on the Naval Fleet at Gibraltar on the 24th/25th of September 1940.

During the second attack a bomb hit the Stella Sirius whilst she was moored. The bomb killed some members of the crew sheltering in the forepeak and set the forward end of the ship on fire. The remaining crew and sailors from adjacent ships assisted the wounded and tried to put out the fire with little success.

As the fire was spreading towards the magazine and a depth charge located in the ASDIC compartment, the decision was made to sink her to avoid an explosion that would damage other vessels. Her Kingston valve was opened and the intake pipe to her condenser split and she quickly flooded and settled on the bottom.

What remains of the wreckage lies on the base of the outer foundation slope of the South mole.

A diver who is researching the wreck has located the graves of two seamen in the North Front Cemetery and will continue to try to locate a grave for Seaman J.H. Wootton.

WRIGHT FREDRICK ARTHUR. 1304125 Private Pioneer Corps.

Fredrick Wright was born in Dudley. He was married to Annie Wright of Lundwood, Barnsley.

At the age of 47, Private Wright died on Tuesday the 7th of January 1941 and was buried in Barnsley (Ardsley) Cemetery in section D, grave 162. He is remembered on the Roll of Honour in the Cudworth West End Working Men's Club.

PALESTINE – 1947 - 1948.

CULLEN DANIEL PATRICK. 4533323 Lance Bombardier 144 (M) H.A.A. Regiment Royal Artillery.

Daniel Patrick Cullen was the son of Michael and Jemima Cullen of 204 Barnsley Road, Cudworth (1919 Electoral Roll).

Lance Bombardier Cullen died on Sunday the 16th of March 1947 while serving in Palestine. He was buried on the 20th of March 1947 in Cudworth Cemetery in grave reference Section J South. Row 1. Grave 7. Father James O' Flynn conducted the service.

JAMES HORACE EDWARD. 19030208 Lance Bombardier Royal Artillery.

Lance Bombardier James enlisted on the 15th of August 1945.

He married Rhoda Padgett at Cudworth St. John's Church on the 18th of January 1947.

He embarked for the Palestine 1947/48 Uprising.

Mrs Rhoda Blackburn (James) states, *"He was killed on the 17th of April 1948, two of his pals were killed on the same day. They were transporting food, ammunition etc., by train between Benghazi & Gaza when the Jews blew up the train. Ted was travelling towards the back of the train so he landed on the ground. As he was getting up he was shot and received multiple gunshot wounds. He is interred in Haifa Cemetery".*

He was 24 years of age.

CHAPTER 6.

CEMETERIES

AND

MEMORIALS.

CEMETERIES and MEMORIALS

ABBEVILLE COMMUNAL CEMETERY
Michelin Map 52, Sect. 7, Ref. 1

Sgt.   J.W. Bromley
Pte.   W. Kirk

Abbeville is on the Paris to Boulogne main road (N1), approximately 80 kilometres south of Boulogne
The Communal Cemetery and extension are located on the left hand side of the road when leaving the town in a northeasterly direction towards Drucat. Commonwealth War Graves Commission signs are displayed within the cemetery.

ACHIET-LE-GRAND COMMUNAL CEMETERY EXT.
Michelin Map 52, Sect. 10, Ref. 55

Pte.   W.A. Spence

A village 19 kilometres south of Arras on the main N17 road from Arras to Bapaume. At Ervillers turn right onto the D9 towards Achiet where a CWGC signpost indicates the way.

ADELAIDE CEMETERY
Michelin Map 53, Sect. 11, Ref. 33

Pte.   J. Eady

The Adelaide Cemetery is situated in the village of Villers-Bretonneux, which lies 16 kilometres east of Amiens on the Amiens to St. Quentin road.

AIRE COMMUNAL CEMETERY
Michelin Map 51, Sect. 14, Ref. 4

Pte.   G. Broardhurst

Aire is on the N43, approximately 14 kilometres south of St. Omer.
The Communal Cemetery is located 0.75 kilometres north of the town with the four commonwealth plots on the east side.

ALAMEIN MEMORIAL
(EL ALAMEIN WAR CEMETERY)

Gnr. G.E. Whiteley

El Alamein village lays approximately 130 kms. west of Alexandria. There are 7,367 burials in the cemetery including 821 unknown. The memorial was designed by Sir Hubert Worthington and bears the names of 11,874 soldiers and airmen who have no known grave, 8,392 in the Western Desert, 184 in Iraq, 116 in Syria and Lebanon and 33 in Persia. The 3,187 missing airmen died not only in these four campaigns but also in Greece, Ethiopia, the French, British and Italian Somalilands, Eritrea and Madagascar.

ALBUERA CEMETERY
Michelin Map 51, Sect. 15, Ref. 90

L/Cpl. F. Doughty
Cpl.   R. Roberts

The village of Bailluel-Sir-Berthoult is 8 kilometres northeast of Arras (D919). The cemetery is located west of the village.

ARRAS MEMORIAL
Michelin Map 51, Sect. 15, Ref. 109

Pte.   A. Blackburn
Pte.   W. Dobson
L/Cpl. H. McNeill
Pte.   W. Meggitt
Pte.   J. Merry
Cpl.   W. Smith
Gnr.   E. Yarrow

The Arras Memorial lies in the Faubourg-d'Amiens Cemetery on the Boulevard du General de Gaulle in the town of Arras. The Memorial was design by Edwin Lutyens and consists of a cloister 25 feet high and 350 feet long.

ATHENS MEMORIAL

Pte. E. Leadbeater

The Athens Memorial lies within Phaleron War Cemetery, which lies a few kilometres to the southeast of Athens on the coast road from Athens to Vouliaghmen, 5 kilometres west of the international airport.

AUCHONVILLERS MILITARY CEMETERY
Michelin Map 53, Sect. 2, Ref. 160
Pte. D. Glover

Travel the D919 from Arras towards Amiens as far as the village of Serre Les Puisieux. (20K from Arras) After a further 3 kilometres turn left following the signs for Auchonvillers. At the crossroads in the centre of the village follow the CWGC signs to the cemetery.

**AUTHUILE MILITARY
CEMETERY
Michelin Map 52, Sect. 9, Ref. 74**
Bdsm. A.H. Nicholson

The village of Authuile lies some 5 kilometres north of the village of Albert. The cemetery is signposted from the main D159 road through the village.

**BAGHDAD NORTH GATE WAR
CEMETERY**
Pte. B. Goulding

The Baghdad North Gate War Cemetery lays 800 metres beyond the North Gate of the City of Baghdad on the southeast side of the road to Baguba. The Commonwealth War Graves Commission strongly advises that the Foreign and Commonwealth Office be contacted before attempting to visit Iraq.

**BAILLEUL COMMUNAL
CEMETERY & Ext.
Michelin Map 51, Sect. 5, Ref. 89**
Pte. E. Allen

Bailleul is a large town in France near to the border with Belgium, on the main road from St. Omer to Lille. From the Grand Place take the leper road and 400 metres along this road is a sign indicating the direction of the cemetery.

**BARD COTTAGE CEMETERY
Michelin Map 51, Sect. 5, Ref. 20**
Gnr. T.H. Harlow
Pte. I. Kenchington

Situated in Ieper, Belgium the cemetery is located on the N369 Diksmuidseweg Road in the direction of Boezinge.

**BARENTHAL MILITARY
CEMETERY**

One of 5 cemeteries situated on the Asiago Plateau in the province of Vicenza, Italy. This cemetery lies 5 kilometres south of the town of Asiago on a minor, narrow road that loops round from the village of Cesuna to Asiago.

Pte. R. Layland

BARI WAR CEMETERY

Spr. W. Eversedge

The cemetery is situated on the outskirts of Bari, Italy in the locality of Carbonara.

**BARLIN COMMUNAL
CEMETERY Ext.
Michelin Map 51, Sect. 14, Ref. 27**
Gnr. H. Taylor

The village of Barlin lays approx. 11 kilometres southwest of Bethune on the D188 road. The Communal Cemetery and extension lie to the north of the village on the D171 road to Houchin.

BARNSLEY (ARDSLEY) CEMETERY

Pte. F.A. Wright

The village of Ardsley lies to the east of Barnsley on the main A635 Barnsley to Doncaster Road. The cemetery is in the grounds of Ardsley Parish Church.

BARNSLEY CEMETERY

Pte. J. Pipe

Barnsley Cemetery lies to the south of the town near to the A61 Barnsley to Sheffield road. Leaving the town centre on the A61 turn left at the second set of traffic lights into Cemetery Road, the cemetery being on the right.

BARNSLEY PALS MEMORIAL.

The Memorial to the Barnsley Pals who fell at the start of the Battle of the Somme on the 1st of July 1916 is located in the Sheffield Memorial Park, at Serre.
The Memorial reads:

1914-1918

13TH / 14TH BATTALIONS
YORK AND LANCASTER
REGIMENT
THE BARNSLEY PALS
DEDICATED
TO THE MEMORY
OF THOSE
WHO FELL HERE
1ST JULY 1916 AT THE START OF THE
BATTLE OF THE SOMME

THEIR NAME LIVETH FOREVER MORE

BEAUVAL COMMUNAL CEMETERY
Michelin Map 53, Sect. 1, Ref. 17
Pte. F. Snowden

The village of Beauval lies on the main N25 road 24 kilometres north of Amiens and 6 kilometres south of Doullens. The cemetery is on the northern side of the village at the end of the Rue de l'Eglise.

BEEHIVE CEMETERY
Michelin Map 51, Sect. 15, Ref. 79
Pte G. Eder

Situated in the village of Willerval 10 kilometres northeast of Arras, the cemetery lies 1 kilometre north of the village in a place called Lorgette.

BERLIN 1939 – 45 WAR CEMETERY

Gnr. W Hyman

The cemetery is in the district of Charlottenburg, 8 kilometres west of Berlin City centre on the Heerstrasse.

BERTRANCOURT MILITARY CEMETERY
Michelin Map 53, Sect. 1, Ref. 18
Sgt. C. Sayers

Bertrancourt village is on the D919 road from Arras to Amiens. Approx. 25 kilometres south of Arras, after passing through the village of Mailly-Maillet turn left, signposted Bertrancourt.

BETHUNE TOWN CEMETERY
Michelin Map 51, Sect. 14, Ref. 19
Cpl. E. Emery

Bethune is 29 kilometres north of Arras. From the town centre turn right in front of the Tribunal, take the second right, and at the bottom of the road turn into a cul-de-sac where the cemetery lies.

BLIGHTY VALLEY COMMUNAL CEMETERY
Michelin Map 52, Sect. 9, Ref. 75
Pte. L.G. Howard
Pte. F. Barnes

Some 4 kilometres north–east of the town of Albert the cemetery lies in a valley between the villages of Authuile and Aveluy to the east side of the D151 road.

BOIS-CARRE BRITISH CEMETERY
Michelin Map 51, Sect. 15, Ref. 88
Gnr. S. Johnson

This cemetery is in the village of Thelus, which lies 7 kilometres north of Arras. It is 1 kilometre east of the village on the D49 road to Bailleul-sir-Berthoult.

BOULOGNE EASTERN CEMETERY
Michelin Map 51, Sect. 1, Ref. 5
Sgt. P. Smith
Pte. G. Hill
Pte. J.M. Buckley

In the district of St. Martin, Boulogne the cemetery is split into two by the Rue de Dringhen just south of the main RN42 road to St. Omer.

BRADFORD (BOWLING) CEMETERY

Pnr. E.K. Howell

Bradford (Bowling) Cemetery, West Yorkshire contains some 151 First World War burials of servicemen killed on active service or who later succumbed to their wounds.

CABARET – ROUGE BRITISH CEMETERY
Michelin Map 53, Sect. 2, Ref. 28
Pte. G.W. Spence

Situated in the village of Souchez 3.5 kilometres north of Arras on the main road to Bethune. The cemetery is 1.5 kilometres south of the village on the west side of the D937 Arras to Bethune road.

CAMBRAI MEMORIAL
Michelin Map 53, Sect. 3, Ref. 44
Cpl. W. Foulstone. M.M.

In the village of Louverval on the north side of the N30 road from Bapaume to Cambrai. The Memorial stands on a terrace in the Louverval Military Cemetery.

CHATHAM NAVAL MEMORIAL

1939 to 1945 Extension.
Gnr. L. Cooper
O.S. J.P. Noon
L.S. J.H. Wootton

The memorial overlooks the town of Chatham and is approached by a steep path from the Town Hall Gardens. Public access is limited to the hours of 0830 to 1700 hrs. A copy of the Memorial Register is kept in the Naval Chapel of Brompton Garrison Church and may be consulted there.
Designed by Sir Robert Lorimer with sculpture by Henry Poole the Memorial is identical to those at Plymouth and Portsmouth. Sir Edward Maufe designed the extension for the Second World War.

COXYDE MILITARY CEMETERY
Michelin Map 51, Sect. 4, Ref. 2
Pte. H.E. Jackson

The cemetery is located 1 kilometre beyond the village of Koksijde, Belgium, on the N396 towards De Panne.
The N396 changes to the N369 Robert Vandammestraat and the cemetery is on the right hand side of this road.

CROONAERT CHAPEL CEMETERY
Michelin Map 51, Sect. 5, Ref. 67
Pte. L. Goldthorpe M.M..

The cemetery is located 6 kilometres south of Ieper Town, Belgium between the villages of Voormezele and Wijtschate on the N331 road.

CROUY BRITISH CEMETERY
Michelin Map 52, Sect. 7, Ref. 6

Gnr. W. Ward

Crouy is a village approx. 16 kilometres north west of Amiens, France, on the west side of the river Somme. The British Cemetery is a little south of the village on the west side of the road to Cavillon.

CUDWORTH (St. John the Baptist) CHURCHYARD

Pte. T. Ball
Pte. W. H. Grocott
Pte. G. Harper
Cpl J. Heaton
A.B. H. Williamson
Dvr. W.L. Barker
A.B. R. Midgley
Pte. P. Burke
Fusilier E. Race
L/Cpl. H. Race
Pte G. Frost
Gnr. B. Lister
Pte. S.G. Grundy
Cpl. A. Bradshaw
Pte. J Shea
Spr. L. Day
Pte. T. Swann
Pte. G. Heaton
Pte. H.J. Tuckwell
L/Bdr. D.P. Cullen
Pte.W. Bonds
Pte. T. Farmery
Gnr. W. Everett
Spr. F. Hutchinson
Sgt. M.G. Hudston
Pte. W.A Goulding
Gnr. E. Kirk
Pte. L. Grieve
A.C/1. J.E. Hyde

Travelling on the A628 Barnsley to Pontefract road Cudworth lays approx. 5 kilometres from Barnsley. On passing through the village the third right turn by the Star Hotel is St. Johns Road. The Church is on the left.

DEARNE (THURNSCOE) CEMETERY

Gnr. S. Conway

Dearne Cemetery is situated in Thurnscoe, South Yorkshire, on the outskirts of the village on Southfield Lane.

DOULLENS COMMUNAL CEMETERY
Michelin Map 53, Sect. 1, Ref. 11
L/Bdr. B. Westmoreland
Pte. J. Lowe

Doullens is a town approximately 30 kilometres north of Amiens, France, on the N25 road to Arras.

DUISANS BRITISH CEMETERY
Michelin Map 53, Sect. 2, Ref. 51
Pte. J.W. Redgate.

The cemetery lies in the village of Etrun but takes its name from the nearer village of Duisans. Both villages are approx. 9 kilometres west of Arras on the D339 road off the N39 Arras to St. Pol route.

DUNKIRK MEMORIAL CEMETERY

The Memorial, designed by Philip Hepworth, stands at the entrance to the British war graves section of Dunkirk Town Cemetery, which lies on the eastern outskirts of the town on the A16 road to Veurne in Belgium. It commemorates those soldiers of the British Expeditionary Force who fell in the 1939-1940 campaign who have no known grave.

Grd. H. Tillotson
Pte. L. Thomas

ELHAM BURIAL GROUND

Gnr. J.W. Peary

Elham is south of Canterbury in Kent

ESQUELBECQ MILITARY CEMETERY
Michelin Map 51, Sect. 4, Ref. 14
Sgt. E. Wright

Esquelbecq is a village near the Belgian border 24 kilometres north of Hazebrouck and the same distance south of Dunkirk. The Military Cemetery is about 1 kilometre west of the village, 200 metres south of the road to Zeggers-Cappel.

ETAPLES MILITARY CEMETERY
Michelin Map 51, Sect. 11, Ref. 12
Pte. C.H. Ellis
Pte. H. White
Pte. W.T. Marsden
L/Cpl. C.E. Hyman

The largest Commonwealth War Graves Commission cemetery in France situated in Pas-de-Calais. Etaples was safe from enemy attack except by air, but accessible by railway from the French and Belgium battlefields.
 Because of this it quickly became the site for a huge concentration of reinforcement camps and military hospitals, which could accommodate up to 22,000 sick and wounded.
A convalescent depot remained there for some months after the Armistice.

EUSTON ROAD CEMETERY
Michelin Map 52, Sect. 9, Ref. 32
Pte. J. McGuigan

The cemetery is situated in the village of Colincamps 11 kilometres north of Albert. From Arras take the D919 road in the direction of Amiens for 28 kilometres. The cemetery is situated about 1 kilometre from the D919 on the right hand side of the road.

FAUBOURG D'AMIENS
CEMETERY (Arras)
Michelin Map 52, Sect. 10, Ref. 1
Pte. C.G. Watson

The cemetery is in the western part of the town of Arras in the Boulevard du General de Gaulle, near the Citadel, approx. 2 kilometres west of the railway station.

FONTENAY - LE - PESNEL WAR
CEMETERY, TESSEL.

Pte. C. Duckworth

The village of Fontenay-le-Pesnel lies 16 kilometres west of Caen on the D9 road towards Caumont L'Evente. The cemetery is 1 kilometre south east of the hamlet of St. Martin on the D139 road to Granville.

GREENHILL CEMETERY,
(GALLIPOLI PENINSULA,
TURKEY)

Pte. L. Kemp

Greenhill and Chocolate Hill (which form together Yilghin Burnu) are adjoining hills about 52 metres above sea level, which rise almost from the eastern shore of the Salt Lake. The cemetery lies on the east side of the Anzac-Suvla road and can be seen from both Suvla and Anzac.

HAIFA MILITARY
CEMETERY, ISRAEL.

L/Bdr. H.E. James

HAZEBROUCK COMMUNAL
CEMETERY
Michelin Map 51, Sect. 4, Ref. 30
Sgt. G.R. King

Hazebrouck is a town approx. 56 kilometres south east of Calais. From Hazebrouck Grand Place follow the D916 Bethune road. The Communal Cemetery is signposted to the right hand side of the road.

HELIOPOLIS WAR CEMETERY

Cpl. J. Richards

Heliopolis is a major suburb of Cairo, Egypt and lies 10 kilometres to the north east of the city centre.

HELLES MEMORIAL.
(GALLIPOLI PENINSULAR, TURKEY)

Pte. A.R. Duckworth
A.B. W. Connick
Pte. R. Clarkson
Pte. T. Swift

HOLTEN CANADIAN WAR CEMETERY

Capt. G. Platt

HOTTON WAR CEMETERY

Sgt. J.M. Wilby

HOTTOT – LES - BAGUES WAR CEMETERY

L/Cpl. H. Jackson

HOYLAND NETHER/HOYLAND LAW

Pte. R. Siddal

The Helles Memorial stands on the tip of the Gallipoli Peninsula. It takes the form of an obelisk over 30 metres high and can be seen by ships passing through the Dardanelles. It commemorates the whole of the Gallipoli campaign and contains the names of over 20,000 of those with no known grave.

Holten is a village 20 kilometres east of the town of Deventer in Holland, on the main A1 motorway from Amsterdam to Bremen in Germany. Leave the A1 at junction 30 and follow the N332 in the direction of Holten. The Canadian War Cemetery contains 1,393 Commonwealth burials of the Second World War.

Hotton, Luxembourg, is located 58 kilometres south east of Namur; Follow the N4 road from Namur to the town of Marche en Famenne and then the N86 road towards Hotton. The cemetery is located 500 metres beyond Hotton on the N86 towards Menil.

The cemetery can be reached from Bayeux by taking the D6 road to the southeast. After 13 kilometres and passing through Tilly-sur-Seules, turn right (westwards) at Juvigny on the D9 road towards Caumont L'Evente. The cemetery is a few hundred metres on the right hand side on rising ground.

Hoyland Nether or Hoyland Law Cemetery lays within the village of Hoyland, near Barnsley, South Yorkshire. On leaving the M1 motorway at junction 36, take the A6135 road towards Hoyland Common. At the traffic lights turn left into the B6096 Hoyland Road, which shortly becomes Hawshaw Lane. St Peter's Church is on the right hand side with the churchyard to the left and right approx. 1

mile from the aforementioned traffic lights.

KANCHANABURI WAR CEMETERY

Gnr. W. Jaques

Kanchanaburi, Thailand is 129 kilometres north west of Bangkok. The cemetery is in the north-eastern part of the town along the Saeng Chuto Road. The graves of those who died during the construction and maintenance of the notorious Burma-Siam railway were transferred from camp burial grounds and isolated sites along the railway into three cemeteries of which Kanchanaburi is one. Colin St. Clair Oakes designed the cemetery.

KEMMEL CHATEAU CEMETERY
Michelin Map 51, Sect. 5, Ref. 71
Pte. B. Smith

Located 8 kilometres south of Ieper, Belgium, on the N331 connecting Ieper to Kemmel.

LARCH WOOD (RAILWAY CUTTING) CEMETERY
Michelin Map 51, Sect. 5, Ref. 49
Pte. M. Ruckledge

The cemetery is located 4 kilometres south east of Ieper Town, Belgium on the N366 road connecting Ieper to Komen.

LES MOERES COMMUNAL CEMETERY

Pte. H. Heath

Les Moeres is a village 13 kilometres east of Dunkerque and 10 kilometres northeast of the small town of Bergues on the Dunkerque to Amiens road.

LIJSSENTHOEK MILITARY CEMETERY
Michelin Map 51, Sect. 5, Ref. 40
Pte. W. Peaker
Pte. E. Fowler

The cemetery is located 12 kilometres west of Ieper, Belgium on the N308 road connecting Ieper to Poperinge. On reaching Poperinge take the ring road R33 to the left and then the N38 Frans-Vlaanderenweg. 800 metres along the N38 turn left into Lenestraat, then right into Boescheepseweg and the cemetery is located 2 kilometres on the right hand side of the road. Sir Reginald Blomfield designed the cemetery.

LIVERPOOL (WEST DERBY).

Liverpool, England, West Derby cemetery.

Bdr. O. Gaskell

LONGUENESSE SOUVENIR CEMETERY
Michelin Map 51, Sect. 3, Ref. 3
Pte. E. Wright
Gnr. A. Colwood

Longuenesse is a commune on the southern outskirts of St. Omer, France some 45 kilometres southeast of Calais. The cemetery is approx. 3 kilometres from St. Omer on the D928 Abbeville road, on the left.

LONSDALE CEMETERY
Michelin Map 53, Sect. 12, Ref. 15
Pte. G.J. Bowering

Lonsdale cemetery is situated in the village of Authuille, Somme, France. The village is 5 kilometres north of the town of Albert on the D151 road to Grandcourt. The cemetery is signposted from the centre of Authille and is 1 kilometre to the east.

LOOS MEMORIAL.
Michelin Map 52, Sect. 2, Ref. 7
Pte. E. Green
Pte. J. Johnson
Pte. R.W. Westbury
L/Sgt. W. Taylor
Sgt. J.J. Goley

Situated in Pas-de-Calais the memorial surrounds the cemetery on three sides and commemorates those Commonwealth servicemen who were killed in the area from 25.09.1915 (The first day of the Battle of Loos) until the Armistice. More than half of the casualties buried in the cemetery are unidentified.

LOWESTOFT NAVAL MEMORIAL

Seaman. K. Fenton

The Lowestoft Naval Memorial is located to the north of the town on the A12 Yarmouth Road, approx. 1 mile north of the harbour. In a prominent position within local authority gardens known as Bellevue Park it was chosen as the site for the Memorial to those men of the Royal Naval Patrol Service who have no grave, other than the sea.

MEDJEZ - EL - BAB

Driver. F. Myatt

Medjez-el-Bab is 60 kilometres west of Tunis, Tunisia. The Memorial stands within the War Cemetery, 3 kilometres west of Medjez-el-Bab on the route P5 to Le Kef.

MERVILLE COMMUNAL CEMETERY
Michelin Map 51, Sect. 14, Ref. 7
Pte. S.J. Wassell
L/Cpl. W. Poskitt
Pte. A. Fenn

The town of Merville lies 15 kilometres north of Bethune and 20 kilometres southeast of Armentieres. The Communal Cemetery is on the northeast side of the town to the north side of the road to Neuf-Berquin.

MIKRA BRITISH CEMETERY

Ordinary Seaman. E. West

The Mikra British Cemetery is situated approximately 8 kilometres south of Thessalonika, Greece in the municipality of Kalamaria. Within the cemetery is the Mikra Memorial commemorating almost 500 nurses, officers and men of the Commonwealth Forces who died when troop transports and hospital ships were lost in the Mediterranean and who have no grave but the sea. They are commemorated here because others who went down in the same vessels were washed ashore and identified and are buried at Thessalonika.

MINTURNO WAR CEMETERY (ITALY)

Minturno is approx. 78 kilometres north of Naples, Italy close to the coast. The cemetery lies several kilometres south of the town on the SS7 road to Naples and is situated in the locality of Marina di Minturno.

Pte. G.A. Bolton
L/Cpl C. Dunhill

MONT HUON MILITARY CEMETERY
Michelin Map 52, Sect. 5, Ref. 2
Pte. H.P. Blackburn

Mont Huon Military Cemetery lies close to the small seaport of Le Treport some 25 kilometres northeast of Dieppe, France. From the town centre follow the Littoral/Dieppe sign and the cemetery stands on the D940. Sir Reginald Blomfield designed the cemetery.

NOTTINGHAM GENERAL CEMETERY

Pte. W. Neville

Nottingham, England.

ORCHARD DUMP CEMETERY
Michelin Map 51, Sect. 15, Ref. 83
L/Cpl. C.H. Hayes

The cemetery lies near the village of Arleux-en-Gohelle on the main Arras to Henin-Lietard D919 road on the left side approx. 1 kilometre from the village of Bailleul-sir-Berthoult.

PHILOSOPHE BRITISH CEMETERY
Michelin Map 53, Sect. 2, Ref. 10
Pte. W. Gelder

Philosophe lies between Bethune and Lens, France on the N43 road. From this road follow the D165E road for 400 metres to a right turn. The cemetery is signed from the N43. Sir Herbert Baker designed the cemetery.

PLOEGSTEERT MEMORIAL

Michelin Map 51, Sect. 5, Ref. 96
Cpl. J. Dent
Pte. W. Waddington

The Memorial stands in the Berks Cemetery Extension some 12.5 kilometres south of Ieper, Belgium, town centre on the N365 road from Ieper to Mesen. The sounding of the Last Post takes place at the Memorial on the first Friday of every month at 1900 hours.
The Memorial commemorates more than 11,000 servicemen of the United Kingdom and South African Forces who died in this sector and have no known grave. The Cemetery, Cemetery Extension and Memorial were designed by H Charlton Bradshaw, with sculpture by Gilbert Ledward

PLYMOUTH NAVAL MEMORIAL

P.O. (R.N.) I. Haskey

Situated centrally on the Hoe looking directly towards Plymouth Sound the Memorial commemorates those members of the Royal Navy who have no known grave, the majority of deaths occurring at sea. The Memorial is identical to those at the two other manning ports Chatham and Portsmouth being designed by Sir Robert Lorimer with sculpture by Henry Poole.

POELCAPELLE BRITISH CEMETERY

Pte. W. Johnson.

Poelcapelle British Cemetery is located 10 kilometres north east of Ieper, Belgium on the Brugseweg N313 road connecting Ieper to Brugge on the right hand side of the road after passing through the village of Poelcapelle.

POND FARM CEMETERY
Michelin Map 51, Sect. 5, Ref. 82
Pte. H. Pearson

The cemetery is located southwest of Ieper, Belgium near the village of Wulvergem. It was designed by Charles Holden.

PONT - DU - HEM MILITARY CEMETERY
Michelin Map 51, Sect.15, Ref. 31
Pte. T. Richards

Pont-du-Hem is a hamlet situated on the main road from La Bassee to Estaires, France on the D947 road 10 kilometres from La Bassee.

PORTSMOUTH NAVAL MEMORIAL

A.B. L. Gillespie
Gnr. W.E. Pygott
Stkr R. Millington
Stkr. H.W. Darnell

The Memorial is situated on Southsea Common overlooking the promenade. It is identical to those at the two other manning ports at Chatham and Plymouth. Designed by Sir Robert Lorimer with sculptures and reliefs by Charles Wheeler, William McMillan and Esmond Burton it commemorates those members of the Royal Navy who had no known grave, the majority of deaths having occurred at sea.

POZIÈRES MEMORIAL TO THE MISSING
Michelin Map 52, Sect. 9, Ref. 68
Pte. S. Clare
Pte. R.A. Morby

Named after a village on the northwest side of the main road from Albert to Bapaume. It contains 2,754 burials, 1,374 of which are unidentified.

PUCHEVILLERS BRITISH CEMETERY
Michelin Map 52, Sect. 8, Ref. 7
Pte. P. Mahers

Puchevillers is a village on the D11 road approx. 19 kilometres northeast of Amiens, France. The first Commonwealth War Graves Commission signpost is by the church in the village. The cemetery was designed by Sir Edwin Lutyens.

RAMBLE WAR CEMETERY

Pte. W.E. Naylor

Ramla (formerly Ramleh) Israel is a small town 12 kilometres southeast of Jaffa. From Tel Aviv proceed along Route One towards Jerusalem. Pass the exit to Ben Gurion airport. Proceed along Route 40 to the 'T' junction with Route 44. Turn right and follow Route 44 towards Lod until the first set of traffic lights. Turn right towards Lod and Ramleh Prison on Route 434. Opposite the prison turn right into a minor road with a supermarket on the right. At the next junction turn right. Take the first left and the cemetery entrance will be found on the right.

RANGOON MEMORIAL. TAUKKYAN WAR CEMETERY

L/Sgt. C.W. Bowen
Rfle. J.H. Wallace
Pte. S. Parkinson

The cemetery is on the PY1 road approx. 35 kilometres north of the city of Yangon (formerly Rangoon) Burma, close to the airport and immediately adjoining the village of Taukkyan. The memorial stands in the centre of the cemetery and is surrounded by the graves of more than 6,000 men whose remains were brought from the battlefield cemeteries and scattered jungle and roadside graves all over Burma.

RANVILLE WAR CEMETERY AND CHURCHYARD

The village of Ranville lies on the D513 northeast of Caen, France. After leaving Caen and travelling 9 kilometres turn left at the village of Hérouvillette towards Ranville. The War Cemetery is on the Rue Des Airbornes.

Sgt. F. Green

REICHSWALD FOREST WAR CEMETERY

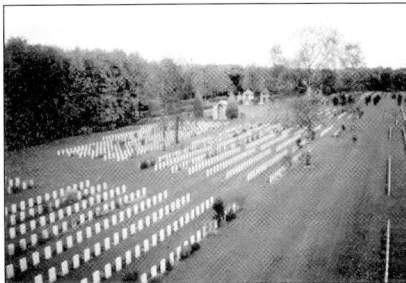

Cpl. A. Millward
L/Cpl. R. Cottam

The cemetery is 5 kilometres southwest of Kleve, Germany. From Kleve town centre take the Hoffmannallee, which becomes the Materbornerallee and enters the Reichswald Forest where it becomes the Grunewaldstrasse. Follow the directions for Gennep and on entering the Reichswald Forest the cemetery is situated 500 metres on the left. The architect was Philip Hepworth, designed by Sir Reginald Blomfield, with sculptures in Portland stone by Gilbert Ledward.

ROCHEFORT COMMUNAL CEMETERY

The town of Rochefort is located on the N86 road in Belgium. From the E411 motorway, which runs between Namur and Luxembourg turn of at junction 23 onto the N94 road in the direction of Dinant.

Pte J. Randle

Follow the N94 to its junction with the N86 and then turn onto the N86 in the direction of Rochefort. From the town centre follow the N803 road and the cemetery is adjacent to the church.

RUNNYMEDE MEMORIAL. (ENGLAND)

Sgt. I.J. Calverley
Sgt. C. Barraclough

This Memorial overlooks the River Thames on Cooper's Hill at Englefield Green between Windsor and Egham on the A308 road, 4 miles from Windsor.
It commemorates over 20,000 airmen who were lost in the Second World War who have no known grave. The structure is in Portland stone and has roofs of Westmoreland green slate.

RUYAULCOURT MILITARY CEMETERY
Michelin Map 53, Sect. 3, Ref. 65
Pte. H. Porter

Ruyaulcourt is a village 11 kilometres east of Bapaume, France on the D7 road and 19 kilometres southwest of Cambrai. The cemetery lies 500 metres north of the village along an unmarked road but signposted to the left by the village church as you enter Ruyaulcourt from Bapaume.

SARIGOL CEMETERY

Pte. O. Goulding

Sarigol is a village 40 kilometres north of Thessalonika, Greece in the direction of Lake Doiran. The cemetery is 3 kilometres out of the village, close to the Civil Cemetery set in farmland. It is signposted and visible from the road.

SERRE ROAD CEMETERY No. 2 (SOMME)
Michelin Map 53, Sect. 2, Ref. 148
Pte. J.B. Clare

The largest cemetery on the Somme with more than 7000 graves, almost 5000 of them unidentified. The last burials took place as late as 1934 following continued clearance of the battlefields after the war.

SHEFFIELD, CITY ROAD CEMETERY

Pte. A. Jackson

Sheffield, England City Road cemetery is a short distance from the City Centre to the left of the A6135 Road to Mosborough and junction 30 of the M1 motorway.

SINGAPORE MEMORIAL. (KRANJI WAR CEMETERY)

Pte. D. Siddall

The Memorial stands within Kranji War Cemetery and bears the names of over 24,000 Second World War casualties of the Commonwealth land and air forces that have no known grave. Included are land forces from the campaigns in Malaya and Indonesia, or those who died in subsequent captivity and airmen who died during operations over the whole of southern and eastern Asia and surrounding seas and oceans.

SKEW BRIDGE CEMETERY (GALLIPOLI PENINSULAR, TURKEY)

Pte. C.E. Wassell

Skew Bridge Cemetery is 2 kilometres northeast of Seddulbahir, Turkey, between the road to Krithia and Kilid Bahr.

SOISSONS MEMORIAL

L/Cpl. W.H. Handley
Pte. E. Evans
Pte. G.H. Lister

The town of Soissons stands on the left bank of the river Aisne, approx. 100 kilometres northeast of Paris, France. The Memorial is to be found in the public square and the memorial register is kept at the Mairie where it may be consulted.

The Memorial commemorates almost 4,000 officers and men who died during the Battles of the Aisne and the Marne who have no known grave. It was designed by G.H. Holt and V.O. Rees with sculpture by Eric Kennington.

SPOILBANK CEMETERY

Michelin Map 51, Sect. 5, Ref. 59
Pte. J. Peaker

Spoilbank Cemetery is located 4.5 kilometres southeast Ieper, Belgium on the N336 road to Komen. It is one of a number of cemeteries in the neighbourhood that bears witness to the fierce fighting of which it was the scene, even under conditions of trench warfare from 1914 to 1918.

SS "KUALA" SECTION OF CIVILIAN WAR DEAD, MALAYA.

Dorothy Hirst (Staff Nurse)

Staff Nurse Dorothy Hirst was killed as the result of enemy action, off Pom Pom Island, on the 14th of February 1942.

ST. POL COMMUNAL CEMETERY EXTENSION
Michelin Map 51, Sect. 13, Ref. 1
Pte. G.A. Morley

The town of St Pol, France, is approx. 29 kilometres southwest of Bethune and 34 kilometres west north west of Arras. Next to the Communal Cemetery the extension is reached by a steep road, Rue de Cimetiere on the north side of the N39 road to Arras.

ST. QUENTIN CABARET MILITARY CEMETERY
Michelin Map 51, Sect. 5, Ref. 92
Pte. W. Starkey

The cemetery is located 10.5 kilometres south of Ieper, Belgium on the N365 road to Wijtschate, Mesen and on to Armentieres. St Quentin Cabaret was an inn near the village of Wulvergem and the front line. At times the Inn was used as battalion headquarters. The cemetery was designed by Charles Holden

ST. SEVER CEMETERY

Michelin Map 52, Sect. 14, Ref. 2
Spr. G. Fisher
Pte. H.H. Ebbage

St Sever cemetery is situated approx. 3 kilometres south of Rouen Cathedral a short distance from the road from Rouen to Elbeuf.

ST. SEVER CEMETERY EXTENSION
Michelin Map 52, Sect. 14, Ref. 2
2nd. Lt. H. Straker

The cemetery and its extension are situated approx. 3 kilometres south of Rouen Cathedral a short distance to the west of the road from Rouen to Elbeuf.

ST. VAAST POST MILITARY CEMETERY
Michelin Map 51, Sect.15, Ref. 38
Pte. A. Bowen
L/Sgt. J.C. Richardson

The cemetery lies near the village of Richebourg-L'Avoue that is 9 kilometres northeast of Bethune, France. From Bethune follow the D171 road towards Armentieres and progress onto the D166 to the outskirts of Richebourg. Turn left into Rue des Charbonniers for approx 2 kilometres and the cemetery is on the right.

STRAND MILITARY CEMETERY
Michelin Map 51, Sect. 5, Ref. 96
Cpl. G. Goose M.M.

The Strand Military Cemetery is 13 kilometres south of Ieper, Belgium on the N365 road connecting Ieper to Wijtschate, Mesen and on to Armentieres. The cemetery is 4 kilometres beyond Mesen immediately before the village of Ploegsteert on the left hand side of the road.

SUCRERIE MILITARY CEMETERY
Michelin Map 52, Sect. 9, Ref. 40
Pte. E. Wilmott
Pte. W.J. Ricketts
Pte. H. Clare
Pte. H.W. Winter
Cpl. W. Joburns

The cemetery lies near the village of Colincamps approx. 16 kilometres north of Albert, France. It is 3 kilometres southeast of the village on the north side of the road from Mailly-Maillet to Puisieux.

TAUKKYAN WAR CEMETERY

Cpl. I. Baugh

The cemetery is outside Yangon (formerly Rangoon) Burma, near the airport and immediately adjoining the village of Taukkyan. It is on the PY1 road approx. 35 kilometres north of the city from which it is easily accessible.

TEHRAN MEMORIAL

Pte. G.S. Stainrod

The Tehran Memorial commemorates casualties of the Indian, United Kingdom and New Zealand Forces who lost their lives during the campaign in Iran (formally Persia) and who have no known grave. It also commemorates those who lost their lives in the neighbouring regions of Russia whose graves are unknown or un-maintainable.

The Memorial is located in Tehran War Cemetery at the southern end of the residential area in the British Embassy compound at Gulhak, 13 kilometres from Tehran.

THIEPVAL MEMORIAL (SOMME)
Michelin Map 52, Sect. 9, Ref. 62

The Battle of the Somme began on 01.07.1916 and by the time the fighting was brought to a close in mid November approx. 125,000 Commonwealth servicemen were dead. The Thiepval Memorial to the missing of the Somme commemorates more than 72,000 men, most of who died in the 1916 Battle, whose graves are unknown.

Pte. J.W. Batty
Pte. A. Chappel
Pte. V. Holmes
Pte. T.W. Powell
L/Cpl. J.W. Thompson
L/Cpl. G. H. Waterfield
L/Cpl. F. Bonds
Pte. J. Jackson
Cpl. E. Joburns
L/Cpl. J.A. Stainrod
Pte. J. Tipping
Pte. J.A. Reece
Pte. J. Brooks
L/Cpl. C.E, Hewitt
L/Cpl. J. Newbury
Cpl. L. Thomas
Pte. R.H. Arnold
Pte. W. Copley
Pte. B.J. Joyner
Pte. F. Teal
Pte R.H. Powell
Pte. J. Cale

TOWER HILL MEMORIAL, LONDON.

The Tower Hill Memorial commemorates men of the Merchant Navy and Fishing Fleets who died in both world wars and have no known grave. It stands on the south side of the garden of Trinity Square, London, close to the Tower of London. The Memorial was designed by Sir Edwin Lutyens with sculpture by Sir William Reid-Dick. The Second World War extension was designed by Sir Edward Maufe with sculpture by Charles Wheeler and bears almost 24,000 names.

Bosun E. Williams
M.S. H. Midgley

TRIPOLI WAR CEMETERY

Bdr. B. Wigglesworth

The cemetery is in the Mansura district of Tripoli, Libia, 2.5 kilometres west of the city centre. It is located at the western end of Sharia Jamahuriya, close to the major roundabout at Bab Gargaresh.

TYNE COT MEMORIAL

Cpl. A. Ogley
L/Cpl. F. Green
Pte. G.S. Holmes
Pte. W. Clay
L/Cpl. C.E. Everett
Pte. H. Andrews
Pte. A. Brook
Pte. W.H. Wright

The Tyne Cot Memorial to the Missing forms the northeastern boundary of Tyne Cot Cemetery that is located 9 kilometres north east of Ieper, Belgium on the N332 road. The Memorial contains nearly 35,000 names of those who have no known grave.

UDEN WAR CEMETERY

Tpr. W. Lake

The town of Uden lies on the main road between Eindhoven and Nijmegen, Netherlands. The cemetery is 350 metres from the town centre and is also signposted from the N265 Uden to Eindhoven road.

VALKENSWAARD WAR CEMETERY

Pte. C.E. Chamberlain

Valkenswaard is located 9 kilometres from the Dutch – Belgian frontier on the main road from Eindhoven to Hasselt in Belgium.

VERCHAIN BRITISH CEMETERY
Michelin Map 53, Sect. 4, Ref. 8
Pte. R.W. Wealthall

In the village of Verchain-Maugre 13 kilometres south of Valenciennes, France the cemetery is 1.5 kilometres northwest of the village on the north side of the road to Monchaux and Thiant.

WARDOUR ROMAN CATHOLIC CEMETERY

Pte. T. Kivell

The Wardour Roman Catholic Cemetery is in Wiltshire, England.

WIMEREUX COMMUNAL CEMETERY
Michelin Map 51, Sect. 1, Ref. 2
Pte. A.I. Goddard

Wimereaux is a small town approx. 5 kilometres north of Boulogne, France. From Boulogne take the A16 road to Calais leaving at junction 4 taking the D242 road to Wimereux. The Commonwealth War Graves are at the rear of the Communal Cemetery.

Y FARM MILITARY CEMETERY
Michelin Map 51, Sect. 15, Ref. 24
Pte. S. Pritchard

Y Farm Military Cemetery lies in the village of Bois-Grenier, Nord, France approx. 4 kilometres south or Armentieres. Leave Bois-Grenier on the D222 in the direction of Fleurbaix. After 1.2 kilometres turn left following the signs for the cemetery which can be found on the right hand side after the farm, approx. 800 metres from the main road.

YPRES (MENIN GATE)
Michelin Map 51, Sect. 5, Ref. 32

Pte. J. Wilde
L/Cpl. J.J. Simpson
Pte. T. Bassett
Pte. A. Allott
Pte. A. Horton
Sgt. D. Hubbard
Pte. R.H. Hann
L/Cpl. F.D. Wright
L/Cpl. T.D. Loft
Rfl. E.W. Horton
Gnr. A.W. Hall

Ypres, now known as Ieper, Belgium is a town in the Province of West Flanders. The Memorial is situated in the eastern side of the town on the road to Menin and Courtrai.

Each night, at 2000 hrs the traffic is stopped under the Menin Gate whilst members of the local Fire Brigade sound the Last Post in the roadway under the Memorials arches.

The Memorial now bears the names of more than 54,000 officers and men whose graves are not known.

Designed by Sir Reginald Blomfield with sculpture by Sir William Reid-Dick it was unveiled by Lord Plumer in July 1927.

ZOUAVE VALLEY CEMETERY

Michelin Map 51, Sect.15, Ref. 78
Spr. W. McNab

Situated in the village of Souchez some 12 kilometres north of Arras on the main road to Bethune, France, the cemetery lies approx. 2 kilometres southeast of the village in a valley extending southwards from Souchez on the western side of Vimy Ridge.

ZUYTPEENE CHURCHYARD

Flt. Sgt. G.A. Wilby

Zuytpeene is a village approx. 27 kilometres south of Dunkirk, and 4 kilometres west of Cassel, which lies on the Dunkirk to Paris road. The War Graves are in a special enclosure near the War Memorial in the north-eastern corner of the churchyard.

CHAPTER 7.

WAR MEDALS

AND

BRAVERY AWARDS.

British War Medals World War One And World War Two

Service Medals Issued in World War One.

British and Commonwealth servicemen and women were awarded a wide variety of medals for their service in World War One. These included medals for gallantry, distinguished service including those bestowed by Allied governments. General service during the wars was recognised by the issue of the 1914 or 1914-15 Star, the British War Medal (1914-1920) and the Victory Medal (1914-1919).

These medals were issued in unprecedented numbers as virtually all service personnel, and civilians who served in officially recognised organisations, all qualified for one of more of these medals.

The usual trio of awards, the 1914 Star (or the 1914-15 Star, if applicable), together with the two service medals became popularly known as 'Pip, Squeak and Wilfred' after characters in a Daily Mail cartoon of the period.

Service Medals Issued in World War Two.

In World War Two the following Stars 1939-45 Star, Burma Star. Africa Star, Atlantic Star, Aircrew Europe Star, France and Germany Star and the Italy Star, War Medal and Defence Medal were awarded, each of these medals having its own qualifying period.

The criteria for award and the dates, services, areas and exceptions concerned are quite elaborate and complicated and would fill several pages. If one reads the entry for the 1939-45 star it will be obvious how intricate this subject is and there are many books on the subject. British Battles and Medals by Major L.L. Gordon and E.C. Joslin covers the subject in more depth than can be covered here and are an excellent source of research. Only the main points regarding these medals have been covered here and we apologise for any discrepancies that may have occurred.

1914 Star and Clasp.

The 1914 Star was awarded to members of the British Expeditionary Force (B.E.F.). This star measures 1 ¾" wide and 2½" from top to bottom having a ring attachment for the suspension ribbon. It has three points; a Crown replaces the uppermost point. On the face are two crossed swords the handles and points protruding from the face of the star. The centre has a scroll with the date 1914 on it there is a small scroll above with the month "AUG" and a scroll at the bottom with the month "NOV". This medal was approved in April 1917 to those who served in France or Belgium between 5th August 1914 and midnight on 22nd /23rd November 1914. In October 1915 the King authorised a Bar for this medal awarded to those who had been under fire in France or Belgium between these two dates. The Bar itself is Bronze and bears the dates " 5th Aug-22nd Nov 1914". Those entitled to this award are allowed to wear a Silver Rose in the centre of the medal ribbon when the medal is not being worn see below. The 1914 Star without the Bar is the same medal in every detail as the medal with the Bar, the ribbon being the same in colour. (See below).

1914 Star Ribbon.
365,622 issued.

Ribbon with Clasp.
145.000 issued.

1914 Star and Bar.

1914-15 STAR.

This Star is identical to the 1914 Star in everyway except that it does not bear on it the scroll having the dates "AUG" "NOV".

The 1914-15 Star was awarded to those who *served* in any theatre of war against the central powers between 5th August 1914 and 31st December 1915 except those who were awarded or eligible for the 1914 Star. The word SERVED is important, as it was not awarded to anyone who visited, passed through or arrived to carry out inspections in these theatres of war.

1914 – 1915 Star.

2,078,183 issued.

THE BRITISH WAR MEDAL.

This medal was issued singly without the Victory Medal in silver and has no bar. Issued to certain regular and mobilized personnel who did not see any fighting. A person "Mentioned in Despatches" who did not qualify for the Victory Medal wore a Bronze Oak Leaf on the medal.

British War Medal in bronze (110,000 issued)

The British War Medal 1914-20 was issued to commemorate the successful conclusion of the war and awarded to those who had served in a theatre of war up to and including the official end of the war in 1920.

Ribbon.

British War Medal.

6,500,000 issued.

Victory Medal.

A bronze medal which was awarded to all those who were entitled to either the 1914 or the 1914–15 Star, and with some exceptions to those who were awarded the British War Medal. It was never issued alone.

The Victory Medal 1914-19 was issued in commemoration of the Allied victory, mostly to those mobilized in any of the fighting services in any of the theatres of operations, or at sea between 5th August 1914 and midnight 11th /12th November 1918 (with some exceptions). Those "Mentioned in Despatches" between 4th August 1914 and 10th August 1920 were allowed to wear a "Bronze Oak Leaf" on the ribbon. (See below.)

Ribbon.

Ribbon with M.I.D.

Victory Medal.
5,725,000 issued

Died for Freedom and Honour.

The plaque shown below was awarded to the family of the serviceman or woman who died in the cause of freedom. It was some times known as "the Death's Head Penny".

1939 – 45 STARS, WAR and DEFENCE MEDALS.

Eight campaign stars were created for the 2nd World War but the maximum any individual can wear is five, none of these medals were named officially according to the Government cost being the prime consideration, but it is possible that the family of the recipient may have had this done which can cause problems when you try to verify a medal. A number of bars were also instituted but only one could be worn on any one of the stars. The criteria for award and the dates, services, areas and exceptions concerned are quite elaborate and complicated and would fill several pages if you read the entry for the 1939-45 star it will be obvious how intricate this subject is and as there are a good number of books on the subject, British Battles and Medals by Major L.L. Gordon and E.C. Joslin for instance, which are available for people to read and cover the subject in more depth than can be covered here and are an excellent source of research. Only the main points to these medals have been covered here with apologies for any discrepancies that may have occurred.

THE 1939-1945 STAR.

Those who were entitled to this Star were also entitled to other Stars on entering the appropriate theatre of operations, except in the case of the Atlantic Star, Air Crew Europe and Africa Star. No one could be awarded more than five Stars and two medals.

1939 – 1945 Star

Atlantic (or France & Germany, or Air Crew Europe Star)

Africa Star

Pacific Star (or Burma Star)

Italy Star

Defence Medal

War Medal

No one was awarded more than one Bar (or Clasp) to any one Campaign Star, nor were they allowed more than one Clasp on any one of the Star ribbons when only the ribbon was worn. Mainly awarded for a minimum of 180 days of operational service between 3rd September 1939 and 2nd September 1945 (60 days for RAF in an operational unit engaged in operations against the enemy). A bar "BATTLE OF BRITAIN" was authorised for fighter aircraft crew that participated in this battle between 10th of July and the 31st of October 1940. The colours of the ribbon symbolize the three Services, the Royal Navy and the Merchant Navy (dark blue), the Army (red) and the Royal Air Force (pale blue).

1939 – 1945 Star.

1939 – 45 Star.

1939 – 45 Ribbon.

1939 – 45 Ribbon with Clasp.

THE AFRICA STAR

No prior award of the 1939-1945 Star is necessary to qualify for this star, which was awarded for one or more day's service in North Africa between the 10th of June 1940 and the 12th of May 1943. Three bars (of which only the first awarded can be worn) were instituted "EIGHTH ARMY", "FIRST ARMY" and "NORTH AFRICA 1942-43". Service with the 8th Army between the 23rd of October 1942 (Battle of El Alamein) and the 12th of May 1943 and service with the 1st Army between the 8th of November 1942 and the 12th of May 1943 qualified one for the first two of these bars. Service between the 23rd of October 1942 and the 12th of May 1943 for those outside of both these armies (i.e. personnel of the 18th Army Group HQ, naval and air force personnel, merchant navy members etc.) was the qualification for the North Africa 1942-43 bar. The ribbon colours represent the desert and the colours of the Royal Navy, Army and RAF.

The Africa Star

Africa Star Ribbon

Africa Star Ribbon
8th Army Clasp

THE AIR CREW EUROPE STAR

This star was awarded for operational flying from UK bases over Europe between the 3rd of September 1939 and the 5th of June 1944. Once again, the criteria for the 1939-1945 Star had to be met before the qualifying period for this star began. The qualifying period for this star was set at 120 days serving as a member of an aircrew in an operational unit, two months for the 1939-1945 Star and a further two months to obtain the Air Crew Europe Star. Bars "ATLANTIC" and "FRANCE AND GERMANY" were created in case the recipient had qualified for those stars, one bar only was allowed on a star. The ribbon colours represent the Air Force (pale blue) and yellow and black represent its continuous day and night operations.

Aircrew Europe Star

Ribbon

THE BURMA STAR

After qualifying for the 1939-1945 Star, service in the area between the 11th of December 1941 and the 2nd of September 1945, service in the Burma Theatre between these dates were the criteria for this star. When the Burma Star itself is being worn the recipient is entitled to wear a bar "PACIFIC" attached to the ribbon. Those who had qualified for the Burma Star and Pacific Star were entitled to wear a Silver Rose on the ribbon of the star first earned when only the ribbon was being worn to this Star. The ribbon colours represent the British and Commonwealth armed forces (blue and red) and the sun (orange).

The Burma Star.

The Burma Star Ribbon.

THE FRANCE AND GERMANY STAR

This star was awarded for operational service in France, Belgium, Holland, Luxembourg or Germany between D-Day and the German surrender, i.e. between 6 June 1944 and 8 May 1945. Prior qualification for the 1939-1945 Star was not required as an entitlement, and the Atlantic Star was denoted by a bar "ATLANTIC". The ribbon colours, besides being those of the Union Jack, represent the national colours of France, Holland and Luxembourg ... little Belgium seems to have been forgotten!

**France and
Germany Star.**

Ribbon.

THE ITALY STAR

Operational service in Sicily or Italy between the 11th of June 1943 (capture of the island of Pantellaria) and the 8th of May 1945 was the main criterion for this star. However, service elsewhere in the Mediterranean, the Aegean, Dodecanese, Corsica, Greece, Sardinia, Yugoslavia, Elba and indeed even the entry into Austrian territory in the later stages of the war, could serve to qualify although for some of these areas time limits were set. The Italy Star was always awarded in addition to other stars so that no bars were instituted for it. Only Royal Navy and Merchant Navy personnel had to qualify for the 1939-1945 Star first; this prior time qualification was not necessary for the other services. The ribbon colours represent the national colours of Italy.

The Italy Star.

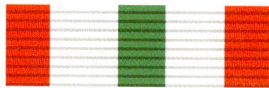

Ribbon.

THE ATLANTIC STAR

Generally awarded for a minimum of 180 days service afloat between the 3rd of September 1939 and the 2nd of September 1945 (60 days for RAF). The star was awarded to commemorate the Battle of the Atlantic and was granted for 6 months service afloat. The qualifying period however, only started from the moment the 1939-1945 Star had been earned. Bars "AIR CREW EUROPE" and "FRANCE AND GERMANY" were created in case the recipient subsequently qualified for those stars. Only one bar can be worn on a star. The ribbon colours are symbolical of the Atlantic Ocean throughout the seasons.

The Atlantic Star.

Ribbon.

THE PACIFIC STAR

Service between the 8th of December 1941 and the 2nd of September 1945 in the Pacific theatre of operations was the requirement for this star although, once again, the 1939-1945 Star had to be fulfilled first. When the recipient later also qualified for the Burma Star, a bar "BURMA" was worn. The ribbon colours represent the jungles and beaches (green and yellow) and the armed forces (dark blue for the Royal Navy, red for the Army and pale blue for the Royal Air Force).

The Pacific Star.

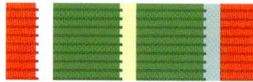

Ribbon.

The War Medal 1939-1945

A minimum of 28 days of service, whether operational or non-operational, in the Armed Forces (including the Merchant Navy when served at sea), sufficed for this medal. The ribbon colours represent the Union Jack. Servicemen who had received a "Mention in Despatches" or the "King's Commendation for Bravery" wore a bronze oak leaf on this medal's ribbon.

The War Medal.
1939 - 1945

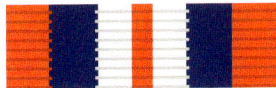

Ribbon.

Ribbon with M.I.D.

The Defence Medal

Various criteria and rules apply for this medal's award also, the main one being service in non-operational areas subjected to air attack or closely threatened for a minimum three years. The ribbon colours are symbolic of the enemy attacks (flame colour) on the British Isles (green) whereas the black stripes represent the blackout during the war years.

**The Defence Medal.
1939 - 1945**

Ribbon.

Distinguished Conduct Medal (DCM).

The Distinguished Conduct Medal

Ribbon

The DCM was instituted in 1854 to recognise "distinguished, gallant and good conduct" by troops in the Crimea. All DCMs are issued named to the recipient, usually with impressed details around the medal's rim.

Nearly 25,000 DCMs were issued during World War One, compared to 1,900 for acts during World War Two. The majority of World War One DCMs have citations in the London Gazette. Since 1939, DCMs are listed in the London Gazette but do not have citations.

Full details of DCMs awarded up to 1914, can be found in the book "The Distinguished Conduct Medal" by P.E. Abbott, published by J.B. Hayward & Son. DCMs awarded during World War One are to be found in a similar publication by R.W. Walker, but no citations are provided.

Contrary to what may be implied by the term "Distinguished Conduct" it should be remembered that this medal was, for NCOs and other ranks, second only to the Victoria Cross.

Following the 1993 review this medal has been replaced by the Conspicuous Gallantry Cross.

The Military Medal.

The Military Medal.

Ribbon.

The MM was instituted in March 1916 as an award for non-officer rank of the Army for acts of bravery. In the First World War the MM was awarded to a few recipients from the Royal Navy and Royal Air Force. Some RAF personnel were awarded the MM during World War Two. All MMs are issued named with the recipient's details impressed around the medal's rim.

During World War One, 115,000 MMs were awarded, with 5,800 first bars and 180 second bars. There was 1 award of the MM and 3 bars. World War Two saw the award of 15,000 MMs with 164 first bars and 2 second bars.

Although all MMs awarded are listed in the London Gazette, the First World War MMs do not have citations. The Second World War MMs generally do have citations.

Following the 1993 review this medal has been replaced by the Military Cross, which is now available

MILITARY DECORATIONS WORLD WAR ONE.

ADDY.   D.C.M.

Regiment: Royal Artillery

Battalion: 347 Battery

Award: **Distinguished Conduct Medal.** 01.07.16

Additional Remarks:

He was the first Cudworth man to receive the D.C.M.

BLOOMFIELD CHARLES ALBERT. M.M.

Rank: Private 1453 Signaller

Regiment: York & Lancaster Regiment

Battalion: 15th Battalion. D Coy

Award: **Military Medal.**

D.O.B.:   20th July 1898. Cudworth.

Occupation: Before enlisting he worked on Midland Railway, Cudworth.

Address: 5, St. Johns Rd Cudworth

Additional Remarks:

Died on the 28th of November 1970.

M.M. presented by Colonel Rideal at Newsham Camp Nr. Blyth, Northumberland 1916.

BRYAN S. D.C.M.

Rank: 240650 C.S.M.

Regiment: King's Own Yorkshire Light Infantry

Award: **Distinguished Conduct Medal.** 03.09.18

Address: Cudworth

Additional Remarks:

For conspicuous gallantry and devotion to duty, when in the attack on a strong point, he personally killed several of the enemy, the subalterns having become casualties he assisted the Company Commander to organise and consolidate, working untiringly throughout the day in complete disregard of danger.

BROOKS G.A. D.C.M.

Rank: Sergeant.
Regiment: Machine Gun Corps.

Award: **Distinguished Conduct Medal.** Aged 24 years.

Address: 45, Albert St. Cudworth

Additional Remarks: Worked at Brierley Colliery. Barnsley Ind. 13.07.1918.

DAVIES C. D.C.M.

Regiment: Royal Engineers.

Award: **Distinguished Conduct Medal.**

Address: Carlton.

Additional Remarks:

CUDWORTH SERGEANT WINS D.C.M.

ONE OF THE BARNSLEY BATTALION "PALS."

We are delighted to learn that Sergeant Davies, of Carlton, who is with the Royal Engineers, "Somewhere in France," has been awarded the D.C.M.

Under date January 30th, 1916, Sapper E. Roberts writes to the Editor: -"Sir, -it is some months since I wrote to you and it was a painful duty then, but this time there is more pleasure in writing to inform you that one of the old Battalion lads has been awarded the D.C.M. for a piece of good work in the field. It is the first honour that has been awarded to one of the Pals, and I might tell you that honours are not easily gained in our work, as it is part of the daily routine to perform tasks that if they were performed in the open, instead of underground more notice would be taken of them. After nearly a year out here things have not gone so badly with us as we have only had three killed, and it is worthy of note that the farthest we have ever been from the enemy was 40 yards, and we have been as near as ten. We had a lot wounded and gassed, but several of those have rejoined. There are about a dozen left in the company, and there are several in other companies.

"I hear that the 1st Barnsley Battalion have landed in Egypt, and I wish them the best of luck, and I am sure the faith of Barnsley people will not be misplaced as they are a fine lot of lads and we shall be hearing of them doing great things. Well, the chap who has won the D.C.M. is Sergeant Davies of Carlton, and I can tell you he well deserved it. He was Corporal when he left the Battalion, but was promoted to Sergeant early as he showed by his ability and daring that he was just the sort of man necessary for the work. I shall now have to close as it is near to darkness and it is not wise to show lights where I am writing. Please convey through your paper my best wishes to the lads in Egypt.

HUNTER.

Rank: Private

Regiment: Kings Own Yorkshire Light Infantry

Award: **Recommended for bravery award** – **(**saved a fellow soldier).

Additional Remarks:

Council meeting Sept. 1917 - Ernest Cooper

FOTHERGILL OLIVER. M.M.

Rank: Private

Award: **Military Medal.**

FOULSTONE WILLIAM. M.M.

Rank: 240658 Corporal

Regiment: Kings Own Yorkshire Light Infantry

Battalion: 2nd/5th Battalion

Award: **Military Medal.**

K.I.A.   Tuesday 27.11.17

Enlisted: Enlisted at South Kirby.

Resting Place: Cambrai Memorial Louverval Panel 8

Occupation: Miner at Monckton Colliery.

Address: 31, Garden Cottages, Pontefract Road, Cudworth

Additional Remarks:
Married 1 child. Marion L. Foulstone
Parents Mr. & Mrs. B. Foulstone.

FOX FRED. D.C.M.

Rank: Private

Regiment: York and Lancaster Regiment

Battalion: 10th Battalion

Award: **Distinguished Conduct Medal and the Russian Medal of St. George (3rd. Class).** 1st to 3rd July 1916

Address: 12, Churchfield Terrace, Cudworth

Additional Remarks:

CUDWORTH HERO HONOURED.
PRESENTED WITH THE D.C.M.
MEMORABLE GATHERING IN THE VILLAGE CLUB.

There was a large gathering in the Cudworth Village Club on Wednesday night to witness the presentation of the Distinguished Conduct Medal to Private Fox, of the 10th Batt, Yorkshire and Lancaster Regiment. Private Fox, who is a well-known Cudworth resident, has also been awarded the Russian Medal of St. George, and this would also have been presented to him on Wednesday night, but unfortunately it did not arrive in time. The splendid idea of having a public presentation emanated from the Cudworth Urban District Council and Mr. R. Taylor, chairman of the Council, presided over the gathering. He was supported on the platform by Mr. S. Gill (Grimethorpe), Sergeant Smith, who is another Cudworth D.C.M., Col. W. E. Raley, and members of the Council.

The Chairman explained the object of the gathering, and called upon Mr.Gill to make the presentation.

Mr. Gill said he thought Private Fox ought really to have been decorated at Buckingham Palace, and to have received the medal from the hands of the King. He remembered Fox for a number of years as a hard-working man who took a deep interest in ambulance and first aid work. He was sure his skill in ambulance work had been of great value to many on the battlefield. Private Fox had done the same as a great many miners, he had been out and done his bit and done it exceedingly well. (Applause.) Mr. Gill expressed his pleasure at meeting their friend Sergeant Smith. (Hear, Hear.) After explaining that only one of the two decorations awarded Private Fox had arrived, Mr. Gill amidst the greatest enthusiasm pinned the Distinguished Conduct Medal on Private Fox's breast.

The singing of " For he's a jolly good fellow," was followed by three cheers given with rare spirit.

Colonel Raley, in announcing that the Russian Medal of St. George (3rd class) had not yet been received read a letter sent to Private Fox by the Adjutant of the 10th Batt. Y & L Regiment, stating that the Commanding Officer wished him to be informed that he had been granted the Russian decoration for work done from the 1st to 3rd July 1916, and also forwarded on to him the congratulations of the Divisional General on his gaining this honour. The letter concluded, "This honour is equal to the Distinguished Conduct Medal, and as you have already been granted that medal you must be very proud of the work you did." (applause.)

Private Fox said he was truly thankful to be there that night, not only because he was glad to be once more with those whom he had been amongst so long. Referring to his past association with ambulance work, Pte. Fox said that whatever it had done for anybody else he had always had the satisfaction of knowing he had done his best. Private Fox went on to say that there were thousands of men who had not been recognised for bravery. Every lad who went over the parapet on July 1st was worthy of a Victoria Cross as big as a Church door. (Applause.) The Army gave you nothing unless you earned it, and he had one consolation that night. He volunteered to do his duty for King and country and the wearing of that medal proved he had done it. (Loud applause.)

At the invitation of the Chairman, Sergt. Smith briefly addressed the gathering and congratulated Private Fox on receiving this great distinction. Any man who got that distinction on the field in France could say that he had won an honour that in any other campaign would have got him the Victoria Cross. (Hear, hear, and applause.)

Colonel Raley said he agreed with Private Fox when he said that every man who went over the trenches on July 1st was entitled to a Victoria Cross as big as a Church door. He was very glad to see that at last there had been taken the objective for which our brave lads in the two Barnsley Battalions, the Sheffield Battalion, and the East Lancashire's, worked on that first of July. They were sent to do an impossible task, but as the "Times" a few days afterwards said, they didn't run, they marched like Guards right away in front of all the machine-gun fire. There was no greater thing in the history of war than the way in which the commands of the Brigade were carried out in the attack, and to day we know that Serre had fallen. It could not be rushed. It had to be virtually surrounded and taken. All honours to those brave lads from Cudworth, Barnsley and neighbourhood who fell on that day, and who fell before or have fallen since. Private Fox had told them that he volunteered when the war began, like so many others. After the retreat from Mons they said, " We are going out to help our fellow countrymen. We are going to help the lads who are fighting for us, and we are going out to see that the Germans are turned back again." It had been a long time coming, said Colonel Raley, but it was coming though it might be slowly. They could not tell how long it would take, but it was coming in the end, and God grant it might come a good deal more speedily than any of us thought. (Hear, hear.) He believed that above all there was a higher hand guiding this war. As Mr. Brace told them when speaking at the Public Hall at Barnsley the other night, if the Germans had only known at the beginning of the war how weak we were they would have been through to Paris and Calais. But there was a hand that turned them back, and we could only thank Providence for what happened then. In a personal appeal to his audience Colonel Raley said they were bound to put up with the inconveniences. Look what Germans, Austrians, French, the poor Serbians and Belgians, look everywhere on the Continent and see what inconveniences those people were putting up with. "Don't let us think of any inconvenience that we may be put to," said the Colonel in conclusion. "Let us think of those dear fellows, our sons, and our brothers, who are doing battle for us out yonder in France, Belgium and elsewhere. Let us determine that so far as we are concerned, whatever little increase in the price of food we may have to pay, whatever inconvenience we may have to undergo, we will do it cheerfully in order that right may prevail and that militarism may be put down and that we may never again in the history of the world see such a dreadful state of carnage as we are subject to to-day." (Loud applause.)

Councillor Duckworth, in moving a vote of thanks to Mr. Gill, said they appreciated his presence with them that night. Councillor Newton seconded, and in doing so also paid a tribute to Private Fox and to the thousands of others who had distinguished themselves on the battlefield.

The resolution was carried, and in responding Mr. Gill, said it had been a great pleasure to him to be able to make the presentation to his old friend.

Councillor W. Maycock moved a vote of thanks to the Chairman, to Colonel Raley and to the Club Committee for placing the room at their disposal free of cost.

Councillor Prince seconded, and this resolution was also carried with acclamation.

Mr. Gardner, the President of the Club, responded, and said the Committee were proud that the room had been used for that purpose.

The Chairman also returned thanks and said that he had been delighted to take the chair on that occasion. Some people had enquired if there was not a citizen in Cudworth capable of presenting the D.C.M. to Private Fox. When this was brought up at the Council meeting he had heard that it was Private Fox's wish that Mr. Gill should present the medal to him. He (Mr. Taylor) said straightaway that the man who had earned by his ability, by his courage and by his bravery, a medal of that description ought to have the opportunity of choosing the person to present the decoration to him. (Hear, hear.) All the Council agreed, and that was the reason why Mr. Gill had been asked to make the presentation.

During the evening an appropriate recitation was given by Councillor H. Maycock, who also spoke a few words of congratulation to Private Fox.

GOLDTHORPE LEWIS. M.M.

Rank :   7380 Private

Regiment: Worcestershire Regiment

Battalion: 10th Battalion

Award: **Military Medal.**

K.I.A.   Friday 13.07.17 aged 37 years. Battle of Messines

D.O.B.: Born in Cudworth

Enlisted: Worcester

Resting Place: Croonaert Chapel Cemetery. Heuvelland   C. 10.

Address: 171, Snydale Road Cudworth.

Additional Remarks:

Married Minnie.

Lewis Goldthorpe lived in a shop at 171, Snydale Road Cudworth and after his death his widow remarried. Her second husband was Wallace Lazenby from Low Cudworth. They had four children and lived on Moorland Terrace.   One of the children was called Lewis, after her first husband.

GOOSE GEORGE. M.M.

Rank: 13/393 Corporal

Regiment: York & Lancaster Regiment

Battalion: 13th (Service) Battalion 1st Barnsley Pals

Award: **Military Medal.** (June 1917) London Gazette 21/10/18

K.I.A.   Monday 30/09/18 aged 30 years. Battle of Messines

D.O.B.: Born in Kinnigrove, Cleveland.

Enlisted: Enlisted at Barnsley 1914

Resting Place: Strand Military Cemetery, Comines-Warneton, Hainaut VIII. D. 9.

Occupation: Miner at Grimethorpe Colliery

Address: 71, St. John's Road Cudworth

Additional Remarks:

Left a wife Alice and 3 children. The son of Harry Goose of Royston Lane, Cudworth. Named on Plaque in Cudworth West End Working Men's Club.

LODGE LUTHER. M.M.

Rank: Private

Award: **Military Medal.**

Additional Remarks:

Awarded for good work on 27th November 1917.

For gallantry while under intense fire, he guided a tank on the morning of the 27th November 1917, when an effort was being made to find a route through a village regardless of the risk he ran. Private Lodge stuck to the tank, which put out of action several machine guns that were inflicting casualties on our men.

NAYLOR E. D.C.M. M.M.

Rank: 241539 Lance Corporal

Regiment: Kings Own Yorkshire Light Infantry

Award: **Distinguished Conduct Medal. Military Medal.** 30.10.18

Address: Cudworth

Additional Remarks:

For conspicuous gallantry and devotion to duty. This N.C.O. was with a defensive patrol, they were heavily bombarded and gassed and two of the patrol were wounded. Unaided, he brought one back safely to his lines and then returned and brought back the other. This was done through a strong concentration of gas and intense shelling. His most gallant conduct and absolute disregard of personal safety set a splendid example to his platoon and undoubtedly saved the lives of his two comrades.

From D.C.M's awarded to the K.O.Y.L.I.

E. Naylor (Cudworth) M.M. (B.Ind. 22.12.1917

O'BRIEN S. D.C.M.

Award: **Distinguished Conduct Medal.**

Address: Cudworth.

PARKER. D.C.M.

Rank: Sergeant

Award: **Distinguished Conduct Medal.** Awarded in public by Col. Fox.

Additional Remarks:

Council meeting Oct. 1917 - Ernest Cooper

PARKES WALTER. D.C.M.

Rank: 1432 Company Sergeant Major

Regiment: York and Lancaster Regiment.

Battalion: 1/5TH Battalion Barnsley Territorials.

Award: **Distinguished Conduct Medal.** July 6th 1916

Address: Rose Villas, 136, Barnsley Rd. Cudworth

Additional Remarks:

Married Rose.

"Company Sergeant Major Parkes was awarded the D.C.M. on July 6th 1916 but he has not personally received the medal. It is hoped to make him the presentation in public when peace is declared and the "boys come home""

Extracted from the Barnsley Chronicle report on Company Sergeant Major Walter Parkes in chapter 8, Prisoners of War.

PHEASANT E.W. M.M.

Rank: Private.

Regiment: York and Lancaster Regiment.

Award: **Military Medal.**

Address: Cudworth.

Additional Remarks:

Rescued colleague under fire.

ROUT A. M.M.

Rank: Corporal

Regiment: Rifle Brigade

Award: **Military Medal.** 23rd December 1915. Aged 21 years

Address: 108, Barnsley Rd, Cudworth

Additional Remarks:

The son of Mrs. James Milne

"He went to France in November 1914. Wounded at Neuve Chappelle. Returned to front in 1915. Last month he was wounded slightly but offered to go back to the front. 4/5 small wounds to the left hand, also hurt by being buried by a shell. He was one of five men from his Battalion who came out alive.

Awarded the M.M. for gallantly holding part of a captured trench by himself, all of his comrades having been killed or wounded". (information from the Barnsley Chronicle, July 1916)

WAUGH HORACE. D.C.M.

Rank: 12770 Private.

Regiment: York & Lancaster Regiment.

Battalion: 7th Battalion.

Award: **Distinguished Conduct Medal.**

D.O.B.: Born in Barnsley, in the second quarter of 1894.

Address: Cudworth.

Additional Remarks:

Horace Waugh was the first Cudworth soldier to receive D.C.M. Private H. Waugh has received the following extract from Battalion Orders by Major W.M.G. Armstrong commanding 7th York & Lancaster Regiment:

23rd December 1915.

Commanding Officer wishes to express his appreciation of the exemplary conduct of 12770 Pte. H. Waugh. This linesman was left in charge of the Signal Station at Lillebeke Lake when the operators went forward on the morning of the 19th inst. Not only did he repair his line under continuous and heavy shell fire from 5 a.m. until the end of the attack and subsequent bombardment, but also sent and received important messages throughout the day. Owing to his action our cable was one of the very few to maintain almost uninterrupted communications during the operations.

WHEATLEY G. M.M.

Rank: Private

Regiment: Scottish Rifles

Award: **Military Medal.**

Enlisted: Grimethorpe.

Occupation: Worked at Grimethorpe Colliery.

Address: 137, Snydale Road, Cudworth

Additional Remarks:

Married with 3 children.

Cudworth Council meeting 10 Nov 1917 - "Private Wheatly, Scottish Rifles has been awarded the military medal (M.M.). Went to France via Dardanelles and Egypt. He has been wounded 3 times.

WILLIAMS J.R.

Rank: Lance Corporal

Occupation: Worked at Grimethorpe Colliery.

Address: Barnsley Road, Cudworth

Additional Remarks:

Reported at Cudworth Council meeting 12.06.1916 - "Lance Corporal J.R. Williams has been wounded on active on June 4th. A letter from his Officer in Charge states that he had been helping injured soldiers who were injured in battle and thought that he would be recommended for a bravery award for the courage and daring he showed while doing his duty to his fellow comrades.

MILITARY DECORATIONS WORLD WAR TWO.

ALLSEBROOK ARTHUR. M.M.

Rank: Guardsman L/Corporal 2657084.

Regiment: Coldstream Guards.

Battalion: 3rd.

Award: **Military Medal.**

D.O.B.:   Baptised at Cudworth 17.03.1915.

Address: 121 Darfield Road. Cudworth 14, Highroyd

Additional Remarks:

The son of John William & Annie Allsebrook of 6, The Avenue, Cudworth.

BAGG CLARENCE E. H. M.M.

Rank: Corporal.

Regiment: M.T. Company Royal Army Service Corps.

Award: **Military Medal.**

P.o.W.

Italy.

Address: 56 Moorland Terrace, Cudworth.

Additional Remarks:

Clarence Bagg was the youngest son of Mr. & the late Mrs. Thomas Bagg, who were Newsagents on Barnsley Road, Cudworth.

Military Medal and Gazetted. 1st January 1944.

Repatriated P.o.W. after 18 months in Italian hands.

He spoke very highly of the Red Cross Society.

BERRYMAN H.E. "Dick" M.M.

Rank: 2570488 Bombardier.

Regiment: Royal Artillery.

Battalion: 347 Battery.

Award: **Military Medal.** 01.02.45 North West Europe Campaign.

D.O.B.:   1918

Address: 10 Newtown Avenue, Cudworth

Additional Remarks:

Married to Bessie Blockley.

CUDWORTH COMMANDO WINS MILITARY MEDAL. (17.02.45)

In 1940 some soldiers were billeted in Cudworth, many of whom married local girls. One, Private Berryman, married Miss B. Blockley, of 10, Newtown Avenue, Cudworth. When on leave last week from Europe, Private Berryman was informed by telegram that he had been awarded the Military Medal for "Devotion to duty on D-day." Although full details are not to hand Private Berryman was one of the first commandos to land in France, and all his officers were killed or wounded. He attended to their wounds and fixed up his wireless, by which means he guided other craft to land.

CUDWORTH BOMBARDIER AWARDED MILITARY MEDAL.

(24.02.45) As briefly intimated last week

Bombardier H. E. Berryman, whose wife lives at 10, Newtown Avenue, Cudworth, has been awarded the Military Medal in the following circumstances. He landed with the Royal Marine Commandos on D-day; he was the forward observer for a naval bombardment unit and his superior officer being mortally wounded, he carried on alone and kept his bombarding ships in action all the afternoon, despite heavy enemy fire from mortars and snipers. Bombardier. H. E. Berryman, R.A. joined the Territorials in July 1938, and was called up at the outbreak of war, being stationed in Cudworth during 1940/41.

His nephew Steve Blockley, who lives in Switzerland, contacted the History Group when researching family tree in Cudworth, and as a result Dick's son Nigel Berryman sent the following photographs and brief history of his father's, H.E. Berryman, life. The History Group expresses its gratitude for this information.

H. E. B. "Dick" BERRYMAN MM. 1918-2002.

Although spending his first 2 weeks in Norfolk, where his father was serving as a sergeant major in the Royal Horse Artillery, Dick grew up in the Devonshire harbour town of Topsham, 3 miles from Exeter on the river Exe.

He had a normal childhood, singing in the church choir and participating in whaler rowing as a member of the sea scouts. For a time he lived in the London South Western Hotel where his maternal grandfather was the licensee. After leaving school at 15 he worked in a gas mantle factory in Exeter, a job that he absolutely loathed, returning to the city on his bike several evenings a week, to take evening classes in literature and art, becoming quite a skilled artist. After about a year of this he departed the hated gas mantle factory and went to live with his Aunt Nell, his father's sister, at Beaconsfield in Buckinghamshire, which was the home of the famous, now defunct, Denham film studios, home of Sir Alexander Korda's London Films. Dick managed an entrée into this glamorous world through a series of menial jobs, clapper boy, receptionist etc. The golden couple Laurence Olivier and Vivien Leigh made a big impression on him, as did seeing Marlene Dietrich in the bath. He acted as a chaperone for the young Indian boy Sabu, star of many oriental epics, including "The Thief Of Baghdad" and "Elephant Boy".

As everyone knows the Thirties were a tumultuous period on the international stage and Dick was well aware of what was going on at Munich and in other European cities. After Munich he felt that war was virtually inevitable. He had been active in the TA and before any declaration of war was made he had followed in his father's footsteps into the Royal Artillery. He rose to the rank of Bombardier, studying all the arts of gunnery including ballistics and land profiling, this last being important when he was trained to operate as a forward observer. His role was to observe fall of shot from a forward-elevated position, reporting back to the gun emplacement by telephone cable or radio.

He trained at various depots and ranges around the country, most significantly, from a personal point of view, Barnsley where he met Bessie at a dance. They were married in 1941.

From a military point of view the most significant posting was probably Papa Westray, one of the more northerly of the Orkney Islands. He was billeted with the local headmaster and spent most of his time enjoying the man's private library. Periodically he would be called into action. Units of the Home Fleet would leave nearby Scapa Flow and sail to the range near Papa Westray and Dick would hone his skills in gunnery guidance, with the aid of naval telegraphers. For the initial phase the armies going ashore on D-Day in Normandy would be supported by naval gunfire. It would be some time before artillery could be landed in significant numbers.

Anticipating forthcoming combined operations Dick joined 41 Commando, his job would be, as part of a small team, to fire ships in support of this Commando at their designated landing area of Luc sur Mer, Sword beach. His unit consisted of Captain Peter Cory Dixon of Liverpool, himself and 2 naval telegraphers ("Tels" as they were called) — apparently the Navy liked their own personnel at the other end of the radio link and the plan was that they should go ashore separately, to avoid possible total loss, and make their way to a pre-arranged rendezvous. Dick drove a jeep from the landing craft onto the beach and, following directions, which he thought were very good, arrived without problem at the meeting place. Captain Dixon joined him but neither of the Tels arrived (one having been killed in his landing craft and the other seriously wounded). Captain Dixon and Dick were sheltering in a trench when a Junkers 88 went across and dropped a stick of anti-personnel bombs, one killing the officer instantly. Apparently this was the only sortie made by Ju 88s on D-Day. (Later Dick managed to get back and check that Captain Dixon's temporary grave was correctly marked. The captain is now in the British cemetery at Douvres-la-Deliverande.)

The unit now consisted of Dick alone, but gunnery support was absolutely essential and he was asked if he felt capable of carrying on, using a Royal Marine radio operator, whom the Navy was prepared to accept. Dick spent the next three weeks directing the fire from ships onto German positions inland of Sword beach, from several different vantage points. He was shot at quite a bit, but survived and after about 3 weeks was withdrawn to England, in preparation for the proposed amphibious assault on Walcheran in Holland. However, he was not called upon again.

Throughout the war Bessie, and then baby Penny, stayed with Arthur and Mary Blockley in Cudworth.

After receiving his MM from King George VI, accompanied by Bessie and Penny, he did not to go back into the film industry, the production side of which had been a possibility, but decided instead to take advantage of the one-year training course for ex servicemen to become a teacher. Throughout his life he was a great believer in young people, and many generations were to benefit from his enthusiasm and encouragement.

He taught first at a multi-aged village school at Stogursey in Somerset, and then at a Secondary Modern and Middle School at Woodlands near Doncaster, latterly as headmaster. Up to his death he was in contact with ex-pupils from all stages of his career.

Following the death of Bessie he had a very happy second marriage to Joan and he died in 2002.

He had been an enthusiastic member of his British Legion Branch and served as chairman.

Although a doughty warrior he was a great believer in contact between peoples and in mending fences. In the I950's Woodlands Secondary Modern had exchange visits with a school in Germany and he welcomed members of German parties to his house, something remembered by his son. He loved travelling in Europe and had a particular affinity with France, enjoying the wine, the fruits de mer (although they didn't always agree with him), and the ambiance of French restaurants. He paid a last visit to Paris some 5 years before his death and enjoyed it thoroughly, despite his failing eyesight robbing him of the pleasure of seeing the paintings by the impressionist masters.

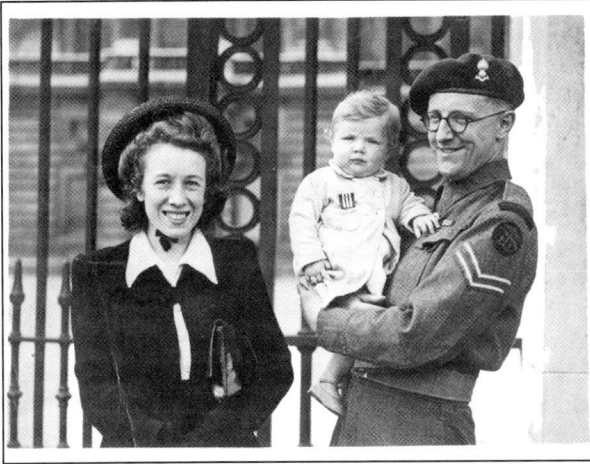

Bombardier H.E. Berryman photographed with his wife Bessie and daughter Penny after receiving the Military Medal.

Bombardier
H.E. Berryman.
(Front)

Bombardier
H.E. Berryman.
(Rear)

CULLEN J.P. (JOE). M.M.

Rank: 2718043 Guardsman.

Regiment: Irish Guards.

Award: **Military Medal.**

Address: Cudworth.

Additional Remarks:

Military Medal 21.12.44 North West Europe Campaign.

SMITH THOMAS. D.C.M.

Rank: Sergeant.

Regiment: York and Lancaster Regiment.

Award: **Distinguished Conduct Medal.**

Additional Remarks:

Aged 25 years.

SWANN KENNETH WARRENDER. D.F.C.

Rank: Squadron Leader.

Service: R.A.F.

Award: **Distinguished Flying Cross.**
22nd April 1944.

D.O.B.: aged 21 years

Address: "Ringbank Kennels," Barnsley Road, Cudworth.

Additional Remarks:

The eldest son of Capt. E. Swann & Mrs. Swann.

He attended Kirk Balk Modern School. (Hoyland) and then Ecclesfield Grammar School.

Reported in the Barnsley Chronicle on the 18th of March 1944 that he had been promoted to Squadron Leader. Squadron Leader Swann was one of the youngest airmen to attain this rank.

On the 22nd of April 1944 the Chronicle reported the award of the D.F.C. as follows:

CUDWORTH SQUADRON LEADER AT PALACE INVESTITURE.

Squadron Leader Kenneth Warrender Swann, who resides at "Ringbank Kennels," Barnsley Road, Cudworth, recently received the Distinguished Flying Cross from the King at Buckingham Palace.

The official citation for the award states that it was for "courage, devotion and tenacity as Captain of aircraft in attacks on Berlin, Essen, Hamburg, Munich and Stettin, during

which his skill and courage in action have been an inspiration to his crew, while his unbounded keenness and enthusiasm have been an example to the whole Squadron".

Squadron Leader Swann was accompanied by his parents and younger brother. His father, Major E. Swann, is in command of "D" 56 W.R. Home Guard.

His brother, Leading Naval Airman G. Derek Swann, is serving in the Fleet Air Arm.

Thus the family are represented in the three Services- Navy, Army and Air Force.

CHAPTER 8.

PRISONERS

OF

WAR.

PRISONERS OF WAR

We have tried to record the men of Cudworth who were taken prisoner in both World Wars while in the service of their country. Very little is recorded of these men except for newspaper cuttings announcing their capture or release. Family members may be able to obtain service records that should at least list where they were taken prisoner, where they were held, and when released. The International Committee of the Red Cross in Geneva keeps lists of all known PoWs of the Second World War.

The following information is of the people that we came across while researching the War dead.

THE FIRST WORLD WAR.

APPLEYARD T.

1st Battalion West Yorkshire Regiment.

19 Albert Street, Cudworth.

P.o.W. Camp.
No. 27 Gefangenenlager, Munster 11, Westphalia.

BENTLEY J.D.

36591.

11th Battalion Leicestershire Regiment.

36 Pontefract Road, Cudworth.

P.o.W. Camp.
2 Co Gefangenenlager, Quidlingburg.

Additional Remarks:

Previously employed by Eastman's Ltd. Butchers.
Private Bentley was a wounded prisoner of war.

BLACKSHAW THOMAS.

31236.

2nd Battalion East Lancashire Regiment.

10 Snydale Road, Cudworth.

P.o.W. Camp.
Gustron in Mecklenburge.

CAWTHROW.

Private.

Additional Remarks:

A report in the Barnsley Chronicle announcing his return home with Pte. Woolston, said that 'they were the first lads to return to Cudworth. They had been working behind the German Lines & would have starved without the kindness of Belgium citizens'.

FREEZER R.W.

Corporal.

4 St. John's Cottages, Cudworth.

P.o.W. Camp.
Engl Kom IX.
Barrack No. 1096 3 Comp
Friedricksfled
Nr. Wesel, Rheinland.

GALLEAR THOMAS.

Private.

York and Lancaster Regiment.

9 Worsley Street, Cudworth.

P.o.W. Camp.
Germany.

GOOSE H.

Corporal.

1st/4th Battalion King's Own Yorkshire Light Infantry.

6 Royston Lane, Cudworth.

P.o.W. Camp.
185 Van Boeize-Laerlann
Den Hagg
Holland.

HOLMES H.

40170.

2nd /6th Battalion North Staffordshire Regiment.

220 Pontefract Road, Cudworth.

P.o.W. Camp.
1077220 Stammlager
Limburg Al

HOLMES WILLIAM HENRY.

King's Own Yorkshire Light Infantry.

Cudworth.

P.o.W. Camp.
Germany.

HOLT H.

Private 3223.

2nd Battalion York and Lancaster Regiment.

12 Eveline Street, Cudworth.

P.o.W. Camp.
No. 998 Batt.
Vogt Stammlager
Parchim.

HUGHES HARRY.

Corporal.

1st/6th Battalion West Yorkshire Regiment.

4 Worsley Street, Cudworth.

P.o.W. Camp.
Camp 22, Barrack 3B
Cottrus.

HOWARD LAWRENCE GEORGE.

Private 24078.

8th Battalion York and Lancaster Regiment.

9 Worsley Street, Cudworth.

P.o.W. Camp.
Unknown.

Additional Remarks:

Lawrence George Howard was the son of George and Lucy Howard 9 St. George's Terrace, Pontefract.
Private Howard was killed in action on Saturday the 1st of July 1916. He is buried in the Blighty Valley Cemetery, grave reference V. E. 38.

MELLOR NOAH.

Private 18997.

2nd Battalion York and Lancaster Regiment.

1 George Street, Cudworth.

P.o.W. Camp.
Camp 80B, Barrack 36A, Group 3.
Dulmen, Westphalia.

Additional Remarks:

Worked at Grimethorpe Colliery.

Enlisted September 1914.

Private Mellor fought at the Battle of Serre (Somme) on the 1st July 1916

He was praised by Commanding Officer for his conduct on a bombing raid of German trenches on the 12th of April 1917.

Noah Mellor had a brother serving in the R.F.A.

MORRELL SYDNEY.

Sapper.

Royal Engineers, Signals.

7 Ainslie Road, Fulwood, Preston. (Previously resided in Cudworth).

P.o.W. Camp.
Germany. (27.05.18)

OSBOURNE GEORGE.

Cudworth.

P.o.W. Camp.
Germany. (Vicar's letter dated May 1915).

PARKES WALTER.

Company Sergeant Major 14/32

14th (Service) Battalion (2nd Barnsley Pals) York and Lancaster Regiment.

Rose Villas, 136 Barnsley Road, Cudworth.

P.o.W. Camp.

Bed No. 2902, Kriegsgefungenlazarett, Alexandrinen Strasse, Berlin, Germany.

Additional Remarks:

The Barnsley Chronicle of the 5th of May 1917 reported a visit by his wife as follows:

CUDWORTH SOLDIER INTERNED.
CAPTURED BY GERMANS WHEN WOUNDED.

"Mrs. Walter Parkes, wife of Company Sergeant Major Parkes, Y & L. Regiment, who resides with her parents at 136, Barnsley Road, Cudworth, has just returned home from a specially-privileged visit to Murren, in Switzerland, where her husband at present is an interned prisoner of war. Formerly her husband was employed at Grimethorpe Colliery, and at the outbreak of war he was in camp at Whitby with the Territorials. He was wounded in the first "Big Push" last July, when a bullet penetrated his left eye and destroyed the sight, damaged his cheek bone, and splintered his shoulder blade. Whilst suffering from these wounds he was taken a prisoner into Germany and received medical treatment; subsequently, with many more soldiers, he was transferred on December 19th last from Germany to Murren, a pretty Alpine village amongst the Alps, in Bernese-Oberland - the land of perpetual snow - where he is now progressing as favourably as can be expected.

Mrs. Parkes, after receiving the necessary permits and vouchers, journeyed to London where she was met by lady guides, escorted to the Y.M.C.A. rooms, and made up a contingent of about 30 wives of soldiers, all of whom were interested in the same errand - " to see our dear husbands" - who were wounded and prisoners of war. In times of peace the journey from London to Switzerland can be done comfortably in a couple of days, but in war time there are so many obstacles to surmount, and risks to avoid, that it took the party of visitors a full week, from the time of leaving home to reaching their destination. When nearing Interlaken the lady guides, realising that some were needing refreshment, questioned the eager wives - "Which is it to be - Tea or Husbands?" - All the party were unanimous - "Our husbands." And so the train carried them to Interlaken East, at which station it was found that the whole of the husbands of the 30 wives had been allowed to come and meet them. And what a meeting it was! Some of the ladies had not seen their husbands for more than two years and they wept for joy at the sight of their loved ones, although many of them were maimed, and permanently disfigured - but they were alive, and in the flesh, and this was strong consolation to the aching hearts.

From Interlaken the mountain train brought the party to Launterbrunnen, where they again changed into a funicular railway car that carried them higher up and nearer the Alps to Murren.

Accommodation was found in the various Hotels of the village, for the soldiers and wives and whilst the food provided was not all that could be desired it was wholesome, and if any of the visitors needed supplementary additions to the menu, it could be from a restaurant near by. For 14 clear days the ladies and their husbands lived together, and as far as possible made things bright and merry, and answered the thousand and one questions put to them by the enquiring husbands. Each day the progress of the Allies on the Western Front is posted up for the wounded prisoners of war to read. There are about 80 men under Sergeant-Major Parkes and their chief duty is fatigue work. He is the only soldier there belonging to Y. & L. Regiment.

We will draw a veil over the day of parting; suffice to say it was a day full of emotion and tears. On arriving in Paris the party found that they could not proceed further because danger lurked in the Channel, and so they were compelled to remain a few days and await the opportunity of crossing the water. Subsequently the signal was given and the party proceeded to Le Havre and during the night a successful crossing was made. On arriving at Southampton one of the lady guides the next morning said: "You all ought to thank God this morning for a safe journey. Whilst we have escaped injury and accident two hospital ships have been torpedoed by the enemy when crossing the Channel at the same time as us." Mrs. Parkes eventually reached Cudworth just a month after the date of her departure and feels grateful and thankful for the privilege she was granted.

It may be added that Coy. Sgt.-Major Parkes was awarded the D.C.M. on July 6th last year, but he has not personally received the medal. It is hoped to make him the presentation in public when Peace is declared and the "boys come home."'

Mr and Mrs Walter Parkes Photographed at Murren.

READER G.

C/o Albert Gallear, Sidcop, Cudworth.

P.o.W. Camp.
Holland.

Additional Remarks:
Information from the Barnsley Chronicle.

WATSON F.

22736

2nd Battalion York and Lancaster Regiment.

78 Manor Road, Cudworth.

P.o.W. Camp.

Stammlager Parchim
Mecklenburg

WIGGLESWORTH ERNEST.

22197

10th Battalion York and Lancaster Regiment.

223 Barnsley Road, Cudworth.

P.o.W. Camp.

Stammlager PR
Holland Ost
Prussion

Additional Remarks:
Previously employed as a platelayer on the railway.
Attested on the 18th of November 1915, approved on the 14th of February 1916 and posted to the 10th Battalion of the York and Lancaster Regiment.
'Missing since 21st of April 1917, now known to have been taken prisoner of war. Aged 19 years, 3 months.

WOOLSTON G.

Private

10th Lincoln Regiment.

11 Bloemfontein Street, Cudworth.

P.o.W. Camp.

Germany.

Additional Remarks:

The Barnsley Chronicle reporting his return home with Pte. Cawthrow, on the 30th of November 1918, said that *'they were the first lads to return to Cudworth. They had been working behind the German Lines & would have starved without the kindness of Belgium citizens'.*

THE SECOND WORLD WAR.

ASTON J. TOM.

Private.

M.T. Company Royal Army Service Corps. (B.E.F.)

56 Moorland Terrace, Cudworth.

P.o.W. Camp.

Stalag XXIB.

Additional Remarks:

Private Tom Aston is on the right.

A later photograph. (note the promotion)

Tom Aston was the son of Mr and Mrs. B. Aston of 56 Moorland Terrace, Cudworth. He first met his wife Violet when she was only thirteen. She and her mother had moved from Newcastle to Yorkshire to join her father. Young Tom happened to be at the bus station, and carried their cases for them. They married at Cudworth, Yorkshire.

Private Aston went missing on the 13th of May 1940 and was known to be a prisoner of war from the 1st of September 1940.

Stalag XXIB was one of the P.O.W. camps in which he was held.

He served on one of Group Captain Douglas Bader's escape committee, who made four escapes from German prison camps during the Second World War.

Before the war he was an RASC member of the supplementary reserve, part of the Territorial Army and was called up just before the war started. He went to Bulford Camp, in Wiltshire, and then went to France with the British Expeditionary Force.

In May 1940 he was with a small convoy heading towards the Maginot Line when it ran into German panzers. The Germans ordered the drivers out of their lorries, blew the vehicles up, then turned the British loose, having no room for prisoners in their tanks.

For a bizarre week they wandered around France, but the German advance was so fast the party had no chance to get back to the BEF, and German soldiers were everywhere. Eventually they were rounded up and started a terrible two-month forced march from Boulogne to the prison camp at Lamsdorf in North Poland. Mr. Aston said that this was one of the untold stories of the war, because he had never seen it in the media.

About 35,000 to 40,000 British and French prisoners marched, six to eight abreast, covering between 22 and 25 kilometres a day. Very little food was provided by the Germans, and then it was usually potato water and pickled cabbage. Once the Germans found two huge crates of toffees. Each man could take two toffees and they had to last 24 hours.

The men were so hungry they ate dandelion leaves from the verges. Sometimes they took fruit and vegetables from the fields and gardens. The men at the front of the column had the easiest pickings, and so the sick and wounded dropped farther and farther back, getting less and less food.

But the British troops always supported, fed, and if necessary, carried their sick and wounded. The French were more inclined to leave their lame ducks, which were sometimes bayoneted to death at the roadside by the guards. The Germans had much more respect for the British.

Eventually they arrived at Lamsdorf where Polish prisoners were still building the camp. Few buildings were ready and the newcomers had to sleep in holes dug in the ground.

After two months, Mr. Aston volunteered for a working party that looked after an SS barracks at Poznan. One day, he managed to smuggle out a complete German uniform from the barracks in a blanket sack, which was supposed to contain rations.

Although there were notices at railway stations that prisoners trying to escape in German uniforms would be shot, he walked unchallenged out of the camp at 2 a.m., carrying no papers and unable to speak a word of German. He walked for six hours, and then passed two small German girls playing at the roadside. They said good morning to him in German, but he impulsively swore at them in English, which he immediately realised was a mistake. A short way down the road, four Polish civilians working for the Germans recaptured him.

For 28 days he was held in a six-by-six-by-four-foot under-ground cell and fed on black bread and water. Every third night he was given a straw palliasse; the other nights it was the bare concrete floor. He also had a Prussian woman jailer, sometimes in uniform and sometimes in civilian clothes, who regularly threatened him with a knife. When he was released from the cell he could hardly walk, and his normal weight of 10 stone had dropped to seven.

Later he was taken to another Stalag and told he was on the German blacklist of prisoners who were not allowed out of camp, but he swapped names and numbers with another prisoner in a working party and was sent to the Bavarian castle of Tittmorning, which he said was similar to Colditz.

The camp had over 200 Allied officers, including some officers of his regiment, the RASC. This was where he met Group Captain Bader. "He was very strict to work for, and wouldn't take any messing about. But he was a very fine officer and masterminded all the escape attempts", recalled Mr. Aston.

Eventually it was Mr. Aston's turn to escape. Other prisoners put him in a rubbish sack and loaded him on a horse-drawn rubbish cart with a German crew, but when they reached the tip outside the camp, the sack burst open as it went out of the cart and the Germans spotted him and it was seven days confinement. This was a lot easier than the first time however, as the officer prisoners smuggled him food.

Surprisingly he was detailed subsequently to another working party in stone quarries on the German-Czech border at Marsdorf. When Mr. Aston found the Germans were mining blue stone there, as a gunpowder ingredient, he had no wish to help their war effort, so he put his finger under the wheel of a rail truck and nearly severed it, in the hope that he would be sent to hospital. But the Germans realised what he had done and kept him working.

Helping to build a one and a quarter mile tunnel under a mountain to another quarry, he again escaped, this time up a rope ladder in a quarter mile deep ventilation shaft.

Free for four days, he was stopped in the road by the Gestapo. He could speak fluent German by then, but without papers he was unable to bluff his way through, and had another 14 days in confinement. He was taken back to work in the Marsdorf quarry, but not in the tunnel.

Not having a secret radio like some camps, they livid in utter limbo and had no idea how the war was progressing. But one-day six Russian planes flew over the quarry and the prisoners' hopes rose.

A week later they set off on another march, but very different from the march of 5 years before from France to Poland. The roles of prisoners and guards were now almost reversed because the captives had plenty of Red Cross parcels by that time, but their captors were running very short of food. All the young German soldiers had long been sent on active service and their guards were old men some of whom could hardly walk. Some of them were not strong enough to carry their rifles and the prisoners carried the weapons for them with a great deal of joking.

This comic opera column marched for some days in aimless fashion, averaging only a few kilometres a day because that was all the oldest guards could manage.

One day they heard American gunfire, and early next morning, Mr. Aston and several other prisoners crept out of the barn where they were sleeping, past the snoring old guards, and walked down a lane. After about an hour they saw a column of vehicles approaching.

They had been cut off from the outside world for so long they did not know that the white stars on the tanks and jeeps showed they were Americans, and they had never heard of jeeps. Uncertain who they were approaching they raised their hands and shouted "Englander!"

The Americans for their part, seeing this dishevelled gaggle of men, thought that they might be Germans and kept them covered with machine guns.

After half an hour, during which other small groups were arriving from the barn, the Americans were convinced of their identity and could not do enough for them. They plied them with tinned food, and then set off for the barn and the remaining sixty or so prisoners. There was no trouble from the old Germans who were just glad to be out of the war.

Their liberators were the 3rd American army, and the prisoners, like Mr. Aston, who could speak good German, rode in their tanks for the final two months of the war, helping them sort out the German prisoners. Most of the Germans were disarmed and turned loose, just as Mr. Aston had been by the Germans in France but the SS men, who were recognizable by the small tattoos under their left arms, whatever uniforms they had managed to change into, were put into lorries coming up behind the tanks. Mr. Aston never heard what happened to them.

With the war almost over, the translator prisoners were flown by American Dakota transports to Belgium where they were picked up by Lancaster bombers. As they crossed the Channel the Captain had the prisoners in the cockpit in turns to see the approaching cliffs of Dover, and most of them burst into tears of joy and relief.

After several years of civvy life, Mr. Aston rejoined the army in 1948, going into the Royal Engineers. He came to the Warminster area for the first time, going to the School of Military Survey, then at Longleats.

In 1952, as a corporal, he was posted to the new territories in Hong Kong on road - building. His feet were still giving him trouble after the forced march in 1940. He went into hospital, and that probably saved his life. While he was away Chinese pirates attacked his unit and several engineers were killed. He was later posted back to the Military School of Survey, which by then was at Hermitage, near Newbury. His final posting before being demobbed for the last time in 1954, was to Perham Down near Andover.

ATHORN FRANK.

Private

9 Royd Avenue, Cudworth.

P.o.W. Camp.

Germany.

BAGG CLARENCE E. H.

Corporal.

M.T. Company Royal Army Service Corps. (B.E.F.)

56 Moorland Terrace, Cudworth.

P.o.W. Camp.

Italy

Additional Remarks:

Taken prisoner of war in Italy, he was repatriated after 18 months in Italian hands. He spoke very highly of the Red Cross Society.

Clarence Bagg was the youngest son of Mr. & the late Mrs. Thomas Bagg who were Newsagents on Barnsley Road, Cudworth.

Corporal Bagg received the Military Medal.

BAINES CHARLES.

12 Beech Avenue, Cudworth.

P.o.W. Camp.

06.10.40

Additional Remarks:

Charles Baines was an army reservist with long service in India.

BRAZIER STANLEY.

AC1.

Enlisted : 1940.

Royal Air Force.

Bloemfontein Street, Cudworth.

P.o.W. Camp.

R.A.F. Camp in Java.

Additional Remarks:

In civilian life Councillor Brazier was on the teaching staff at Snydale Road School, Cudworth. His brother, Leonard, was in the Army Pay Corps. B.N.A.F.

Stanley Brazier was the youngest member of the Cudworth Urban District Council.

After joining the R.A.F. in 1940, he went to serve in the Far East in 1941.

His parents, Mr. And Mrs. T. Brazier of Bloemfontein Street, Cudworth, last heard of him on February 21st 1942, when he sent a telegram from Java saying he was safe. Airman Brazier was held in the R.A.F. P.O.W. Camp in Java.

On December 30th 1944, after a year and 10 months absence of news, their anxiety was then eased by the receipt of a postcard which stated: *"won't it be wonderful when we meet again? Our camp is well equipped and our daily life is very pleasant. The Japanese treat us well. Never worry or feel uneasy"*

Stanley Braziers' P.o.W. experience seriously affected his life including bouts of malaria and he had great difficulty with his sight.

He became the Head of Snydale Road Junior Mixed School and was greatly respected throughout the village.

CLIFFORD THOMAS HENRY.

Private

York and Lancaster Regiment.

Additional Remarks:

Private Clifford was reported in the Barnsley Chronicle on the 20th of July 1940 as having been taken a prisoner of war.

CONWAY STANLEY.

Gunner 1520665

2 Bty. 1 Searchlight Regiment Royal Artillery.

64 Lunn Road, Cudworth.

P.o.W. Camp.

Stalag XXIB

Additional Remarks:

Stanley Conway was the youngest son of George Patrick and Elizabeth Conway of 64 Lunn Road, Cudworth. He was known locally as "Tom".

Gunner Conway was taken prisoner at Dunkirk in April 1940 and was held in Stalag VIII. On repatriation a German Doctor gave him a pint of his own blood and accompanied him to the boat for England so that he could get home to see his mother before he died.

A Cudworth Variety Concert was held at the Catholic Club in aid of Norman Stacey and Stanley Conway, repatriated prisoners of war.

Stanley Conway died in hospital before the concert took place, but it was agreed that the project should be carried through, his mother to receive his share. There was a good company of talented artistes, all of whom gave their services free.

Gunner Conway died on Tuesday the 18th of January 1944 and is buried in the Dearne (Thurnscoe) Cemetery in section E. 1. R.C. grave 43. He was 24 years old.

His brother Driver J. Conway R.A. also of 64, Lunn Rd. was a Dunkirk evacuee.

GOULDING ERNEST.

Gunner.

Searchlight Regiment, Royal Artillery.

7 Lunn Road, Cudworth.

P.o.W. Camp.

September 1940.

Additional Remarks:

Ernest Goulding was the eldest son of Mr and Mrs H. Goulding of 7 Lunn Road, Cudworth.

He was posted as missing while serving overseas in April 1940 and was known to be a prisoner of war in September 1940.

HEMMINGWAY JAMES VERNOR.

Private.

Kings Own Yorkshire Light Infantry (transferred to the Durham Light Infantry).

High Royd, Cudworth.

P.o.W.

1940.

Additional Remarks:

James Hemmingway was the son of Mr and Mrs George Hemmingway of High Royd, Cudworth. Prior to joining the Army he worked as a screen hand at Brierley Colliery.

While serving in France he was listed as a prisoner of war in 1940.

HOOPER VERNOR.

Able Seaman, Royal Navy.

Cudworth.

P.o.W.

1941.

Reggio, Italy.

Additional Remarks:

In September 1941 he was taken prisoner in the desert after bombing had sunk his ship, H.M.S. Hereward, off Crete.

He was repatriated and sent to Canada to recuperate.

JARVIS E.

Private

Argyle and Sutherland Highlanders.

40 or 24 Pontefract Road, Cudworth.

Additional Remarks:

He was the son of Mr and Mrs E. Jarvis of 40 Pontefract Road, Cudworth.

Private E. Jarvis was confirmed as a P.O.W. after being missing in the Middle East.

JARVIS HORACE.

Private

Argyle and Sutherland Highlanders.

40 (24) Pontefract, Cudworth.

Additional Remarks:

Private H. Jarvis was the son of Mr and Mrs E. Jarvis of 40 Pontefract Road, Cudworth.

He had been serving overseas since 1939, he was listed as a prisoner of war.

LAWRENCE ROBERT JULIAN.

Corporal.

Royal Air Force.

56 Moorland Terrace, Cudworth.

P.o.W. Camp.

Taken prisoner in Crete.

Stalags IID, VIIIB and 334

Additional Remarks:

The Barnsley Chronicle reported his return home as follows:

"BACK IN THIS COUNTRY.

Cudworth Prisoner Who Was Captured At Crete.

Corporal Robert Julian Lawrence (26), R.A.F., who was taken prisoner by the Germans in Crete, has arrived back in this country. News to that effect reached his mother last week at 14, The Green, Cudworth. Cpl. Lawrence was educated at Cudworth Schools, and before joining the R.A.F. in July 1937, was employed by Newton Bros. He was a popular member of St. John's Church, being a choirboy and server. He was also in the local Church Company of boy scouts.

He went overseas and while in the Middle East formed an R.A.F. choir. He then went to Greece, was evacuated to Crete, and here he was captured. He was prisoner in Stalags IID, VIIIB and 334, and while in the latter camp formed a choir. For his work and interest he was presented with two conductor's batons: one by the camp commandant and the other by the men. These were brought back home to Cudworth by Mr. Hiram Marrison, a repatriated prisoner of war, who has been back in Cudworth several months. Corporal Lawrence arrived in England on Tuesday, 10th April."

LINDLEY CYRIL.

Private 4345978

4th East Yorkshire Regiment.

P.o.W. Camp.

Campo P.G. 73.
Posta Militare 3200
Italy.

Additional Remarks:

Reported missing in the Middle East on the 4th of June 1942.

His mother received a letter on the 2nd of September 1942 that he was a prisoner of war in Italy.

Cyril Lindley was repatriated on the 4th of June 1945.

Discharged at Beverley, he had served in the army from the 15th of January 1940 to 29th of March 1946. These dates have been taken from his "Soldiers Release Book", however Private Lindleys "Record of Service" shows the 2nd of July 1946 as the final date.

MAIN ARTHUR.

Private

19 Newtown Avenue, Cudworth.

P.o.W. Camp.

Taken prisoner at Tobruk.
Prisoner in Italy for 13 months.
Released from Stalag IV F.

Additional Remarks:

A report in the Barnsley Chronicle on the 28th of April 1945 reads:

"CUDWORTH SOLDIER WHO WAS CAPTURED AT TOBRUK.

Private Arthur Main (28), who married Miss Ethel Berry of 19, Newtown Avenue, Cudworth, arrived home from Germany last Friday, to greet his only child, Freda (4 years and 3 months) whom he had never seen. Pte. Main who prior to joining up in March 1940, worked at Messrs. Booth Ltd., hosiery manufacturers, Ilkeston, went abroad in August 1940. He was captured at Tobruk in June 1942, and after 13 months in Italy was transferred to Germany. He was eventually released from Stalag IV. F., by the Americans and arrived back in England on Wednesday, April 18th 1945."

Arthur Main was a member of the Cudworth Salvation Army and later emigrated to Australia.

MARRISON HIRAM.

Private

York And Lancaster Regiment. Transferred to The Argyle and Sutherland Highlanders.

200 Barnsley Road, Cudworth.

P.o.W. Camp.

Stalag XXIB

Additional Remarks:

He was a surface worker at Grimethorpe Colliery.

Private Marrison also served in Egypt and Crete.

"Cudworth Man Saw Bombed Areas in Germany.

Looking fit and happy and wearing the medals given them in the liner Gripsholm, a large number of the less severely wounded repatriated prisoners of war went on leave on Tuesday, and a party of 160 left a R.A.M.C. depot in Hampshire.

Private Hiram Marrison (29), of 200, Barnsley Rd., Cudworth, one of the returned prisoners of war, gave this picture of Germany to day:

"The Germans are always asking when the invasion is going to come off. They will never speak if there are two together, but if you can get one alone he will tell you 'We are finished'.

When we were first taken prisoner the Hitler salute was being given all day long. Now you hardly see it. You can buy a Second Class Iron Cross souvenir for 20 cigarettes."

Marrison was captured in Crete and was taken to a prison near Munich.

"We have heard plenty of our boys' air raids," he said. "There was great excitement in the camp every time they came over. We were 30 miles from Munich and the explosions shook the barracks."

"The R.A.F. boys are doing a grand job. Their bombs never came anywhere near the camp. German civilians used to get into trenches outside the camp for safety."

"Passing through Germany on the repatriation train we passed several bombed areas. One German officer made a speech on the radio. He said: "This is the war of Churchill. He is killing women and children. Tell your people what Churchill is doing. We are your friends.""

Extract from the Barnsley Chronicle - 5th June 1944.

Hiram Marrison was well known in Cudworth when he worked at the Rock Cinema. No child that attended the Saturday matinees would forget him, not even the cowboy who rode his imaginary horse home after every performance and who eventually became a national/world celebrity.

MITCHELL ROBERT.

Driver.

September 1938.

Royal Army Service Corps.

George Street, Cudworth.

Additional Remarks:

Robert Mitchell was married with one daughter and lived at George Street, Cudworth. He was employed as a bus driver and enlisted in September 1938.

Driver Mitchell went missing whilst with the British Expeditionary Forces and was last heard of in May 1940. He was not known to be a prisoner of war until the 31st of August 1940.

NEALE GERALD W.

Trooper 4347489.

44th Royal Tank Regiment.

Address. Post Office, 246, Barnsley Road, Cudworth.

PoW. Camp.

Germany.

Additional Remarks:

Trooper Neale fought in the relief of El Alamein, the invasion of Italy and failed to reach Monte Casino due to the tanks being bogged down in heavy ground. The Regiment returned to England for the D Day landings.

He was taken prisoner at Calne in France and transported by cattle truck to Germany where he worked down a coal mine for eighteen months.

When the Americans advanced the prisoners were taken on the Death March round Poland in snowstorms and temperatures below zero. The Russian prisoners were treated badly, just pulled out and shot at random. Anyone who could not keep up was also shot. Gerald, unable to walk, was helped along for a day by his mates; they saved his life.

The German soldiers ran away across fields when the American Tanks came in view.

Gerald Neale returned to England and was a driving instructor on tanks at Barnard Castle.

He was chosen to drive a tank at the Victory Parade.

Trooper Neale was discharged on the 27th of June 1946.

SHENTON THOMAS.

Private

Durham Light Infantry.

23 Moorland Terrace, Cudworth.

P.o.W. Camp.

Germany, Stalag 8 B.

Additional Remarks:

Thomas Shenton, who lived at 23 Moorland Terrace, Cudworth, worked as a haulage hand at Grimethorpe Colliery.

Private Shenton, serving with the British Expeditionary Forces, was reported missing in May 1940 at the age of twenty-one. He had been captured at Dunkirk, and taken to work in the coalmines on the Polish/German border. Thomas Shenton was repatriated in 1945.

He was killed at Monk Bretton Colliery on New Years day in 1967 while living at 28 Moorland Terrace, Cudworth.

STACEY NORMAN.

Private 4619772

Cudworth.

Additional Remarks:

Norman Stacey was the fifth son of Mr and Mrs Ernest Stacey of Snydale Road, Cudworth. He was married with one child.

Private Stacey served with the B.E.F. in 1940.

It was reported in the Barnsley Chronicle in January 1944:

Cudworth.

"A Variety Concert was held at the Catholic Club last week in aid of Norman Stacey and Stanley Conway, repatriated prisoners of war. Since the concert was originally planned Stanley Conway has died in Hospital, but it was agreed that the project should be carried through, his mother to receive his share. There was a good company of talented artistes, all of whom gave their services free."

RELATIVES IN CUDWORTH.

The criteria for inclusion in this book was set as either being 'Born in Cudworth' or 'Resided at Cudworth', however an exception has been made for Desmond Lumb because of his connection to Cudworth and the insight into the life of a prisoner of war given by the photographs and letters loaned by his relatives living in Cudworth. We thank them for the privilege of seeing the documents etc.

LUMB DESMOND S.W.

Lieutenant

The East Yorkshire Regiment.

Warmfield near Wakefield. Relatives in Cudworth.

P.o.W. Camp.

Italy. PG. 35P M.3400.

Weinsburg, Germany. P.o.W. Number 2232/12.

Additional Remarks:

Lieutenant Lumb lived at Warmfield, near Wakefield. He had a sister, Mrs K. Ward, who lived in Belmont Avenue, Darfield Road, Cudworth and relatives still reside in the village.

Lieutenant Lumb was reported missing in the Middle East on the 4th of June 1942.

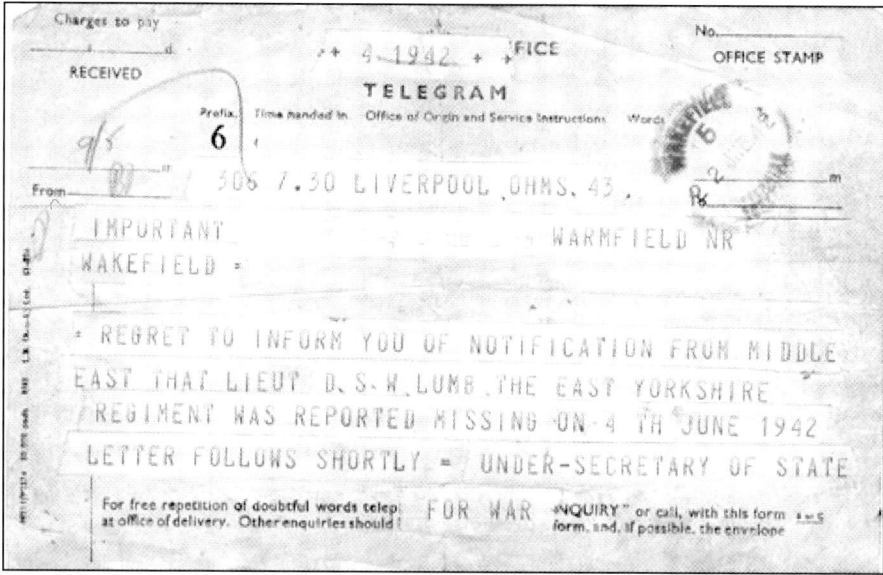

Desmond Lumb had been taken prisoner and was held by the Italians in P.O.W. Camp P.G. 35 P. M.3400.

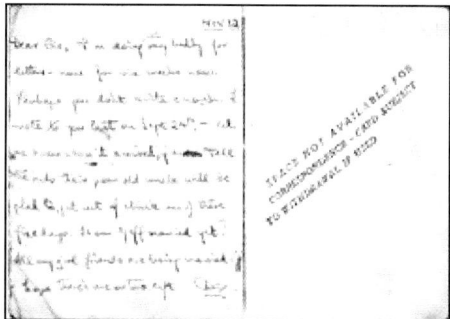

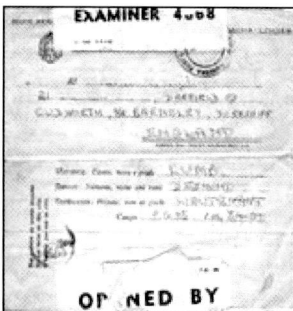

The following letter was sent to Desmond's sister on March the 25th from the same camp and though there is no complete postmark it is safe to presume that the year was 1943 as by November of that year Lieutenant Lumb was in a German camp.

Dear Bis, I received your Feb 16ᵗʰ letter on   MARCH 25
March 11ᵗʰ. This is the first chance I've had of writing
an Air-Mail letter to you, as we write only one a
fortnight and I sent the first one home. I had your
Jan 30ᵗʰ letter on March 4ᵗʰ and I sent you a card on
Jan 21ˢᵗ. Yesterday I had one from Ban dated Feb 13ᵗʰ
She says I won't know our Mally, she's grown so
much. I'm hoping that she wins her scholarship –
nothing could please me more. I'm glad Peter
likes going to school – I sometimes find it hard to
realise that I've a nephew nearly six years old.
The mail has been very slow recently, though I
keep getting the odd one from various people. The
main news seems to be that everyone is getting
married – I hope there are a few girls left. I'm
still very well – I've spent most of today sitting
reading in the sun. Red X parcel today tomorrow, so
I'll have at least one good feed. We find the
news interesting these days and hope for all that
you must be wanting. We are certainly not pessimistic.
Tomorrow we have a show of three one-act plays. We
have concerts once a fortnight and they are very fine
– you should see the girls with bass voices. Hope
you're all well, see you soon,   Des

A Christmas/Birthday postcard sent to his mother on the 23rd of November 1943 was
from the German Prisoner of War camp Oflag V A. His P.o.W. number is given as
2232/12. A 'Declaration of Parole' document dated from the 4th of September 1944 to
the 17th of April 1945 shows him to be still held at the same camp in Bung. No. 12.
Room No. 4.

P.W.No. 2232... Rank. OBLT... Name. LUMB........ Initials. P.J.W.

Hut. No. 12.... Room No. 4....

"DECLARATION ON PAROLE"

I hereby promise that on walks, recorded overleaf, I am allowed to have outside Oflag V A, I shall not escape and do nothing that might either facilitate or support my own escape or that of other Ps. O. W.

Especially I promise not to do anything on the occasion of walks that might be injurious in any respect to the interests of the German Reich.

I have been warned that on the walks I have to obey the orders of the accompanying German, that I must endeavour to keep strictly reserved and that I am forbidden to have any intercourse by word or by signs with other Ps.O.W. or civilians.

P.W.No. 2232 .. Signature. Peter Lumb .S...

Front of Declaration of Parole.

LIST OF WALKS.

PAROLE GIVEN IN TERMS OF UNDERTAKING OVERSEAS.

Date.	Time Out.	P.W.'s Signature.	Time In.	Duty Officer's Signature.
4.9.44	1445 hrs	Dell. humb. Lt.	17.00	
12.9.44				
13.9.44	1445	Dell humb Lt.	17.30	
14.9.44	1445	Dell humb. Lt.	17.30	
30.9.44	1500	Dell humb Lt		
13.10.44	1440	Dell humb Lt	16.45	
24.10.44	1415	Dell humb Lt.	17.00	
29.12.44	0900	Dell humb Lt.	17.00	
10.1.45	1415	Dell humb Lt	16.00	
		Dell	16.00	
15.2.45			16.00	
14.2.45	1430	Dell humb Lt.	16.00	
19.2.45	1430	Dell humb Lt.	16.00	
27.2.45	1430	Dell humb Lt.	16.00	
17.4.45	0945	Dell humb Lt	11.30	

Record of Walks.

(Twelve in seven months)

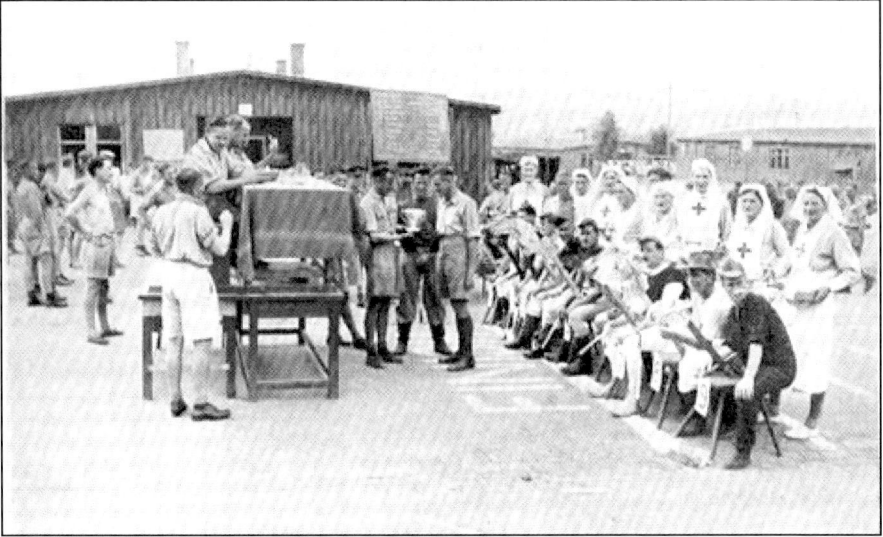

PoW Camp 1944

Weinsburg, Germany.
(Written on the back of photograph)

Gatehouse Café.

Above photographs were taken during a visit to the camp by Red Cross nurses in 1944. The Germans were still giving Lieutenant Lumb parole for walks on the 17th of April 1945.

Lieutenant Desmond Lumb was appointed Acting Captain on the 30th of March 1946. He was released from service on the 2nd of August 1946 with the honorary rank of Lieutenant.

Front Row.   Back Row ← R

. GOODHART.   LT. FYALL.-
    England.   South Africa.

LT. F. GREER.   Padré P.G. GUINNESS
    New Zealand.   England.

LT. R. TAYLOR   Jan.C Lamprecht.
    England.   South Africa.

CAPT. A.J.F. JOHNSTONE   LT. D.S.W. LUMB.
    Indian Army.   England.

CAPT. P. SCHOFIELD.   LT. J.L. STARK.
    Indian Army.   England.

CAPT. J. MARTIN.   LT. P.A. TITTERTON.
    South Africa.   England.

Group Photograph taken at Weinsburg Camp, Germany.

OFLAG VA.

CHAPTER 9.

REGIMENTS.

The following is a short description of most of the Regiments in which the men from Cudworth served during the First and Second World Wars.

It is in no way meant to cover the whole of the history of these famous Regiments as we would not have the space to do this, there are however many excellent regimental histories available should the reader require to know more about the individual Regiments.

York and Lancaster Regiment. (65th 84th Regiments of Foot)

The Regiment was raised in 1756 as the 2nd Battalion 12th Foot, but was re-designated as 65th Regiment of Foot on the 15th of June 1758. In August 1782 it became the 65th (2nd Yorkshire North Riding) Regiment of Foot. On the 1st of July 1881 it became the 1st Battalion of the York and Lancaster Regiment.

The 2nd Battalion was raised on the 2nd of November 1793 as the 84th Regiment of Foot. In 1809 it was re-designated as the 84th (York and Lancaster) Regiment of Foot. On the 1st of July 1881 became the 2nd Battalion of the Regiment.

During the 1st World War the Regiment raised 22 Battalions who served with distinction and gained 59 Battle Honours. A total of 57,000 men of all ranks joined these Battalions, 48,650 of them were casualties, 8,814 of them died. 72 out of every 100 men were wounded or killed. There were 1,190 gallantry awards to all ranks including four Victoria Crosses. After the Great War, the well under strength 1st Battalion was sent to Salonika in March 1919 and then home to England. The "new" Battalions of the Y & L were disbanded and sent home after hostilities ended. In 1922 through to 1926 the York and Lancaster Regiment was part of the occupation Army of the Rhine. The Regiment then came home until 1936 when it was sent back to Egypt and then to Palestine for the Arab-Jewish war. In December of 1936, they were sent home again to Fulford Barracks, York and stayed there until 1939.

During the Second World War the York and Lancaster Regiment served in at least 5 different divisions in Battalion strength. They fought in the following theatres Norway, Normandy, Operation Market Garden (Arnhem), Crete, North Africa, Sicily, Italy, Burma, Dunkirk, Rhine, Syria, and many others. They raised 11 Battalions including an anti-aircraft and an armoured Battalion. The Battle Honours awarded to the Regiment in the Second World War were, Fontenay, Antwerp-Turnhout Canal, Tobruk 1941, Mine de Bedjenane, Sicily, Salerno, Minturno, Crete, North Arakan, and Chindits 1944. Only one VC was won. This was by Corporal John Wm Harper of the 4th (Hallamshire) Battalion. After the War, some of the Battalions stayed in Germany as part of the Army of Occupation.

Kings Own Yorkshire Light Infantry (51st 105th Regiments of Foot)

The 51st Regiment of Foot was raised in 1755 within the West Riding of Yorkshire and has been associated with this area ever since. The East India Company in 1839 raised a new Regiment, the Second Madras Light Infantry.

After the Indian Mutiny of 1857 this Regiment was re-designated as the 105th Foot (Madras Light Infantry).

The Cardwell reforms of 1881 saw the 51st 105th Regiments of Foot amalgamated to form the Kings Own Light Infantry (South Yorkshire Regiment), the Depot being at Pontefract.

During the First World War this Regiment had thirteen Battalions on active service and lost a total of 9,447 members. The 2nd Battalion of the K.O.Y.L.I. was the first Battalion to into action at Le Cateau and as a result suffered 600 casualties, half of whom were killed. Service Battalions were raised by the Regiment who joined Kitchener's New Armies and by the end of 1915; most of these Battalions were in action in France. 8 Victoria Crosses were won and Captain Bentley won 4 Military Crosses. They were awarded 59 battle honours.

After the First World War the K.O.Y.L.I. served in Mesopotamia and then took up duties as part of the Army of Occupation in Germany.

World War Two saw the 1st Battalion of the K.O.Y.L.I going to France in 1939, but soon moved to Norway after the German invasion of that country. It returned to England after a very gallant rearguard action at Kvam. In 1942 the Battalion went to India and on to Iraq, Persia and Syria before taking part in the invasion of Sicily. It landed in the toe of Italy with the 8th Army and advanced up the east coast — the Sangro, the Garigliano and Minterno before being withdrawn and used as re-enforcements in the Anzio bridgehead. After the fall of Rome it went to Palestine, and in March 1945 to N.W. Europe for the final battles of the war.

The 2nd Battalion of the K.O.Y.L.I. was still in Burma when the Japanese invaded in January 1942. The next hectic five months were spent covering the Army's retreat into upper Burma and then finally, into India. Some notable actions were fought at the Sittang and Saiween rivers and around the oil fields.

On arrival in India only three trucks were required to lift the whole Battalion. After re-forming in India and training for the assault on Malaya, the war ended. This is just a short account of some of the battalions that served and fought with this famous Regiment during the Second World War.

The Regiment ceased to be The Kings Own Yorkshire Light Infantry after amalgamation with the Light Infantry on the 10th of July 1968.

Duke of Wellington's Regiment (West Riding)

The Cardwell reforms of 1881 saw the amalgamation of the 33rd Regiment of Foot with that of the 76th Regiment of Foot; it was with both these Regiments the Duke Of Wellington had been closely associated. The Regiment was raised on the 12th of February 1702 as the Earl of Huntingdon's Regiment of Foot and throughout the years it was known by the names of its Colonels. 1751 brought about the numbering of regiments and it was at this time they became the 33rd Regiment of Foot. It was in 1853 that they took the Crest and Motto of the Duke of Wellington as their Cap Badge.

The 76th Foot was raised on the 12.10. 1787. It was re-designated in 1803 as the 76th (Hindustan) Regiment of Foot; this subtitle however was dropped in 1812.

In 1881 the 76th became the 2nd Battalion of the Duke of Wellington's Regiment.

In all, this Regiment had 21 Battalions serving during the First World War. 5 Victoria Crosses were awarded, 63 Battle Honours were won and over 8,000 men of all ranks gave their lives. During this war to end all wars, 14 out of the 21 Battalions of this Regiment were engaged on active service on the Western Front, in Italy and in Gallipoli.

September 1939 saw the Duke of Wellington's Regiment immediately being despatched to France with the British Expeditionary Forces and later becoming part of the Dunkirk evacuations. It was during this operation that the 'Dukes' formed part of the rearguard action that covered the embarkation of the remainder of the British troops before eventually returning to England themselves.

During the Second World War the 'Dukes' as they are known fought in all the major theatres of war except the Middle East and the Pacific. The Regiment was awarded 23 Battle Honours. In the Second World War battalions of the regiment took part in the campaigns of Dunkirk, North West Europe, North Africa, Italy and Burma.

They did at sometime in the 2nd World War bear the additional title "Chindit Column 76".

In late 1942 the 1st Battalion of the Duke of Wellington's Regiment joined the 1st Army in Tunisia and fought with distinction at the assault of Djebel Bou Aoukaz. A short time later the 1st Battalion suffered 114 casualties (31 killed), with the 8th Battalion also suffering similar losses. After a period of in theatre training, the 1st Battalion moved to Italy in December 1943 in preparation for the key landings behind enemy lines in January the following year. The Battalion landed at Anzio on the 23rd of December having a hard time holding the beachhead and resisting persistent German counter attacks. The Dukes suffered heavily, losing 39 officers and 921 other ranks. The 1st

Battalion of the Duke of Wellington's Regiment remained in Italy for most of the remainder of the war.

Peshawar India was where the 2nd Battalion D.W.R. found themselves during the early part of the war. They were however rapidly deployed in February 1942 to Rangoon, Burma to face the ever-increasing threat of the Japanese Army. Shortly after their landing they were sent forward to join the 17th Indian Division. Here, the job of the Battalion was to defend the bridge crossing the Sittang River, which formed part of the last natural obstacle protecting Rangoon from the advancing Japanese Army. The one remaining bridge however at Mokpalin had to be destroyed to prevent it falling into the hands of the enemy. This left much of the division, which included the majority of 2nd Bn. D.W.R., on the wrong side of the river. It was during the action around the Mokpalin Bridge area that the Battalion suffered over 100 fatalities, including the Commanding Officer who was killed after successfully swimming the 800 metre wide river.

On reaching the other side of the river, the 2nd Battalion D.W.R. took part in the infamous 700-mile withdrawal to Imphal; finally reaching their destination on 22nd May 1942. In 1944 they were assigned to the 23rd Brigade – "Wingate's Chindits". The Duke of Wellington's Regiment were awarded 23 Battle Honours – 10 of which were added to the Colours. 2 Victoria Crosses were won by members of the Regiment for their conspicuous bravery.

The Green Howards (Alexandra, Princess of Wales's Own Yorkshire Regiment).

This Regiment was raised on the 20.11.1688 as Francis Lutterell's Regiment of Foot. It was in 1744 that the Regiment became known as the Green Howards. At this time Regiments were called after the colonels so it was therefore called the Howard Regiment. There were however two colonels with the name Howard, so to remove any confusion, as the Regiment wore green facings on their uniform it was only natural that they became the Green Howards. In 1747 they were ranked as the 19th of Foot. On the 31.8.1782 they were re-designated as the 19th (The 1st Yorkshire North Riding) Regiment of Foot. In 1785 they were subtitled "The 1st Yorkshire North Riding-Princess of Wales's Own". The Cardwell reforms of 1881 brought about the title "The Princess of Wales's Own (Yorkshire Regiment)", then in 1902 they were re-designated as Alexandra Princess of Wales's Own (Yorkshire Regiment) and finally on the 1st of January 1921 they became, The Green Howards (Alexandra, Princess of Wales's Own Yorkshire Regiment).

During the First World War 24 Battalions of this Regiment were raised, 12 officers and men were awarded the Victoria Cross. There were over 65,000 men serving with the Green Howards. Over 7,500 of these lost their lives and almost 24,000 were wounded. The Regiment was awarded 56 Battle Honours.

In the Second World War 12 Battalions of this Regiment were raised, serving in all the principal theatres. The Green Howards had 2 Battalions being the first to land on D-Day. The Regiment gained 25 Battle Honours; they won 3 Victoria Crosses, 19 Distinguished Service Orders, 50 Military Crosses, 16 Distinguished Conduct Medals and 92 Military Medals.

Durham Light Infantry (68th Regiment of Foot).

Raised on the 25th of August 1756 as the 2nd Battalion, 23rd Regiment of Foot it was re-designated on the 15th of June 1758 as the 68th Regiment of Foot. 1782 saw it as the 68th (Durham) Regiment of Foot then it became the 68th (Durham) Regiment of Foot (Light Infantry). Under the Cardwell reforms of 1881 it was re-designated as the 1st Battalion Durham Light Infantry. The Durham Light Infantry, after many years of distinguished service, on the 10th July 1968 became the 4th Battalion The Light Infantry.

The 1st Battalion served throughout the war on the North West frontier of India, whilst the 2nd Battalion was in France from 1914 onwards. Other Battalions of this Regiment the 5th, 6th, 7th, 8th, and 9th went to France in April of 1915. There were 13 Service Battalions raised by this famous Regiment, which served in France Egypt and Italy.

During the First World War this Regiment raised no fewer than 37 Battalions all of which were recruited from the County of Durham. 6 Victoria Crosses were awarded and no fewer than 12,606 members of the Regiment were killed in action or died of wounds. In World War One 18 Battalions of the Regiment won 51 Battle Honours, 2 Victoria Crosses and suffered 3,000 fatal casualties.

During the Second World War 18 Battalions of the Durham Light Infantry won 51 Battle Honours 2 Victoria Crosses and suffered the loss of 3000 men who paid the ultimate sacrifice. The 1st Battalion found itself fighting in the Western Desert at El Alamein and Mersa Matruh, the Mediterranean and Italy. They also served at Capuzzo, Tobruk and on the Island of Cos. In 1940 there were six Battalions in France.

The 2nd Battalion found themselves fighting with the 14th Army in Burma where they gained a major Honour at the Battle of Kohima. On D-Day there were five Battalions in Normandy, all in the front line at the same time.

West Yorkshire Regiment (The Prince of Wales's Own).

On the 22nd of June 1685 this Regiment was raised at Canterbury and named Sir Edward Hales's Regiment of Foot, as all Regiments of this time they were named after their Colonel until 1751, this saw them ranked as the 14th Regiment of Foot. On the 31st of August 1782 it became the 14th (Bedfordshire) Regiment of Foot. Further changes in designation took place; they also served as Marines in 1805, then changing in May 1809 to the 14th (The Buckinghamshire) Regiment of Foot. On the 6th June 1876 they became the 14th (Buckinghamshire-The Prince of Wales's Own Regiment of Foot). The reforms of 1881 re-named it as The Prince of Wales's Own (West Yorkshire Regiment). On the 1st of January 1921 it was re-designated as The West Yorkshire Regiment (The Prince of Wales's Own).

On the outbreak of the First World War this Regiment consisted of two regular Battalions the 1st and 2nd, two special reserve Battalions the 3rd and 4th and four territorial Battalions the 5th, 6th, 7th and 8th, the Regiment eventually raising 31 Battalions many of these serving in most of the theatres of war.

This Regiment served with great distinction during the Second World War serving as they did in the First World War in many theatres of war. The first Battalion served in Burma on the Arakan Range, where they were involved in severe fighting against the Japanese and in the Western Desert at the Reweisat Ridge area, where the Regiment again gave great service. It is reported that Field Marshall Montgomery referred to the Regiment as "My Yorkshire Lads. You can't beat them". They also gave great service In Iceland, Norway, Dutch East Indies, and France.

On 25th April 1958 two great Regiments, The East Yorkshire Regiment (The Duke of York's Own) and The West Yorkshire Regiment were amalgamated to form The Prince of Wales's Own Regiment of Yorkshire.

East Lancashire Regiment (30th & 59th Regiment of Foot).

This famous Regiment was raised in 1702 as Thomas Saunderson's Regiment of Marines. Through the following years as with other Regiments of this time it was known by the name of the Colonel commanding it. This carried on until 1747 when they were numbered as the 30th Regiment of Foot and by 1782 they had become the 30th (The Cambridgeshire) Regiment of Foot. On the 1st of July 1881 they were amalgamated with 59th Foot raised in 1755 to become the 1st and 2nd Battalions East Lancashire Regiment. In 1881, the 1st Battalion became The West Lancashire Regiment, but soon afterwards received the title of The East Lancashire Regiment. Two further amalgamations would take place, the first on the 1st of July 1958 when it joined with the South Lancashire Regiment (The Prince of Wales's Volunteers) to form the Lancashire Regiment (Prince of Wales's Volunteers). The final amalgamation took place on the 25th March 1970 when it joined with The Loyal Regiment (North Lancashire) to become The Queen's Lancashire Regiment.

During the First World War the East Lancashire Regiment raised 17 Battalions fighting with great distinction in all theatres of the war.

The Royal Engineers.

There are many early records of the Royal Engineers, beginning with Edward III who formed a Corps of Engineers in 1346 for the siege of Calais.

The Royal Engineers have a long history that would be difficult to equal in any armed service in the world. The 'Engineers' can claim direct descent from the military engineers brought to England by William the Conqueror and an unbroken record of service to the Crown since then.

1716 saw the first permanent Corps of Royal Engineers formed on this occasion by Officers only. Some 56 years later, when the first permanent unit of other ranks was formed at Gibraltar in 1772 and they were known as 'Soldier Artificers'.

In 1856 it was combined under the present title of the Corps of Royal Engineers. The R.A.F. started life as the Air Battalion Royal Engineers. Also under the umbrella of the Royal Engineers was the mechanical transport, which used steam traction engines during the Boer War.

An officer of the Royal Engineers commanded the Tank Corps formed in France in 1916. 'Signals' was another branch of the R.E. until it was formed into a separate Corps in 1920. The varied activities of this Corps were brought into prominence in the war of 1914-1918. The experiences and knowledge gained from this conflict also served them well in 1939-1945. During this war they were responsible for many and varied duties, Lines of communication, airfield construction, the construction of roads and bridges, bomb disposals are among the list of duties for this Corps that are too numerous to list here. As warfare became more reliant on the development of mechanised weapons in WWI and WW2, the Royal Engineers expanded to cover all manner of technologies. In WWI these responsibilities included gas and chemical warfare, air defence searchlights, tunnelling, mining, meteorology, postal services and wireless communications.

In WW2 Sappers led the way in breaching enemy minefields, and the Luftwaffe blitz early in the war brought a new responsibility - bomb disposal, a field in which 55 officers and 339 soldiers were killed and 13 George Crosses were won. The invasion of Normandy and the passage into Germany could not have been possible without the efforts of the Royal Engineers, whose skill in building bridges and harbours enabled their fellow soldiers to do their job.

The Royal Scots Greys.

This Regiment was raised in 1678 as the Royal Regiment of Scots Dragoons and consisted of 3 troops. In 1681 further troops were raised, and combined with the original three troops to form the Royal Regiment of Scots Dragoons. In 1694, ranked as the 4th Dragoons the entire Regiment rode on grey horses. They were known unofficially at this period as the Scots Greys.

In 1681 King Charles II, by Royal Warrant, authorised the raising of three more troops and formed the six troops into a regiment that was styled the "Royal Regiment of Scots Dragoons." The regiment wore coats of stone grey cloth.

In the year 1751 they became the 2nd Royal North British Dragoons

In 1768 the Greys were ordered to wear black bearskin caps with the Thistle within the circle of St. Andrew and the motto "Nemo me impune lacessit" on the front.

At Waterloo, Sergeant Ewart of the Greys captured the "Eagle" of the 45th French Infantry. For services in this campaign the Greys received Royal permission to bear on their guidon the badge of an eagle and the word " Waterloo."

Further changes took place and in 1921 this Regiment was restyled The Royal Scots Greys (2nd Dragoons).

In the war of 1914-1918 the Greys took part in all the major battles on the Western Front and marched into Germany with the guidon at their head.

At the outbreak of the 1939-1945 war, the regiment was in Palestine. In 1941, when half the regiment fought in the Syrian campaign as lorried infantry, the Greys ceased to be "Cavalry of the Line" and joined the Royal Armoured Corps.

The Greys took a leading part in the fighting at Alamein and throughout the 1,500 miles to Tripoli, which they captured with the New Zealand Division. After serving in the Italian campaign, the regiment took part in severe fighting in Normandy and in the pursuit of the enemy across France and the Low Countries into Germany. On 2nd May 1945, when the port of Wismar on the Baltic was captured, the Greys were the first British troops to meet the Russians.

The Royal Regiment of Artillery.

Royal Regiment of Artillery
raised in 1716

Royal Horse Artillery
formed in 1793

It was in the year 1716, under Royal Warrant that two companies of artillery, each consisting of 100 men, were to be formed at the Woolwich Warren later to become the Royal Arsenal. This was to ensure that a regular force of Gunners was available when needed.

This Regiment was expanded quickly in the 18th Century and they served in every theatre and garrison throughout the world.

In 1793 the Royal Horse Artillery had been formed to provide much greater mobility in the field, it soon became part of the role in supporting the Cavalry, performing so well that it became an elite part of the Regiment.

In the 19th Century this Regiment was heavily engaged in the Crimean and South African wars. It was also involved in India alongside the separate Artilleries of the Honourable East India Company, being amalgamated after the Indian Mutiny.

The 1st July 1899 saw the Royal Artillery divided into two separate branches that of mounted and dismounted. The decision was however reversed in 1924 when the two branches were amalgamated into a single Corps 'The Royal Artillery'.

'The war of 1914-18 was an artillery war. Artillery was the battle-winner. Artillery was what caused the greatest loss of life, the most dreadful wounds, and the deepest fear. Throughout the First World War the regiment expanded to 50 R.H.A. Batteries. By the end of the war they were hit by the inevitable reductions and by 1936 the strength was of three Brigades and five un-brigaded batteries, giving a total of 14 batteries. In 1940 however the batteries were mechanised, except for a ceremonial troop R.H.A. in London (The Riding Troop).

The largest arm of the artillery, the Royal Field Artillery was responsible for the lighter, smaller calibre guns and howitzers deployed close to the front line.

The Royal Garrison Artillery was responsible for the heavy, large calibre guns and howitzers that were positioned some way behind the front line.

The Royal Horse Artillery was responsible for light, mobile guns that provided firepower in support of the cavalry and the infantry.

The Oxford and Buckinghamshire Light Infantry (43rd 52nd)

This Regiment came into being in 1741 as the 54th Foot. In 1748 it was re-designated as the 43rd Regiment of Foot.

In 1881 after the Haldane reforms these two Regiments became the 1st and 2nd Battalions of the Oxfordshire Light Infantry.

1908 saw a further change in Regimental title when the Regiment became the Oxford and Buckinghamshire Light Infantry.

During the First World War the Oxfordshire and Buckinghamshire Light Infantry consisted of two Regular Battalions, four Territorial Battalions, four New Army Service Battalions, (this title denoted war raised Battalions) and two Garrison Battalions.

The 1st Battalion (43rd) fought in Mesopotamia (later Iraq), from 1915 assisting in the seizing of Amara and fighting at the battle of Es Sinn, north of Kut-El-Amara and again at Ctesiphon near Baghdad, Outnumbered, the British forces withdrew to Kut but were besieged by the Turks and after four months were starved into surrender. Only 90 of the 300 members of the Battalion taken prisoner survived the harsh conditions of captivity.

The 2nd Battalion (52nd) and most of the Territorial battalions fought on the Western Front.

Arriving in France in August 1914 it reached Mons on the 23rd. This Regiment was involved in the retreat from Mons. This Battalion marched 227 miles to the south of the River Marne. Advancing north to the River Aisne; it took over 100 prisoners and was in action at Soupir, north of the Aisne.

In the Somme battles, the Regiment suffered 153 officer and 2,800 other rank casualties.

The other Battalions of the Regiment also served with distinction throughout the First World War on the Western Front, in Salonika, northern Greece, Bulgaria and the Italian Front. In all 5878 members of The Oxfordshire and Buckinghamshire Light Infantry died in the Great War and gained 59 Battle Honours and two Victoria Crosses.

The Oxfordshire and Buckinghamshire Light Infantry raised nine battalions during the Second World War.

The Regiment was involved in France from September 1939, including the evacuation from Dunkirk. They saw service in many theatres of war in North West Europe 1944-1945, Italy (Monte Cassino) and then Iraq.

The 7th Battalion casualties were such that the Battalion was once again reduced to 2 very weak rifle companies - 1 of which was only 20 strong - and it was disbanded in January 1945.

In 1942 the 6th Battalion went to India, moving from there to Burma in March 1944.

Royal Army Service Corps.

In 1794 by Royal Warrant the Royal Waggoner's was formed. In 1855 it became the Land Transport Corps, re-designated as the Military Train in 1856. It carried this title until 1869 when it became the Army Service Corps. General Sir Redvers Buller V.C Quarter Master General gave approval that supply and transport should become the responsibility of a single military unit, and a fully combatant Army Service Corps was formed in 1889.

At the beginning of the First World War, the Corps strength stood at 6,500, but by the time of the Armistice they registered 325,000 of all ranks. It was in 1918 that the Corps was re-designated as the Royal Army Service Corps.

The Second World War brought with it many familiar difficulties and technical challenges. 1942 brought about a change when the R.A.S.C. heavy workshops were transferred to the R.E.M.E. The Corps was to be seen in all theatres of war covering Dunkirk, North Africa, Sicily, Normandy and in Burma where R.A.S.C. Airborne units were raised.

It was noted by the end of the war that 1 in every 10 soldiers wore the R.A.S.C. Cap Badge.

The Royal Army Medical Corps.

This Regiment was formed in 1898 with the amalgamation of the Medical Staff and the Medical Staff Corps. The Royal Army Medical Corps was formed by Royal Warrant on 23rd June 1898. Prior to that date medical organisation within the British Army can trace its formal origins back to 1660 and the formation of the Standing Regular Army. Each regiment of infantry and cavalry had a "Regimental Surgeon" and his assistant, eventually titled the "Assistant Surgeon". In 1815, after Waterloo, the Army Medical Department underwent great reorganisation under Sir James McGregor but it would be forty years before the British Army was called on again to fight a war of such a large scale, (the Crimean War) and unfortunately by then the lessons learnt after Waterloo had been forgotten. After the Crimean War there was great reorganisation within the Medical Services including the formation of a Corps of medically trained soldiers, the Medical Staff Corps. By 1898 there were two distinct organisations within the Army Medical Services, the "Medical Staff Corps" and the "Medical Staff", the officers. They were reorganised into one Corps a year prior to the Anglo Boer War, which saw the new Corps fully committed. After the war there was once again great reorganisation within the R.A.M.C. so by 1914 there was established a very proficient system of casualty treatment and evacuation. The 20th Century saw the R.A.M.C. serving during all the wars and campaigns to which the British Army was committed and gaining high honours and awards as they did so. Today the R.A.M.C. continues to provide a high standard of support to the British Army in its many operations, worldwide.

The Rifle Brigade (The Prince Consort's Own).

An experimental Corps of Riflemen was raised in Sussex in 1800 wearing a uniform of green. This new unit led an assault on the Spanish Coast in August, some two months after this; they ceased to be experimental becoming the Rifle Corps.

1803 saw a change in title when it became the 95th or Rifle Regiment. A second Battalion was raised in Canterbury in 1805. They served in the Peninsular War and at Quatre Bras, and in 1815 the 1st and 2nd Battalions were at Waterloo.

1815 they were renamed The Rifle Brigade at the recommendation of the Duke of Wellington for service at Waterloo and the Peninsular Wars. It took part in many wars during Queen Victoria's reign - South Africa, The Crimea, The Indian Mutiny and The Boer War.

During the First World War the Rifle Brigade raised 21 Battalions. In August 1914 they fought at Le- Cateau and in the retreat from Mons, acting as rear guard they assisted in covering the retreat, marching more than 160 miles in 10 days. It was after the battle of the Aisne that the Battalion settled into trench warfare. Many Battalions of this Regiment were involved in different theatres of the war. During the First World War this Regiment suffered the loss of 11,500 men, either killed in action or dying of wounds, after four years of hard fighting. The Rifle Brigade were awarded 52 Battle Honours, 10 Victoria Crosses and a further 1743 decorations for bravery.

In 1920 the title became The Rifle Brigade (The Prince Consorts Own).

In World War Two the Rifle Brigade raised 6 Battalions. The 1st Battalion was at Tidworth whilst the 2nd Battalion was serving in Palestine.

The Black Watch (Royal Highland Regiment) (42nd 73rd)

This famous Regiment was raised in 1725 from Highlanders who had remained loyal to George I throughout the Jacobite Rebellion of 1715. While keeping peace and order in the Highlands, the wearing of their dark coloured Tartan during the night watches, led to them becoming known as The Black Watch. In 1739 they were amalgamated into the 43rd Regiment of Foot, 1751 saw another change when they became the 42nd Highland Regiment of Foot. Other changes took place in the Regimental title and a second Battalion was raised in 1779 and was titled the 73rd Highland Regiment of Foot. With the Haldane report of 1881 the 42nd and 73rd Regiments of Foot were amalgamated to become the 1st and 2nd Battalions of the Royal Highlanders (The Black Watch).

During the First World War the Regiment raised further Battalions the 8th Battalion was bestowed with the Croix de Guerre the highest honour in France for gallantry shown in July of 1918 at the village of CHAMBRECY. 1922 saw the Regiment become officially known as The Black Watch (The Royal Highlanders) this title lasting until 1937 when the Regiment took on the title it has at the present, becoming The Black Watch (The Royal Highland Regiment).

At the outbreak of World War Two the Regiment consisted of 9 Battalions and 6 of these were on active service throughout the war. They embarked for France on the 5th of October 1939 as part of the 4th Division serving until March 1940, at which time they were on the Belgium Border where they joined the 51st Highland Division. June the 11th saw the 1st Battalion at St. Valery, where the main part of the Division, which included the 1st Battalion Black Watch, found themselves with no food or ammunition, or any chance of escape and they had no option but to surrender. This Battalion was reformed and after two years of hard training in the north of Scotland they set sail for the Middle East in the summer of 1942 taking part in the Battle of El Alamein. The Regiment served in many theatres of war including Burma ("Wingate's Chindits"), Italy, Normandy and the Ardennes Offensive. The regiment served with great distinction.

The Royal Hampshire Regiment.

Nothing is truly gone until it is forgotten.

In 1702 it was raised as Meredith's Regiment and in 1731 became the 37th Foot and in 1786 as the 67th Foot. The reforms of 1881 made them the 1st and 2nd Battalions of the Hampshire Regiment. In 1881 The 37th North Hampshire Regiment & the 67th South Hampshire Regime united to form the 1st & 2nd Battalions the Hampshire Regiment, the 37th to be the 1st Battalion and the 67th to be the 2nd Battalion attaining the title 'Royal' in 1946

During World War One the Hampshire Regiment raised a total of 32 Battalions from its establishment of 2 regular, 1 reserve and 11 territorial Battalions. The Regiment won 3 Victoria Crosses but lost a total of 7,580 men as casualties.

In World War Two, on June 6th 1944 "The Hampshire's", "The Devon's", and "The Dorset's", formed one of the Spearheads that landed on the Arromanches Beach. They were to be preceded by amphibious and flail tanks to clear mines. Things did not go as planned, - tanks bogged down on the beach and were hit by defensive fire. The Hampshire's hit the beach at 07. 25 hrs, and were the first British Infantry to land in France. By the end of the day they had cleared Arromanches itself within two miles of their landing point, having forced the enemy to retreat inland, even though they lacked much of the expected support. Almost two hundred officers and men had been lost, but the Germans never took a Hampshire prisoner.

On the 1st of August 1944, Minden Day, two months after landing, the Hampshire's helped force the enemy's surrender of Villers Bocage. The Corps Commandant General Horrocks congratulated the Hampshire's at which time they were withdrawn with the rest of the 50th Division from the front line on August the 4th. Only four days later they were back in action in the climactic battle of Normandy to close the Falaise Gap, through which the enemy was withdrawing.

The sweep across France began, and a few days later the allies were in Belgium. 'C' Company of the 1st Hampshire's was the first British Infantry to enter. There were still great battles to come - Arnhem, the Ardennes and the Reichswald Forest.

At the end of the War 2,094 of the Regiment had given their lives for their country.

The South Lancashire Regiment (The Prince of Wales's Volunteers).

This Regiment was raised in 1717 as Philip's Regiment when Regiments carried the name of their Colonel. In 1751 it became the 40th Foot and in 1793 the 82nd, or Prince of Wales's Volunteers Regiment. In 1881 these two Regiments became the 1st and 2nd Battalions of the Prince of Wales's Volunteers (South Lancashire Regiment).

This famous Regiment served with honour and great distinction in World War One and World War Two.

Worcestershire Regiment (29th 36th Foot).

This Regiment was raised in 1694 as Farrington's Regiment and became the 29th Foot in 1701. In 1751 Charlemont's Regiment became the 36th Foot. These two Regiments became the 1st and 2nd Battalions of the Worcestershire Regiment in 1881.

At the outbreak of World War One the Regiment had 4 regular Battalions, 2 Militia and 2 territorial Battalions expanding to 22 Battalions. There were 130, Officers and men who fought in this war, 9,463 of them who paid the ultimate price. This Regiment was awarded 9 Victoria Crosses.

During World War Two the Regiment was in Palestine. The 7th and 8th Battalions were at Dunkirk in 1940 suffering heavy casualties.

The 1st Battalion was serving in the Western Desert and was at the battle of Gazala and the defence of Tobruk it was here that many of the Battalion were taken prisoner.

This Battalion landed in France on D Day and fought throughout Western Europe 1944-1945.

The 2nd Battalion was in India and Burma taking part in one of the greatest forced marches covering 400 miles in just six weeks. The 7th Battalion was also in Burma and took part in the recapture of this Country in 1944.

The Cheshire Regiment (22nd Foot)

In 1689, Henry Howard the 7th Duke of Norfolk raised and equipped a new Regiment taking the title The Duke of Norfolk Regiment.

The Regiment served in Ireland 1689, Jamaica 1702, Minorca 1726 and by the year 1751 the Regiment had been titled the 22nd Regiment of Foot, keeping this number until the Haldane reforms, then being titled the Cheshire Regiment.

At the beginning of the 1st World War this Regiment had two regular Battalions the 1st and 2nd and four territorial Battalions the 4th, 5th, 6th, 7th. New Army Battalions were raised and by the end of the war 38 Battalions were in being. The 1st Battalion of the Regiment was part of the British Expeditionary Force. From the 24th August 1914 the Regiments served in every major action in France.

They were awarded many Battle Honours and 8,420 of their ranks were either Killed in Action, Died of Wounds or Disease. Battalions from this Regiment served on the Western Front France and Belgium and Gallipoli.

The outbreak of the Second World War found this Regiment serving on the Franco Belgium border being eventually evacuated from Dunkirk in May 1940. The Second Battalion also saw service in North Africa, being involved in January of 1941 as support to the 6th Australian Division in the capture of the town and perimeter of Tobruk.

The Cheshire Regiment was also present at the following actions: - Malta, North West Europe, Sicily, 'D'. Day Landings at Normandy and in Italy.

The North Staffordshire Regiment (38th 80th Foot).

They were raised in 1756 as the 2nd Battalion the 11th Foot, (becoming the 64th Foot in 1758) and as the 98th Foot in 1824.

These two Regiments became the 1st and 2nd Battalions of the (Prince of Wales's) North Staffordshire Regiment in 1881. From this time the Regiment went through many changes in their numbers and Regimental titles. This lasted until May 1881 when they were styled The South Staffordshire Regiment (The Prince of Wales's). This title however only lasted a matter of two months until July 1881 when they were re-designated as The North Staffordshire Regiment (The Prince of Wales's), this being part of the Cardwell reforms.

During the Great War 1914-1918 this Regiment raised 18 Battalions, the 1st Battalion going to France in 1914 and spending the whole war in France and Flanders.

The 2nd Battalion were kept in India on service in the North West Frontier. This Regiment also took part in the Gallipoli Campaign. The Regiment was awarded 4 V.C.'s

In the Second World War the Regiment raised an extra four Battalions, the 1st Battalion seeing service in 1943 at Arakan in Burma.

The 2nd Battalion of this Regiment were part of the original B.E.F. who went to France, being evacuated from Dunkirk in 1940 later serving with the 1st Army in the North African Campaign and also took part in the Anzio landings Italy.

The Cameronians (Scottish Rifles) (26th 90th Foot).

This Regiment was raised in 1687 as the Earl of Angus's Regiment going through various changes in their Regimental titles until the reforms of July 1881 (The Cardwell Reforms) when the Regimental title became The Cameronians (Scottish Rifles).

In the First World War the 1st and 2nd Territorial and Service Battalions served with great distinction.

The outbreak of the Second World War saw the 1st Battalion in India, remaining there for two years. On the 17th of February 1942 the Battalion embarked for Burma, arriving during the battle of the Sittang River. They took part in the very hard fought battle of Pegu.

While serving in Burma it became part of the "CHINDITS" and operated behind the Japanese lines.

The 2nd Battalion was part of the 5th British Infantry Division, going to France in September 1939, it was withdrawn from Dunkirk in 1940. It was the reserve Battalion for the Madagascar landings, although the fighting was brief. It then embarked for India for training. In August 1942 it went to Persia and then in February 1943 it went to Syria with the 8th Army. On July the 3rd it embarked at Suez, landing in Sicily as the follow up Battalion. July 10th 1943 to September 1943 the 2nd Battalion was involved in the landings in Italy, it also served in Belgium.

The Buffs (Royal East Kent Regiment).

This famous Regiment can trace its origins back to Captain Morgan's Company, which was made up of volunteers from the City of London in 1572. It saw service in the Netherlands in 1664, the Spanish War of Succession, and the Peninsular War of the 1800's.

In the First World War the Buffs eventually numbered 10 Battalions and they were involved in every theatre of the War. At the end of the Great War 5,688 Buffs had paid the ultimate sacrifice.

The Second World War had the 1st Battalion serving in Egypt, Tunisia and Italy, whilst the 2nd Battalion was at Dunkirk, Egypt, Persia, India and Burma. The 4th Battalion served at Dunkirk, Malta and Leros, the 5th Battalion being at Dunkirk, Algeria, Tunisia, Sicily, Egypt and Austria. The 7th Battalion of this Regiment was converted to Armour becoming 141 Regiment Royal Armoured Corps (The Buffs).

The Machine Gun Corps.

After making numerous enquiries it was found that this arm of the British Army had lost most of the documents relating to it. They were destroyed during the blitz of London in 1940.

During the First World War the British Army was operating with the Infantry Battalions and Cavalry having only two machine gun sections attached to them, each having only two machine guns. By November however this was increased by the formation of a Motor Machine Gun Section. This was administered by the Royal Artillery and consisted of Motor Cycle mounted machine gun batteries. A Machine Gun School was then opened in France.

It was found that more than two guns per Battalion were required to make effective use of this weapon, so larger units were created with men specially trained in the tactics required to use this weapon to its maximum.

The Machine Gun Corps was authorised in October of 1915 with units attached to the Infantry and Cavalry, with the addition of a Motor Machine Gun Corps and a Heavy Machine Gun Corps.

The Infantry Branch was the largest.

The Motorised Branch took under its wing the Motor Machine Gun Section consisting of motorcycles, light armoured gun batteries, and light car patrols.

The Heavy Section was formed in March of 1916 and was re-designated the Heavy Branch in November of the same year. The men belonging to this branch were to crew the first tanks in the Action at Flers. In July of 1917 the Heavy Branch separated from The Machine Gun Corps to become The Tank Corps.

During this period of its history 170,000 officers and men served with 62,000 becoming casualties. Of them 12,498 were killed in action or died of wounds.

The Royal Munster Fusiliers (101st 104th).

This Regiment was formed with the amalgamation of the 101st and 104th Regiments of Foot,

There have been five Regiments numbered 101st over the years. The fifth raising of the 101st Regiment of Foot came from the 1st Bengal European Fusiliers. This Regiment was about to become extinct, but was transferred to the service of the Queen with the title 101st (Royal Bengal Fusiliers). Over years of service many title changes took place.

In 1881 when the Cardwell Territorial reforms took place throughout the British Army the 101st (Bengal Fusiliers) became the 1st Battalion The Royal Munster Fusiliers.

During the First World War this Regiment was raised to 11 Battalions and was part of the 86th Brigade in the 29th Division.

April of 1915 they landed at Helles Beach Gallipoli where they sustained so many casualties they were amalgamated with the 1st Battalion Royal Dublin Fusiliers resuming their own identity in May 1915. They withdrew from Gallipoli and went to Egypt to rest, arriving in France March 1916.

A second Regiment was formed as the 104th Regiment of Foot in 1761 as with other Regiments it was involved in many conflicts and title changes over many years, being raised and disbanded. After the Indian Mutiny the number 104 was assigned to the 2nd Bengal Fusiliers, which then became the 104th (Bengal Fusiliers). This Regiment, originally on the East India Company roll, was raised during the first Afghan War. It had been formed at Hazeerabagh July 1839. Further changes took place until the reforms of 1881 when they finally became the 2nd Battalion The Royal Munster Fusiliers.

The First World War saw this Battalion stationed in Aldershot. They were to become part of the 1st Guards Brigade. As part of the original British Expeditionary Force they went to France and were transferred to the 3rd Brigade in the 1st Division completing the war in the 150th Division. The 3rd, 4th, 5th, 6th, 7th, 8th, 9th, Service Battalions also saw service in the First World War.

This Regiment was disbanded in 1922 and as Munster was part of Ireland they returned to Eire on the formation of Southern Ireland.

The Coldstream Guards

World War One.

On August Bank Holiday 1914, Great Britain declared war on Germany and the Coldstream Guards were immediately involved. The 1st Battalion, as part of 1st Guards Brigade, and the 2nd and 3rd Battalions, as part of 4th Guards Brigade, all moved to France immediately. The Regiment suffered heavily throughout the war: On 29th of October 1914 at Gheluvelt, for example, the 1st Battalion suffered so many casualties that it had no officers left and only 80 men. Four days later, after reinforcement, it had once more been reduced to no officers and only 120 men. This Regiment took part in many of the war's most significant engagements, including the Retreat from Mons. The First World War brought significant change to the Coldstream Guards, including an additional, 4th, Battalion. The men of the Guards Brigade had always been called "Privates" but on 22 November 1918 the King granted them the title of "Guardsmen" as a mark of respect from His Majesty, in appreciation and pride in the exemplary services rendered by the Brigade of Guards during the war".

World War Two.

On the outbreak of World War Two in 1939, the 1st and 2nd Battalions, despite being woefully under-equipped (in common with the rest of the Army), took to the field with the British Expeditionary Force in France. During the following six years the Coldstream Guards fought throughout Europe and North Africa: France 1939 - 40, Egypt 1939 -42, North Africa 1942, Italy 1943 - 45, Normandy to Baltic 1944 - 45. The battles are too numerous to detail in this brief account, but during the war the Regiment served as dismounted Infantry and also as Armoured Battalions (equipped with Sherman and Churchill tanks). Throughout the war they amply lived up to the Regimental motto of "Second to None". Two additional battalions, the 4th and 5th, were also raised during the war.

The Grenadier Guards.

World War One

The outbreak of the First World War in August 1914 saw the 1st Battalion as part of 20th Infantry Brigade, 7th Division (IV Corps) and the 2nd Battalion - which, after being brought up to war strength was the first to embark - in 4th Brigade, 2nd Division (I Corps) of the British Expeditionary Force.

The Guards Division was formed in August 1915 with four Grenadier Guards Battalions and later in the war a Guards Machine Gun Battalion was formed. This Regiment took part in many engagements during the First World War and it would be impossible to cover all of the Battalions involved. Suffice it to say that they all served with distinction and honour.

In all, the Regiment gained 45 battle honours, lost 490 officers and 15,512 other ranks killed, wounded or missing

World War Two.

In 1939 the Regiment mobilised and three Battalions went to France, to be stationed on the Franco-Belgian border. Returning to England in 1940 via Dunkirk the Battalions were reorganised and re-equipped.

In 1942 the Guards Armoured Division was formed, the 1st Battalion (as motorised infantry) and 2nd Battalion in Covenanter tanks - later Crusaders, then Sherman tanks.

North Africa in 1942, the Tunisian Campaign 1942-1943, Normandy and North West Europe 1944-1945

The 5th Battalion on 22nd January 1944 landed near Anzio on the west coast of Italy and to the rear of the German lines. Capturing positions some miles inland, the Battalion resisted severe enemy counter attacks, during which Major Sidney won the Regiment's second Victoria Cross of the war, and 20 officers and 577 other ranks fell, but the positions were eventually lost. The Battalion re-embarked and became part of the 6th South African Armoured Division. After fighting its way through Italy, the Battalion was returned to England, being disbanded on 11th May 1945.

The Guards Armoured Division and 1st and 2nd Battalions Grenadier Guards arrived in Normandy in June 1944, pushed inland and were soon heavily engaged.

At Nijmegen a mass parachute drop of Allied troops took place on 17th September 1944 to seize bridges spanning the waterways and thus speeding the Allied advance. The

Guards Armoured Division formed the spearhead of the British Army, which was advancing up one narrow road into Holland to link up with these airborne troop forward drops. At Nijmegen the road bridge and rail bridge over the River Waal were still intact. The Guards Armoured Division entered Nijmegen and cleared the town of Germans. The German defences to the road bridge were stormed by two companies of the 1st Battalion, supported by tanks manned by the 2nd Battalion. A small detachment of tanks of the 2nd Battalion then rushed the bridge and, under heavy fire, reached the far end. Their position was consolidated and the important bridge was in Allied hands.